PARENTS OF TLC'S *19 Kids & Counting*

A LOVE THAT
MULTIPLIES

AN UP-CLOSE VIEW OF
HOW THEY MAKE IT WORK

MICHELLE &
JIM BOB DUGGAR

HOWARD BOOKS
A DIVISION OF SIMON & SCHUSTER, INC.
New York · Nashville · London · Toronto · Sydney · New Delhi

During our growing up years Jim Bob and I both overlooked a lot of the sacrifices our parents made to provide for us emotionally, physically, and spiritually. We want to publicly acknowledge with a grateful heart all that they have poured into our lives. Their love, guidance, and many times sleepless nights have formed who we are today.

Thank you, Mom and Dad,
Ethel and Garrett Ruark,
Mary and J. L. Duggar

Howard Books
A Division of Simon & Schuster, Inc.
1230 Avenue of the Americas
New York, NY 10020

First Howard Books trade paperback edition March 2012

HOWARD and colophon are trademarks of Simon & Schuster, Inc.

For information about special discounts for bulk purchases, please contact Simon & Schuster Special Sales at 1-866-506-1949 or business@simonandschuster.com.

The Simon & Schuster Speakers Bureau can bring authors to your live event. For more information or to book an event, contact the Simon & Schuster Speakers Bureau at 1-866-248-3049 or visit our website at www.simonspeakers.com.

Edited by Sue Ann Jones

Designed by Stephanie D. Walker—www.water2winedesign.com

Manufactured in the United States of America

10 9 8 7 6 5 4

The Library of Congress cataloged the hardcover edition as follows:

Duggar, Michelle.
    A love that multiplies / Michelle and Jim Bob Duggar.
        p. cm.
    Includes bibliographical references.
    1. Duggar, Jim Bob—Family. 2. Duggar, Michelle—Family. 3. Families—United States. 4. Newborn infants—United States. 5. Family size—United States. 6. Child rearing—United States. 7. Christian life—United States. I. Duggar, Jim Bob. II. Title.
    HQ536.D864 2011
    277.3'082085—dc22

2010053829

ISBN 978-1-4391-8381-6
ISBN 978-1-4391-9063-0 (pbk)
ISBN 978-1-4516-0616-4 (ebook)

• Contents •

Acknowledgments iv
Our Biggest Test Begins v

PART 1 • Little Baby, Big Challenges 1

1 • Little Eyes Watching 3
2 • More Babies on the Way 17
3 • A Surprising Test Begins 25
4 • Praying Without Ceasing 41
5 • Miracles and Milestones 49
6 • Difficult Priorities 65

PART 2 • Shaping Hearts and Minds 73

7 • Living Under the Microscope 75
8 • Opportunities to Reach Out to Others 87
9 • Developing a Servant Heart 103
10 • Making Faith Fun 115

PART 3 • Big Hope for Our Children's Future 137

11 • Homeschool, Duggar Style 139
12 • Vocations, Goals, and Roles 149
13 • Daily Training, Tips, and Practicalities 165
14 • Life Is a Classroom 185

PART 4 • Big Hearts, Full of Love 199

15 • Protecting and Cherishing Our Relationships 201
16 • Michelle's Heart for Children and Moms 213
17 • Jim Bob's Lifelong Hobby 239
18 • Do the Duggars Date? 257

• P.S. Answering the Big Question 273
• Resources 275
• Notes 281

ACKNOWLEDGMENTS

We are ever grateful to the many people God has brought into our lives and who have encouraged us spiritually throughout our marriage. Pastor Cliff Palmer, Pastor Don Elmore, Pastor Clark Wilson, Dr. Ed Wheat, Dr. Bill Gothard, Dr. S. M. Davis, and Jim Sammons, thank you for your counsel and wisdom. We also appreciate the courage of Eileen O'Neil with TLC/Discovery channels and our producer, Sean Overbeeke, along with our film crew friends at Figure 8 Films in stepping out to share our family's life with viewers around the world.

Sue Ann Jones receives our enormous gratitude for her careful, thoughtful writing in helping us tell our story. As well, we owe many thanks to the publishing team at Howard Books/Simon & Schuster for their vision, including Philis Boultinghouse, Becky Nesbitt, Jessica Wong, and Jonathan Merkh. We are so thankful for our literary agent, Leslie Nunn Reed, who reached out to us five years ago, encouraging us to write, and has guided us through the whole process.

Especially, we want to thank our children for seeking God's will for your lives, working together, and being each other's best friends. You are a blessing from the Lord. We count it all joy to be your parents!

• Our Biggest Test Begins •

Friday, December 4, 2009

As another happy, pre-Christmas day began, the Duggar household was bustling with busyness.

Our seventeen children still living at home hopped out of their beds early to get ready for the arrival of a film crew coming to do a story about our supersized family. This one, from Australia, was coming to do a segment for a television newsmagazine there.

The children got dressed, brushed their teeth, combed their hair, and came downstairs for breakfast. The younger ones put on their notecard-sized chore packs, which list and remind them of their responsibilities and activities for the day. Besides household chores, each child would spend time on homeschool assignments and music practice for upcoming performances: a Christmas pageant sponsored by their music teachers, a harp recital at the mall, and then a piano and violin recital.

Ten of the older children were planning next week's mission trip to El Salvador with Jim Bob and thinking about what they had to pack and what gifts would be needed for the children they would see there.

The Australian TV production team arrived, and after we introduced our family and showed them around the house, they began videotaping the day's many activities. The children enjoyed meeting this crew and marveled at their beautiful Australian accents; the kids asked them as many questions about their country as they asked about our family.

As we went through the day, Michelle, twenty-four and a half weeks pregnant with baby number nineteen, started experiencing a lot of pain. Years before, she'd had a kidney stone that caused excruciating pain, similar to what she was experiencing now, so she thought maybe another stone was starting to pass. She slipped away to rest in the afternoon, but by that evening, when the production crew had left for the day, the pain had become unbearable.

Jim Bob called Michelle's doctor, who recommended that she come to the hospital for some tests. Grandma Duggar was staying with us at the time, and she stepped in to watch the kids while we were away. We told everyone we would be home in a few hours and headed out the door.

There was no indication that our happy lives were about to be turned upside down, that our relationship with each other would be challenged, or that our strong faith would be sorely tested.

We had no idea that within twenty-four hours our children would gather around their somber-faced daddy and hear him tell them the most frightening news imaginable: their mama's life and the life of the new baby were in grave danger.

"Pray hard," Jim Bob would tell them as tears welled up in his eyes. "Pray to God for Mama and for the baby; pray like you've never prayed before!"

PART 1

Little Baby, Big Challenges

Fear thou not; for I am with thee: be not dismayed;
for I am thy God: I will strengthen thee;
yea, I will help thee.

—Isaiah 41:10a

1

• Little Eyes Watching •

Lo, children are an heritage of the Lord:
and the fruit of the womb is his reward.
—Psalm 127:2

We believe that children are a blessing from God, and twenty-two years ago, in the fifth year of our marriage, we decided to let Him decide how big our family would be. By early 2009, He had given us eight daughters and ten sons—eighteen wonderful children—and an amazing life filled with enduring love, incredible joy, and fun-filled adventure. We were amazed at how God had entrusted us with so many blessings.

Sure, there were challenges along the way. We had endured some very stressful times in our marriage, when feeble income and overwhelming work and responsibilities had threatened to tear apart our dreams for our family. And we had suffered hard losses, including the death of Michelle's mother. But with faith and prayer we had survived all those difficult times, and as 2009 began, we felt confident that *nothing* could ever shake our relationship with God or with each other.

We never dreamed that by the time 2009 ended, we would find ourselves living in a whirlwind of fear, anxiety, and turmoil. Now, a year after the overwhelming challenge that turned our lives upside down, we're writing this book to share what we've learned from the experience and also to share how our faith in God and the Bible principles we live by have sustained and guided us through a traumatic season of our lives, one that may not be over yet.

This is the story of how we survived the upheaval that swept through our family—and how we manage our family in everyday life. Because of the audience that watches our large family move through daily life on the TLC reality series *19 Kids and Counting,* we have had many people express interest in our faith, principles, and experiences. We hope this book answers some of the many questions we receive in hundreds of e-mails and letters every day from people telling us they watch our show or they've read our previous book, *The Duggars: 20 and Counting* (a number based on our then eighteen children and ourselves). We are very conservative Christians, and many of the writers introduce themselves by telling us how different they are from us: "I'm Jewish . . ." "I'm Muslim . . ." "I'm an atheist . . ." "I'm a flaming liberal . . ."

Sometimes they go on to say that they don't share any of our beliefs and they think our parenting practices are outdated, narrow-minded, misguided, ridiculous, and a host of other adjectives, some of them too harsh to print here.

And yet the majority of the letters—even from those whose beliefs are different from ours—also tell us that they like the end product of what we do and believe: a close-knit, love-filled family bustling with well-behaved, respectful, fun-loving, adventurous, and smart children who cherish their parents and siblings and show courtesy and kindness to those they meet.

One of the most frequent comments was that we'd never experienced "real life," with all its hardships, challenges, setbacks, and pain. The truth was, we'd been through plenty of hard experiences, but none as difficult as those we've experienced in the last two years. In this book we hope to communicate how the faith and principles that guided us through all the good times have kept us strong through the bad times too. Our hope is that through our story you'll find ideas for enriching your own family's life together, building love, joy, wisdom, and strength that will see you through good times and bad.

We're not parenting experts. We don't have all the answers; we're still learning every day. These are just the guidelines we follow, the practices that work for us. Since we're unable to respond to the hundreds of daily inquiries that come to us, we hope this book will provide answers and insights that will not only answer your questions about the Duggars but will also inspire you to look for ways to become the best possible parent and role model to your own children.

DIFFERENT NOW

As we write, our family's life seems to have returned to something like normal after experiencing events that turned our world upside down. But we are different people now than we were when 2009 began. We've experienced firsthand how quickly and cataclysmically everything can change, and now we value even more the beliefs and principles that sustained us through our ordeal—not only in matters of faith and of the heart but also of the home.

In the chapters to come we'll share how our parenting methods worked, failed, or evolved under duress. In reading about our experiences, perhaps you'll find ideas for developing your own household systems for managing things like schedules and organization. As you learn about our child-rearing practices, maybe you'll gain insights about how to shape your own children's hearts and minds lovingly and effectively.

Our primary goal in this book is to encourage you to recognize the God-given blessings in your own life and help you find ways to fill your family with everyday joy as well as lay a foundation of faith that will sustain you through difficult times. In short, we want to help you find ways to infuse your family with faith, fun, and hope for a bright future.

JIM BOB'S DAD MOVES IN

During our nearly twenty-seven years of marriage, God has given us constant joy through our big, expanding family; but to keep life interesting, He's also sent plenty of challenges our way. For example, in our first book, we described how we coped with having five children under age five when we lived in a nine-hundred-square-foot home that was also the sales office for our used-car business.

Now we live in a seven-thousand-square-foot home, but we still live frugally, and we still encounter challenges, as well as joy, on a daily basis. We finished our first book in October 2008, when our joy about the marriage of our firstborn child, Josh, to the delightful Anna Keller was tempered by the sober awareness that my (Jim Bob's) dad, J. L. Duggar, had been diagnosed with a terminal illness, an advancing brain tumor.

When we built our home in northwest Arkansas (a nearly four-year family project completed in 2006), we intentionally included a handicap-accessible living area for family members who might need our assistance as they coped with health issues. Shortly after we moved into the house, that guest area had been put to good use by Michelle's dad when he lived with us following a terrible car crash with a drug-impaired driver. He stayed a year and then moved back home to Ohio to live with Michelle's siblings, leaving the guest area ready for the next time it was needed.

A few months later, my dad was diagnosed with a medulloblastoma—a brain tumor. This stage of our lives began one day when Dad felt a little knot on the back of his head. He thought at first it was a bug bite, but when the "bite" got bigger instead of going away, he went to a dermatologist, who sent him to another specialist, who sent him to another specialist, until finally the tumor was identified. The doctor who diagnosed the problem told us he'd never seen anyone survive past about age fifty with that kind of tumor. Dad was seventy-one when he was diagnosed.

His doctors said the tumor had started in his brain and had eaten through his skull to protrude out the back of his head, causing the bump. One surgery was performed, but the surgeons said they couldn't remove the entire tumor without causing brain damage. Dad chose not to go through chemotherapy and radiation; he wanted to avoid the side effects of those treatments so he could enjoy being with his family and especially his grandchildren during the remainder of his days here on earth.

For a while Dad's overall health held steady, but gradually his condition began deteriorating. We welcomed him and Mom into our guest

Our kids love celebrating our family's special days together, including Grandma and Grandpa Duggar's forty-eighth wedding anniversary.

room, and while Mom insisted on providing almost all of Dad's daily care and devotedly worked to preserve his dignity, our children loved having them there to play games, listen to stories, go on outings, and share meals with us.

It was truly a joy to have my parents living with us, even though it was hard on all of us to see Dad's health steadily fail over the next eighteen months. Mom put him on a special diet that she credits with prolonging his life and keeping him active for much longer than anyone expected. In addition, a wonderful physician friend, Dr. Doty Murphy, came to our home frequently to manage the IV treatments that kept him from getting dehydrated.

Dad remained active, but nothing could stop the inevitable growth of the tumor. When it extended into the part of the brain controlling motor skills, the change seemed to happen overnight. One day Dad was at the park with Grandma and the kids. The next day he could no longer stand or feed himself.

COMPOUNDING PROBLEMS

By January 2009, Dad was unable to speak. But he remained an important part of our family; we visited his bedside often, and whenever he felt up to it, we wheeled him out to the living room or to the dining table to join us for family time. The kids interacted with him whenever he felt like coming out. They would sit and carry on conversations with him, even though he couldn't respond, telling him about their music lessons or the new phonics sounds they were learning or some funny thing one of them had seen or done.

Then a major ice storm struck our area, possibly the worst in northwest Arkansas history. Many homes and vehicles were damaged or destroyed by falling trees. Without power, businesses couldn't open. Schools were closed. The governor declared our area a disaster area, and residents struggled to recover from an estimated seventy-seven million dollars' worth of damage.

Our yard turned into a giant ice rink (a wonderful thing, our middle six boys would tell you, when they were allowed to go out), and throughout the region ice-crusted power lines either fell on their own or were brought down by ice-coated trees falling on them. Huge limbs from the massive shade trees in our yard broke off and fell to the ground, littering our lawn with gigantic ice sculptures.

Roads were closed, and simply being outside was hazardous, with trees or limbs constantly falling and power lines dangling or already on the ground. But our devoted film crew, which for several months had been videotaping our family for the TLC reality series, called to say they were heading our way, determined to capture the Duggar family's reaction to the weather-induced woes and wonder.

That was a blessing for us because just as the power went out and trees started falling, Michelle realized we were running short of diapers. She called associate producer David Felter and asked if he could pick up some diapers on the way.

David, a single guy who'd never been anywhere near a discount store's baby department, gamely made the purchase and headed our way with producer Sean Overbeeke. They drove around a ROAD CLOSED sign only to end up in a ditch a little later. Passing firefighters pulled them out and set them on their way again, and eventually they slid down our driveway, delivered the diapers, and started filming.

To our younger kids, having the power go out was a grand adventure. Our family almost never watches broadcast TV, so nobody missed that at all, and if you're a little boy with a bunch of younger brothers, what can be more fun than having to use the bathroom by flashlight? The kids were excused from doing most of their schoolwork because there was no power to run the computers, and they found creative ways of entertaining themselves, as always, whether it was Rollerblading through the living room or conducting circus acts such as balancing a stick horse on their noses.

On the other hand, to Michelle, the mother of a newborn (our eighteenth child, Jordyn Grace, had been born about a month earlier, on December 18, 2008) as well as the sixteen other children then living at home, having no electricity wasn't all that wonderful. Exciting, yes, just not the ideal.

And this wasn't just a short little power outage. No, power was out throughout our region, and at the Duggar home, for *nine* long days!

WATCHING DADDY'S RESPONSE

Thankfully, I (Michelle) am married to a creative and smart husband who's also a devoted father. He knew that lots of little eyes were watching how he would cope with the ice-storm disaster, and his optimism and good humor never waned throughout that long, difficult time. Jim Bob rarely gets rattled; he's always rock solid in his beliefs and in working toward the parenting goals we have set for ourselves. He looks at everything as an opportunity to teach our children something new. The ice storm was no exception.

We hold to the truths of the Bible, in which the apostle Paul wrote, "I have learned, in whatsoever state I am, therewith to be content" (Philippians 4:11). How could we teach our children those words and then show frustration, fear, anger, or some other destructive emotion when an ice storm made our lives a little more complicated?

Seeing the vast amounts of damage to the trees in our yard, Jim Bob might have had a few moments when he felt completely overwhelmed, wondering, *How am I going to get this huge mess cleaned up? What if the power stays off for several days? How can I get my family through this calamity?* But those little eyes watching him never saw him hesitate. Instead they saw him thank God that everyone was safe, fed, and relatively warm, and then ask Him for strength and wisdom to meet the challenge. And through it all, the smile on his face and the love sparkling in his eyes never faded.

However, one thing *did* change. There have been very few times when Jim Bob has done *anything* without one or two kids in tow, especially work outside, but on that first icy morning he told everyone to stay put while he cautiously stepped out onto the frozen yard to assess the damage. What he saw was breathtaking. Everywhere he looked, the ground was covered with frozen trees, limbs, and power lines creating a massive, impenetrable thicket of ice.

Normally, our home would at least have had radiant floor heat, thanks to the nine thousand feet of Vanguard PEX pipe embedded under the floor tile that was connected to our outdoor wood-burning furnace, but a few days earlier, a part on that system had malfunctioned and we were still waiting for its replacement when the ice storm struck. With no electricity to power the forced-air fans on either the wood-fueled or natural-gas furnaces, our house was quickly growing cold. That situation would have been stressful enough under ordinary conditions, but we had a sick, bedridden grandfather and a newborn baby to think of, in addition to the twenty-one other family members living in our house (ourselves and Grandma Duggar plus our sixteen other living-at-home children, in addition to Josh and Anna, who fled their frozen home in town to seek refuge with us).

We were all looking to Jim Bob to figure out how we would survive this trial, knowing that he was relying on the One who had all the answers. Thus we moved through the icy day with a sense of adventure rather than fear.

Later that first morning Jim Bob made another trip outside, carefully maneuvering over the ice to the storage shed in our backyard. He retrieved a small generator and fired it up on the front porch to operate the furnace fans, which brought a little relief from the steadily increasing cold. But he quickly realized we would need more fuel to keep the generator running—it had to be refilled about every ninety minutes—so he asked Josh and our next-oldest son, John-David, to try to get to town to buy gasoline. They were gone several hours, not only because they had to drive so slowly on the ice, even in a four-wheel-drive truck, but also because so few service stations were open. Power was out everywhere, which meant that only stations with generators could operate their pumps. It took them a long time to find one that was open.

While they were gone, we looked out the windows and watched in amazement as frozen limbs fell minute by minute and splintered trees covered our property—and stared at the utility pole leaning precari-

The weight of the ice caused dozens of trees to fall on our property.

ously in our backyard, the broken line coming out of the box dangling ominously in midair. Then, while some of the children watched, a huge tree fell on the storage shed where the generator had been stored, totally crushing it.

When he saw the destroyed building he'd just entered a short while earlier, Jim Bob's mood momentarily changed. He sat the children down at our long dining table and earnestly explained how dangerous their outside world had suddenly become. No one, he said, was to step foot outside until he gave the okay—and that might be several days away. "Just like that tree that fell squashed the shed, a tree or limb could fall and squash *you*. I love y'all, and I don't want anyone to get hurt, so *no one* goes outside until I say so," he said, his eyes focusing on each child in turn and waiting for an acknowledgment.

One day passed and then another. We normally do eight to eleven loads of laundry a day, and by day three, with none of our four washers and four dryers running, the mountain of dirty clothes in our laundry room threatened to equal the mountain of ice-covered debris outside our house.

Then Jim Bob had a brilliant idea. He carefully walked, slid, and skidded his way over the ice field to the shop building several hundred yards away where we park our bus. Ever so slowly, he navigated the giant vehicle up and down the hills in our driveway and cautiously pulled it up next to our frozen-over house. He turned on the bus's generator and plugged in some electrical cords, and in what seemed like a wonderful miracle, we were able to power one washer, one dryer, two furnace fans, and several strings of low-wattage LED Christmas lights to provide some nighttime illumination. Our home filled with a web of electric cords snaking along the floors and stairs.

It still wasn't easy to catch up with the forty loads of laundry that had accumulated and then keep up with the ever-growing pile of dirty clothes, but by running the single washer and dryer constantly we made progress, slowly but surely.

The outdoor temperatures were so cold we simply lifted the garage door on our home's massive pantry (the space that would be an ordinary garage in other homes is a pantry in ours) so that the food in our three large chest freezers stayed frozen. Fortunately we still had water, and our cooktops and ovens run on gas, so we could still cook.

"Isn't this something?" Jim Bob asked the children one night as we all settled under the glow of the Christmas lights strung around our eighteen-foot-long dining table. "Even though we don't have power, we can still enjoy a healthy, hot meal, and we're all together and safe. We have so much to be thankful for!"

A Perfect Time for Company

We thanked God for His blessings and His protection during the ice storm, and we asked Him to keep us strong and hold us close during the difficulties we knew were coming: not just during the complications from the ice storm but also Grandpa Duggar's declining health. Dr. Murphy faithfully continued to come to our home to check on Grandpa and set up his IVs, despite the icy conditions. On one of those cold, hard days, he warned us that Grandpa was failing fast and might have less than a month left to live.

About that same time we worriedly noticed that Grandpa wasn't the only one having health problems. Our six-week-old baby, Jordyn Grace, had what first seemed like nothing more than a runny nose for a day; we assumed she'd been infected with the same minor cold symptoms that had passed through the rest of the children a few days earlier. But when you're just a month old, a minor cold can progress into a serious respiratory problem in the blink of an eye, and that's what

On the second day of a major ice storm, our baby, Jordyn, had to be hospitalized due to a respiratory problem. In this photo, Jordyn is about one year old.

happened to Jordyn. On the second day of the ice storm, her minor symptoms suddenly evolved into a struggle to breathe. A woman who's mothered eighteen children recognizes when one of her little ones is in distress, and that evening, I (Michelle) knew it was time to head for the emergency room.

When doctors at the hospital in Springdale said Jordyn needed to be admitted for observation and respiratory treatments we couldn't provide at home, especially since we had only limited power provided by the generators, we both stayed with her. Jordyn was struggling to breathe, and we didn't feel comfortable having just one of us stay with her; with two of us there, one could attend to Jordyn while the other slept or grabbed a bite to eat. We often rely on "tag-team" parenting when things get too difficult for one parent to handle alone.

So we called home and made arrangements with the older children and with Grandma Duggar, who quickly offered to step into the supervisory role (no wonder our children long ago nicknamed her Super Grandma!). While her main focus would be tending to Grandpa Duggar's needs, she would be there to support our older children as they kept the household running.

A few days later, while driving through the winter wonderland to return home after Jordyn was discharged, one of our older kids called with a brilliant idea. Since many of the roads were impassable and we were holed up in a giant igloo with limited power and a horde of little kids who couldn't play outside, they suggested that we invite our friends Gil and Kelly Bates and their seventeen children to come visit from Tennessee!

We quickly agreed. And no, we hadn't completely lost our minds. You see, the Bateses are another huge family who share our conservative Christian beliefs and parenting philosophies, and they're among our very closest friends.

Best of all, they own a tree-trimming service!

Gil had told Jim Bob recently that the middle of winter is typically the slowest time for their business. "Come to northwest Arkansas," Jim Bob now told Gil on the phone. "With all the ice-storm damage, there's enough business here to keep you busy for weeks!"

They took us up on our offer and arrived a few days later, when the roads had cleared, and we were delighted to see them. Our boys moved out of their large, dormitory-style room into our bus, parked outside, giving the Bateses a big room and bathrooms of their own. Our youngest children were deliriously happy to have some of their favorite friends to play with; all the older girls gathered comfortably in the kitchen to chat, cook, and bake, and the Bates and Duggar older boys went to work under Gil's direction cleaning up the tree debris from our yard and at several other homes and businesses in our area as well.

John-David and Josh had already used a rented backhoe to clear away some of the debris from our driveway, but Gil and his teenagers taught our older boys and Jim Bob a lot about how to safely trim standing trees. The rest of us watched in awe as they fearlessly climbed the tallest trees, tethered to a safety line, cutting and clearing damaged limbs as they moved about the treetops as easily as monkeys.

Now, before we knew it, our yard was cleaned up, the dangerous tree limbs removed. The still-frozen hill in front of our house was perfect for sledding. Jim Bob retrieved a pile of old signs left over from his unsuccessful run for the U.S. Senate a few years earlier, and the children quickly transformed them into slick toboggans that skidded down the icy hill at lightning speed.

Northwest Arkansas was still trapped in an ice locker, but at the Duggar home there was, as always, plenty of fun to be found.

BIG NEWS AT THE BIRTHDAY PARTY

The power was still out and the Bateses were still with us when Grandpa Duggar's seventy-third birthday rolled around on February 3. Grandpa felt well enough to be lifted out of his bed and onto one of our rolling office chairs for an appearance in the living room. Jana had baked his favorite banana cake and the kids had decorated the table with happy birthday banners and streamers.

There was lots of laughter but also lots of tears. We all knew this would be Grandpa's last birthday, and although we were at peace, knowing he would happily spend the rest of eternity in heaven with Jesus, we also knew how much we would miss him as part of our daily lives here on earth. By then the tumor had taken away his ability to speak, smile, walk, stand, or move his arms, but we sensed his happiness to be among us, surrounded by the family he loved. With him seated at the

GRANDPA DUGGAR'S FAVORITE BANANA CAKE

1 box yellow cake mix (plus ingredients specified on box)
2 boxes vanilla pudding mix (plus milk specified on box)
5 bananas

Prepare yellow cake as directed and bake. In a bowl, prepare pudding as directed on box. Pour pudding over cake. Slice bananas and lay slices on top of cake. Refrigerate until cold, about 1 hour. Serve and enjoy!

DUGGAR SIZE IT!

Use 1 industrial-size cake pan (or two 9 x 13 pans)

2 boxes yellow cake mix (plus ingredients specified on box)
4 boxes vanilla pudding (plus milk specified on box)
8 bananas

head of the table as my mom fed him his birthday cake and ice cream, we were sadly aware that he was living his final days. And our children were watching it happen—and watching the way we responded to that sad, slow decline toward death.

Grandpa's last birthday was another momentous occasion for our family. The TLC film crew lined us all up in birth order—the Bateses and their sixteen children (Kelly was pregnant with their seventeenth), and the Duggars with our eighteen children plus daughter-in-law Anna.

The camera slowly panned over one set of smiling faces and then the other, and just when we thought the shot was completed, Josh cleared his throat and said, "Everybody, Anna and I have an announcement . . ."

Josh and Anna surprised everyone when they announced they were expecting our first "grand-Duggar."

2

• More Babies on the Way •

God blessed them, and God said unto them,
Be fruitful, and multiply.
—Genesis 1:28

Mackynzie Renee Duggar, our first grandchild, was born October 8, 2009. What a joyful event that was for all of us! If you believe, as the Bible says, that children are a blessing from God, then having a big family *and* a grandchild is simply over the top.

Amazingly, a couple of months before we celebrated Mackynzie's birth in October, we celebrated some exciting news of our own. In August 2009, when baby Jordyn was just six months old, Michelle asked me (Jim Bob), "Honey, could I talk to you about something?" She led me into our bathroom and shared a wonderful surprise. "You're a father again," she told me. An early-pregnancy test showed a positive reading. We were expecting another baby!

You probably won't believe *this*, but I could hardly believe *that*. It just wasn't on my radar for possibilities at the time. I knew that having another baby was completely possible—God had proven that again and again. But the timing was really surprising.

Jordyn had been born December 18, 2008. We choose to follow some Old Testament directives about when intimate relations between a husband and wife should resume after childbirth. After the birth of a male baby, couples were told to abstain for forty days, and after the birth of a female baby, eighty days— almost three months (see Leviticus 12:2–5; 15:19). As Christians we aren't bound by Old Testament law, but we've found that some of the practices laid down all those years ago for our biblical ancestors still have merit today. This is

A family portrait with our first grandchild, Mackynzie Renee Duggar, born to Josh and Anna on October 8, 2009.

simply one of the practices we choose to follow. So our intimate relationship hadn't resumed until March 2009.

In August, Michelle was still breast-feeding Jordyn, which works as a natural means of birth control for some mothers, but not for Michelle. Now she'd gotten pregnant again, and we were delighted to know that another baby would be joining us in March 2010, when Jordyn was fifteen months old, which is a fairly short time between Duggar births (normally Michelle can get pregnant again around nine months after the previous birth; this time she was pregnant again after only five months).

I try to be a good listener and confidante, but I do have one serious weakness: I'm totally unable to keep good news a secret for long. So even though we planned to wait a little while before telling the rest of our children that a new brother or sister was on the way, I spilled the beans much earlier than I had intended.

It happened that very afternoon. We had just bought a giant roll of black plastic sheeting, twelve feet by one hundred feet, to put under the concrete slab we were going to pour for a basketball court in our backyard. It was a hot, muggy day in northwest Arkansas, and all around me were sweaty little kids looking for a fun way to cool off.

One of the parenting ideas we try to practice is to keep our children on their toes, never knowing when some fun, new adventure is about to unfold for them. That day I looked at the black plastic, looked at the kids, and said, "I've got an idea."

"What is it, Daddy?"

"What are we gonna do? Are we going somewhere?"

"Are we going to the park? Should we get everyone on the bus?"

"Are we gonna have an ice cream party?" (I assume this question came from the messiest Duggar when he saw me looking at the big rolls of plastic sheeting.)

I love building my children's anticipation and enthusiasm. I smiled at them and said, "I've got a surprise."

"Daddy's making a surprise! Hey, everybody!" The first scouts tore off toward the house to raise the alarm.

I pulled out my cell phone and called John-David, who was working nearby at one of our rental properties. I asked him to bring the backhoe to the house.

"Daddy told John-David to bring the backhoe!"

"What are we gonna do, Daddy?"

"Why do you need the backhoe?"

The tribe watched in wonder as I directed John-David where to dig. He scooped out a

The Duggar kids were beside themselves with curiosity and excitement as John-David used the backhoe to help create Dad's big surprise.

shallow hole at the foot of our sloping front lawn. Then we unrolled the black plastic all the way down the front-yard hill, brought out the garden hose, and greased up the plastic with Dawn dishwashing liquid and water. Voilà! A poor-man's water slide and swimming pool.

The kids rushed inside to put on their swim clothes—modest swimwear that covers everything from shoulders to knees. In a matter of

FAVORITE DUGGAR FAMILY SNACKS

Some favorite snacks at the Duggar home are: dill pickles (everyone's favorite!); canned green beans spread on a plate and spritzed with vinegar; black olives (which make great fingertip decor before they're eaten); frozen-and-thawed or canned peas or corn eaten as finger food (they especially enjoy eating them frozen, without thawing, in the hot summertime!); as well as carrot and celery sticks, apple wedges, and banana slices (with peanut butter), orange slices, lemons, and limes. (Yes, lemons and limes! It's not uncommon for someone to spend his or her own money at the grocery store to buy them. The only condition is that as soon as the kids eat them they have to go brush their teeth to remove the fruit's acid.)

We also freeze blueberries, strawberries, seedless grapes, and banana slices (to name a few) to create yummy frozen treats. We buy large bags of mixed frozen fruit as a special treat.

Since we've had at least one toddler in the house now going on twenty years, we have daily snack times that are two hours before the scheduled lunch and dinner meals, and then another snack time at 8:00 p.m. before bath, Bible time, and bedtime.

moments, everyone was slipping and sliding and having a great time, and I was right there in the middle of them, slipping, sliding, and shrieking with joy just like they were.

Carrying fresh-from-a-nap Jordyn on her hip, Michelle came outside to watch the children having the time of their lives. I quietly asked Michelle if this might be a good time to spring the news to the kids about the new baby we were expecting. She smiled and nodded, so we gathered up all the kids and told them we had a surprise to share. When we broke the news, the children gasped, flashed wide smiles, clapped their hands, and cheered, understanding the amazing blessing we'd been given.

PREPARING FOR A NEW GENERATION

It was fun for me (Michelle) to be pregnant at the same time as our daughter-in-law, Anna. Jim Bob and I, along with Josh and Anna, even went to a couple of doctor's appointments together. Jim Bob told the receptionist, "My wife's having a baby—and my baby's having a baby."

Since their marriage, Josh and

Anna had been living in a small home they rent in nearby Fayetteville, about eight miles away from us, and they work together at Josh's car lot, where they sell pre-owned cars to support themselves. Once Josh left our home, the heart ties between us remained strong, but the apron strings were cut. We had done our best to prepare him for adulthood and family responsibilities, and as soon as he and Anna said, "I do," they were financially on their own.

From the beginning, however, they were already a step ahead of where we were when we started out. After we were married in 1984 we lived in a mortgaged, nineteen-thousand-dollar fixer-upper home and sold used cars out of the front yard, in addition to Jim Bob's job at a grocery store. Then we moved to an even smaller home on a busy street where we could have a real used-car lot out front.

For a while I ran the car lot during the day, relaying customers' questions by phone to Jim Bob at the grocery store or, later, on the wrecker after he had left the grocery store and started a towing service.

Josh and Anna were following a similar path with a couple of important differences. For one, they are committed to living debt-free, a concept that we didn't adopt until a few years into our marriage. And they've kept their home and business separate, rather than turning their front yard into a car lot (something that newer zoning codes don't allow anyway).

But they've chosen, on their own, to adopt one idea that both Anna's and Josh's parents followed. They're letting God decide how many children they'll have in their family; they even included that promise in their wedding vows.

Two months after they were married, Josh and Anna joined Jim Bob and several of our children on a December mission trip to El Salvador. While the rest of the family members came home healthy, Josh and Anna managed to contract mononucleosis while they were there. Despite that setback, by early February, when we gathered during the ice storm to celebrate Grandpa Duggar's birthday, they were far enough along to confirm Anna's pregnancy.

Josh not only got to break the news to the rest of the family, the day before he had the privilege of letting Anna know she was pregnant! She had already gone through several early-pregnancy-test kits only to be disappointed by negative results. She couldn't bear to go through the suspense and possible disappointment again. So she asked Josh to look at the test stick first and tell her what it said. She left it in a cup in the bathroom for him and then busied herself in the kitchen.

As the film crew's cameras rolled, Josh checked the test and then settled down beside Anna on the couch. "I have some news for you, babe," he told her gently. "You've joined the mommy team!"

PREPARING FOR PARENTHOOD

One of the joys of owning a car lot is getting to drive all sorts of fun vehicles. In all our family's history, we've never owned a *new* car, but we've had lots of interesting ones. When Anna's mom and sisters flew from Florida for the baby shower our girls and I hosted for her, Josh picked them up at the airport in a limo he'd recently traded for!

Jim Bob has taught our children that the secret to successful buying and selling is to always buy big items, like used cars and equipment, for a bargain price so that later the purchases can be resold for a price that lets the next buyer get a good deal while you make a fair profit. He tells them, "You make your money when you *buy* something!"

Following that guideline, Josh uses his astute business sense (we'll tell you more about that later in the book) to buy all sorts of vehicles for his pre-owned car lot, things he knows he can resell. He follows other advice Jim Bob teaches the family: "Always negotiate to buy items at a price you could instantly get back if you decide to wholesale it."

As a result, at various times Josh has owned, through the car lot, everything from Jaguars and high-end SUVs to Hondas and Toyotas. His lot can hold cars he's bought at auctions or from new-car stores that they got as trade-ins, as well as older clunkers that individuals have traded to Josh when buying newer vehicles.

Unfortunately, when they were on their way to their first prenatal appointment with Anna's obstetrician, they were driving one of the latter—a pickup truck that broke down on the highway!

Josh had traded for the truck the day before. He drove it home that night, and it had run fine. The next morning he'd had a little trouble starting it, but once it got going it seemed to be all right. But then, on their way to the doctor's office, the pickup started lurching and hesitating until finally Josh steered the sputtering vehicle into a parking lot on the side of the highway, where it coughed another time or two and finally died.

A short while later, they finally arrived at the doctor's office—riding in John-David's tow truck!

Josh is blessed to have a wife who's unflappably patient and understanding. She's shown those qualities repeatedly in the two-plus years they've been married. And as we write, she is pregnant again with our second grandchild.

EARLY ARRIVAL

Josh jokes that he's chronically late for almost everything, but his firstborn daughter may be the one who'll break that mold. One morning more than a week before the baby's due date, Anna woke up in labor.

When Josh called with the news that baby Mackynzie was on her way, we were with the rest of the family attending one of our favorite yearly family events: the Advanced Training Institute Homeschool Conference at the ALERT Academy in Big Sandy, Texas. Jim Bob excitedly passed on the news to me, and I immediately started repacking my suitcase. No doubt Anna would have preferred to have her own mother and one or more of her own sisters to be with her as she gave birth to her and Josh's first child, but in their absence I was delighted to be able to assist—assuming I could get there in time!

We talked it over with Josh and Anna, and with our older daughters, and it was decided that Jill would fly home with me. Within an hour or so of Josh's call, we were in the car, and Jim Bob was driving us to the nearest airport. As our plane landed in northwest Arkansas, I called Josh to see how Anna was progressing.

Michelle and our daughter-in-law, Anna, had fun being pregnant at the same time.

"You need to hurry!" Josh told us.

They had decided to do a home birth, and Jill and I walked through the door just as Anna started to push. She was so calm and focused, breathing through the contractions and coping bravely with the pain. Josh was excited but as steady as a rock. Watching him (which you can do on the TV series videos), it's hard to believe he's a first-time dad, joyfully catching his baby girl as she made her entrance into the world.

Mackynzie Renee Duggar was here! What an amazing moment that was in so many wonderful ways. We'd just become grandparents, incredibly blessed by God to watch the creation of another generation.

Meanwhile, in the Texas campground where the rest of the family was attending the homeschool conference, Jim Bob hurriedly packed up all the gear, loaded all the children, and headed home. He couldn't wait to see his first grandchild, and he glowed when a friend said, "Congratulations, Grandpa!"

It was a wonderful milestone in our lives. And in a few more months, Lord willing, we'd be going through childbirth again ourselves, welcoming the nineteenth child into the Duggar family.

3

• A Surprising Test Begins •

Our roller-coaster year rolled along. January's ice storm and Grandpa Duggar's death in mid-February had gotten 2009 off to a rocky start, but Michelle's positive pregnancy test in August and Mackynzie's birth in October lifted our spirits and filled our hearts with joy. In our big, active family, it seems there's a major or minor crisis about every thirty minutes, but most of 2009's crises seemed to get resolved according to our most frequent advice: wait a minute; it'll pass.

Then came Thanksgiving, when we welcomed family members from near and far to join us. The house was full of loved ones sharing happy sounds, delicious aromas, and a rich sense of thankfulness and contentedness.

And with Thanksgiving came . . . a stomach virus. Or was it the flu? *Something* was sweeping through the family, infecting one child after another. Fearful that we were all coming down with the H1N1 virus—swine flu—which was causing such concern around the country at that time, we took the first couple of young patients to the doctor. Tests showed it wasn't swine flu but some other kind of virus.

The illness progressed through the whole family, knocking each one of us out of commission for about three days each. When I (Michelle)

BROCCOLI CHEESE SOUP

An easy way to feed a crowd on a cold
winter day.

7 pounds frozen broccoli
2 pounds Velveeta processed cheese
1 quart whipping cream
Enough water to cover and cook broccoli
1 cup cornstarch mixed with cold water
   to thicken after soup is hot

In a large soup pot, cook broccoli first. Add Velveeta and whipping
cream. Heat on low until cheese is
melted, stirring constantly. Slowly stir
in cornstarch blended with cold water
to thicken. Serves a crowd!

looked at five-year-old Jackson's
throat and saw white spots, I nearly
panicked. "We've got strep!" I told
Jim Bob.

Back to the doctor we went, taking not only Jackson but also eleven-
month-old Jordyn, who was showing
symptoms of sore throat and fever.
Again the tests came back negative
for what we feared most. The doctor
said the problem was the Coxsackie
virus rather than streptococcus. The
potential complications weren't as
severe, but many of the symptoms
were the same.

By the time the virus had run its
course through the Duggar household, fifteen of the seventeen chil-
dren living at home had been sick, as well as Jim Bob and me. We were
wiped out! A friend asked how we were holding up, and I told her, "I
don't know whether to say our nights are long or short. We're not getting a lot of sleep at our house!"

I didn't keep track of
how many boxes of tis-
sues and Popsicles we
went through, but it had
to be dozens. The last
patient recovered just as
everything was gearing
up for Christmas—and
a host of other activities.
The biggest thing on
our calendar was an up-

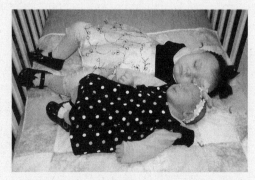

*Our daughter Jordyn (top) loved having her new
niece, Mackynzie, come to our house for "napovers."*

coming Christian mission trip that would take ten of our older children and me (Jim Bob) to El Salvador. We'd made similar trips to that area of El Salvador in the past, but this year a hurricane, along with its aftermath of mud slides and rock slides, had destroyed thousands of the crude shacks occupied by families in the poor villages we would be visiting. We were going to help rebuild homes; plus, with our friend Todd Hertzberg and his family, we had committed to bringing wrapped gifts in our checked luggage for the 250 children who had already been invited to a Christmas party at one of the other poor communities.

A few days before we were scheduled to leave, I gathered a half dozen of the middle Duggar children who would be going on the trip and headed to a local discount store to meet the Hertzbergs and do some shopping. It was a joy to see our children diligently searching for special gifts for the El Salvadoran children, piling several shopping carts high. Following our assigned list, they picked out, for example, eighteen gifts for ten-year-old boys and twelve gifts for nine-year-old girls. Then we went to the Samaritan Thrift Store and picked up hundreds of clothing items that were being donated. The children stuffed the clothes in big, military-style duffle bags to take to El Salvador.

All our children sing and play musical instruments. Here (from left to right), Joy-Anna, Jedidiah, Jason, Jinger, Jeremiah, and Josiah are ready for a Christmas recital.

The children also were preparing for musical Christmas recitals and programs, we were meeting with out-of-town editors about starting this book, and the Australian film crew was scheduled to spend the first weekend in December with us, shooting video to broadcast in early 2010 on the popular TV newsmagazine *Sunday Night.* There were still homeschool lessons to be taught, more than twenty people to feed (film crews and other visitors in our home at mealtime are always invited to join us), and lots of tender hearts and minds needing attention.

We managed to slip out on the evening of December 3 for a double-date dinner with some friends, heading to one of our favorite casual restaurants that serves the most delicious sweet-potato fries. Oh, they were good!

And a few hours later, oh, how I (Michelle) regretted eating them! I had indigestion. The kidney stones that have bothered me on and off for years often flare up when I get dehydrated, and when back pain joined my indigestion, I assumed that's what was happening. Tossing and turning and walking the floor throughout the night, I knew that eating those greasy sweet-potato fries had been a mistake.

A LONG, HARD ABSENCE BEGINS

That Friday morning, December 4, we had to get up earlier than usual because the Australian team was scheduled to arrive in time for breakfast at eight thirty. They showed up as planned. We all gathered around the long dining table, pleased to get acquainted with these new friends who'd come so far to meet us. Afterward we gave the crew a tour of the house, settled in for some quick interviews, and then went about our normal day (if any day is ever normal in the Duggar household!) while they did their filming.

I (Michelle) had hoped that as

I had to give up some of the food I enjoy, like fried chicken and mashed potatoes, when my kidney stones and gallstones flared up.

time went by the indigestion and kidney-stone discomfort would ease, but instead it worsened. I'm constantly aware that my mood and disposition set the tone for our home, so my goal is always to maintain a pleasant, optimistic demeanor, knowing that all those little eyes are watching me. But the back pain seemed to increase steadily, coming in waves; whenever it intensified, I slipped away to our bedroom to curl up on the bed. Then I tried lying back on my recliner, seeking a position that would ease my misery. Meanwhile, Jim Bob and the older children covered for me, leading the family through its daily schedule and helping the film crew with whatever it needed.

By that evening the pain exceeded what I was able to bear. After Jim Bob talked to the doctor on the phone and explained my symptoms, she recommended we come to Mercy Hospital in Rogers. We quickly headed out.

I could never have imagined that it would be nearly two weeks before I would see our family again—or that seven months would pass before I was home again.

Praying for Peace

At the hospital tests revealed a gallstone the size of a marble—and possibly those suspected kidney stones as well.

Jim Bob spent the night with me in the hospital, leaving Super Grandma and our older children in charge of the family. The next morning, I was resting as comfortably as possible, and we were encouraged by the doctors telling us that, even if I needed surgery to eliminate the gallstone, there were precedents of that being done during pregnancy without serious consequences. We prayed continually and hoped for the best.

As the day passed, my pain increased despite the antibiotics prescribed to treat the gallstone. I began experiencing nausea and my blood pressure was rising. Then another scary complication occurred: I started having contractions.

I was terrified as I realized what was happening. My due date was still more than three and a half months away. Only twenty-four and a half weeks into my pregnancy was way too early for this child to be born. The thoughts that went through my mind were tormenting: *Is my baby going to die? Am I going to die?* My fear caused my blood pressure to soar, which also increased the contractions.

I asked God for peace. I wanted to do everything I could to keep my baby safe, and that meant I had to stay calm.

Meanwhile, my doctors were becoming increasingly concerned. They knew if I continued to have contractions, everything would get worse. Tests were showing protein in my urine and elevated blood pressure—conditions that could indicate preeclampsia, a serious, and possibly fatal, complication of pregnancy.

They were doing everything they could to stop, or at least delay, my labor. But they also gave me two injections of steroids designed to improve the baby's lungs in case a premature birth did occur. The injec-

I'm blessed to have so many wonderful daughters to help and encourage me. From left to right: Jinger holding Jennifer, Michelle, Jessa, Joy-Anna (front), Jana, and Jill holding Johannah. Not shown: Jordyn and Josie and daughter-in-law, Anna.

tions created an optimal delivery "window" for a premature birth. To have the best impact on the baby's lungs, the steroids need to be in the mother's system at least forty-eight hours before delivery, and they are usually effective for seven days.

We kept praying and thinking that if only my blood pressure would stabilize, maybe the baby could be born much closer to the expected due date, March 18.

Jill and Jinger came to the hospital to help. They fed me ice chips and did whatever they could think of to make me comfortable. I know it was hard for the girls to see their mother in such distress, praying aloud and asking God, "Please protect our baby. Please let the baby survive, Lord." But if they felt fearful they didn't let it show. They prayed with me. We all knew that anxiety could make my blood pressure rise even more, so they also prayed that I would find peace in the midst of this life storm.

The day passed slowly, and my situation didn't improve. That evening the doctors told Jim Bob, "Michelle needs to be at a hospital with a neonatal intensive care unit, in case we can't get the contractions stopped and the baby has to be delivered early."

They said they were going to call an air-evac service but needed to know where we wanted to go. Our choices were Springfield, Missouri, or Little Rock, Arkansas, both about two hundred miles away. Because we were more familiar with Little Rock, that's the option we chose.

It all felt like a bad dream, a situation that was slipping out of control. We kept praying, "Oh God, please have mercy on us. Please stop Michelle's pain. Please stabilize her blood pressure. Please let our baby live!"

About an hour later, an Angel One Flight helicopter, sent from the University of Arkansas Medical Sciences (UAMS) Hospital in Little Rock, landed on Mercy's helipad.

FLYING UNDER THE STARS

Jim Bob asked to ride in the helicopter with me, but of course that's not allowed; there isn't enough room. As the helicopter was being dispatched from Little Rock to Rogers, he hurried back home to break the news to the children and pack a suitcase. He called ahead and asked our oldest daughter, Jana, to go with him. He knew he had at least a three-hour drive to Little Rock, and he wanted to try to get there before I arrived in the helicopter.

The air ambulance arrived at Mercy Hospital, and it took about thirty minutes to transfer all the monitors and other equipment and get me loaded and stabilized. Jim Bob had left to get a head start on the helicopter, but Jill had stayed behind at the hospital to see me off. Jessa had picked up Jinger earlier, and John-David had come to drive Jill home.

It broke my heart to think of my two precious children, Jill and John-David, standing alone in the parking lot, watching their mother fly away in that helicopter. I knew it had to be an almost overwhelming sight for them, especially for Jill, who'd been with me throughout the day and knew how terribly sick I was and how close we were to losing the baby.

As soon as the helicopter roared off into the night sky, they headed home. By the time they got there, Jim Bob and Jana were almost two hours into their drive to Little Rock. They'd left after he gathered our children and Grandma Duggar around him and urgently asked them to pray.

"This is really serious," he had said, wiping away his own tears as he looked into each loved one's worried face. "There's a chance our baby might not make it. There's a chance we could lose the baby—and Mama too."

Not wanting to frighten his family but at the same time preparing them in case the unthinkable happened, Jim Bob looked at those dear ones gathered around him and urged them to pray hard, begging for

God's mercy on Mama and the baby. Then he hugged each one, and he and Jana headed out the door and into the night.

The helicopter flew under a spectacular canopy of stars in a beautiful evening, crisp, cold, and clear. Whenever I opened my eyes, I looked up into the confident faces of the respiratory therapist, Buck, and flight nurse, Cindy.

"Have you ever ridden in a helicopter before?" one of them asked me.

"As a matter of fact . . . just last week," I told them. Our film crew had chartered one for some aerial shots of our property, and they had invited all of us to take a ride. I didn't even bother telling Buck and Cindy that I'm terribly prone to motion sickness. As ill as I was, it didn't seem possible that things could get worse.

Then I saw the tiny incubator tucked into a cramped space in the aircraft and knew I was wrong.

IT'S A GIRL!

Back at the house, the children, plus Grandma Duggar, Josh and Anna, and baby Mackynzie, gathered under the colorful Christmas decorations strung along the banister and upstairs catwalk and spent the rest of the evening in prayer. Later Jill told us that the youngest kids asked again and again what was happening. Why is Mama sick? Why did she have to fly in the helicopter? Why did Daddy and Jana have to leave? Why, why, why?

"We were scattered all over the living room, some sitting on the chairs and couches, some on our knees, everyone praying," Jill said.

During Jim Bob and Jana's drive to Little Rock they alternated between praying together and calling friends, asking them to pray too.

I (Jim Bob) was driving over the Arkansas River coming into Little Rock when I happened to look up and see a helicopter fly right over the highway in front of us. "Jana, there goes Mama's helicopter," I said.

I pushed the accelerator a little harder as we watched the chopper descend out of sight in the direction of UAMS Hospital. We arrived there just a few minutes after Michelle was wheeled into her room. The staff member who greeted us didn't ask our names. "Hello, Mr. Duggar," she said. "You're looking for your wife, right?"

We teach our children the biblical directives to "pray without ceasing" and "in everything give thanks" (1 Thessalonians 5:17–18). The first thing Michelle, Jana, and I did when we were able to be together again was to pray, thanking God for the dedicated and skillful people who'd brought us safely to that point and asking His mercy on us and our unborn child in the days ahead.

Some of the first tests performed were ultrasounds to assess Michelle's gallbladder. With a smile, one of the technicians provided us with a little additional information. The next morning, Sunday, December 6, I called the family back home and told Jill, "Round up everyone tonight at six, and we'll send you all a message on the computer."

Sitting together on Michelle's hospital bed, we recorded a short piece of video and e-mailed it back to the family. Our goal was to reassure our children and also to share a wonderful little tidbit of news.

At 6:00 p.m., the older kids set up one of the laptop computers on the kitchen counter, and everyone gathered around it. Then they downloaded our video message and were delighted to hear about their next sibling . . .

"It's a girl!" we told them.

"A girl!" they all exclaimed together, cheering long and loud.

EL SALVADOR

By Monday, Michelle seemed to be improving slightly; antibiotics seemed to be reducing the inflammation in her gallbladder. She was feeling a little better—although she was still prone to frequent blood-pressure spikes that zapped every ounce of her strength and gave her a splitting headache.

With Michelle's health somewhat stabilized, the next issue to be addressed was the mission trip to El Salvador. Ten of our oldest children and I had nonrefundable airline tickets to fly there the next morning from Northwest Arkansas Regional Airport in Fayetteville.

No question about it, I wasn't leaving Michelle. But what about the kids? The trip meant a lot to them. It had been a highlight in the lives of those who had already been to El Salvador; most of them had been two times before. Serving the impoverished people we met there had made an unforgettable impact on them and reinforced the ministry mind-set we wanted them to have. And in addition to the "ordinary" work they planned to do assisting with clothing and food distribution, the children had been asked to help with cleanup operations following a tragic hurricane that had struck the region the month before, causing, among other damage, a devastating rock slide that had destroyed everything in its miles-long path.

We heard story after story describing residents there who'd lost everything. Here was a chance to make a difficult situation better for a group of devastated people. Back at our house in Springdale, twenty huge duffle bags were already packed with donated clothes and brand-new Christmas gifts for more than two hundred children.

If our group of fifteen didn't go—ten Duggar children (from the oldest set of twins, then age nineteen, through the youngest set of twins, then age ten), plus our cousin Amy and her friend Zach, and our friends Mandy, Heidi, and Amara Query—the children who'd already been invited to the little church's Christmas party wouldn't have a Christmas at all. And that was one of our group's top priorities in making the trip: spreading the true meaning of Christmas, sharing the Gospel, and demonstrating a Christlike servant's heart by doing the difficult work that needed to be done.

There were also security issues to consider. We knew this was a part of the world where gang activity, robberies, and other situations could change conditions from safe to dangerous in a matter of seconds. Almost every store or restaurant of any size has at least one guard standing at the entrance with a shotgun. But some of our kids and I had been to El Salvador three times with the same group leaders who had organized and would be supervising this next mission; I trusted them to watch over our children this time.

Michelle and I talked it over—and, of course, prayed about it, asking for God's guidance.

It was a hard decision for all of us; we were hesitant to let them go, and we knew the kids were nervous about being so far away from their mother when she was seriously ill. Yet we all perceived that it was God's will that they should go, and we truly believe the safest place to be is in the center of God's will. Gradually, as we made our decision, a peace covered us.

The next morning at ten o'clock, twins Jana and John-David, Jill, Jessa, Jinger, Joseph, Josiah, Joy-Anna, and twins Jedediah and Jeremiah, plus their cousin and friends, boarded a plane at Northwest Arkansas Airport and headed to El Salvador.

A FAMILY SCATTERED

That day and the next, my (Michelle's) vital signs showed some improvement, although I still felt miserable most of the time. Whenever my blood pressure spiked, I endured terrible headaches. When the doctors learned of my family history of aneurysms, they immediately ordered an MRI, a normally painless procedure that turned out to be an agonizing ordeal for me.

The twenty-minute test in the small, tubelike chamber required that I lie perfectly still—despite the turbulent gymnastics of the baby inside me. The baby did *not* like the loud, pounding sound of the MRI as it created the image the doctors needed to see. She kicked, squirmed, and jumped inside me, responding to the noise as I tried to hold myself perfectly still while twisted slightly onto my left side, a position that would ensure that she continued to get plenty of oxygen.

It was all I could do to keep from crying my urgent prayers aloud as the pain in my head and back intensified and tears rolled off my cheeks while the thunderous test continued: *Please, God! Help me get through this without moving. Please, God! Protect our baby's little ears. Please, God! Keep her heart rate strong and my blood pressure steady. Please, God! Hold us both in Your hands.*

When the test was over and I was wheeled back to my hospital room, I cried and cried and cried, both from relief that the difficult procedure was over, and because my head was pounding—and also, I think, because the whole situation just seemed to momentarily smother me. I was sad to be so far away from my children—the little ones back home, missing their mama, and the older ones fifteen hundred miles away in another country. I didn't know what the future held, didn't even know if I would survive this ordeal. For a few moments, the situation seemed overwhelming. But in order to cry I had to draw in big gulps of air, and the deep breaths sent sharp pains shooting up my back.

"I'm at the end of myself," I sobbed to Jim Bob. "I feel so miserable, and I hurt so bad, and I can't even cry without hurting more."

Holding my hand, Jim Bob cried for me.

Optimism Before the Crash

What a gift it was when the doctors came later to say the MRI revealed no signs of aneurysms. *Thank You, God!*

For a while that Tuesday and Wednesday, my vital signs showed a slight improvement, and when we talked to the kids in El Salvador Wednesday night, I was glad we could tell them that I was doing better. It felt good to hear the relief in their voices—and it warmed our hearts to hear their excitement, and their emotions, as they described the work they were doing and the people they were meeting.

We were also relieved to hear that the governor of the province where the mission work was being done had sent a seven-man military escort to protect the group's comings and goings. God had provided greater security than we could have ever imagined.

Ten-year-old Jed, making his second trip to El Salvador, cried a little bit when he talked to me, but not because he was homesick. "Mama, this is so special," he said, his voice breaking. "We got to go and help the children at an orphanage, and we helped dig mud out of some families' homes, and we helped rebuild some houses. I want to come back next year. I think God might be calling me to be a missionary someday, Mama."

I told him, "Jed, you're a missionary right now, wherever you are. You're serving God right now as you help those children and families."

What a special moment that was for this mama and her boy, hundreds of miles apart but connected heart to heart.

We hung up from the phone call Wednesday feeling very glad we'd let our children go.

The 2009 mission trip to El Salvador was the second for twins Jedidiah and Jeremiah.

The improvement in my symptoms gave us hope that I might be on the road to recovery and that I could carry the baby full term, even though we knew my condition was still precarious.

Then, on Thursday, December 10, the world seemed to crash in upon us.

Suddenly I felt flushed and consumed by heat. My head seemed ready to explode. I knew my blood pressure was soaring, even before the nurse checked it. During the previous week I'd had rounds of illness when pain, nausea, and despair seemed to conspire to make me miserable, but those previous episodes seemed mild compared with what was happening now.

I truly thought I could be dying.

Medical personnel bustled around me, responding to what had obviously become full-blown preeclampsia. The darkness seemed to be closing in around me. And yet, somehow, it was a shock to both Jim

Bob and me when the doctor came in and said, "We have to take the baby—now, within the next thirty minutes."

It was too soon! Too early for our baby, then at just twenty-five weeks, four days gestation. But I was at the point where my out-of-control blood pressure made a stroke or seizure, or even death, a strong possibility. The only cure for preeclampsia is to deliver the baby.

The doctor's statement made it clear that we had no choice. Still, we asked for a moment alone to pray.

"Father, if this is not Your will for us, please show us," we prayed. "Give us a sign by having Michelle's blood pressure come down. Please, God, make Your will clear to us."

The nurse came in and checked my blood pressure again. Instead of going down, it had skyrocketed.

The nurse's name was Lisa, and as she stood at my bedside, looking over the monitors, I read concern in her face. I grabbed her arm. "Am I going to die?" I asked her.

"No, honey. You're not going to die. We're going to take good care of you and your baby."

Jim Bob had stepped into the hall to talk with the doctor, and when he came back into the room, I saw the same look of concern on his face and tears filling his eyes.

And then the transport team arrived and wheeled me away.

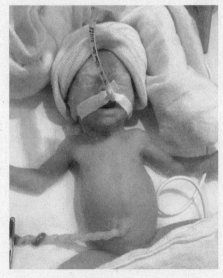

Josie Brooklyn Duggar weighed just twenty-two ounces when she was born three and a half months premature.

4

• Praying Without Ceasing •

As thou knowest not what is the way of the spirit,
nor how the bones do grow in the womb of her that is with child:
even so thou knowest not the works of God who maketh all.
—Ecclesiastes 11:5

Josie Brooklyn Duggar was born at 6:27 p.m. on Thursday, December 10, 2009, at UAMS Hospital in Little Rock—two hundred miles from home, three and a half months ahead of her due date. She was twelve inches long and weighed twenty-two ounces. Her head was the size of a billiard ball; she could have worn her daddy's wedding band on her thigh.

She came out kicking and flailing her arms—a good sign, doctors said. Jim Bob managed to record Josie's birth on a tiny video camera, and when the neonatal team whisked her away to the neonatal intensive care unit (NICU), he followed, filming the first few minutes of her life.

Meanwhile, immediately after Josie was born, the neonatal team intubated her, started IVs, enclosed her in an incubator, and then wheeled her by my bed in the recovery room on their way to the NICU.

Because of the spinal block I'd been given for the C-section, I couldn't sit up—or even lift my head. But they positioned her near enough that I could roll my head slightly to the side and see my precious girl.

She looked like a perfectly formed baby, but she was so tiny and fragile it took my breath away. Our precious gift from God had a soft, downy cap of dark blonde hair, and her skin was so transparent it seemed that every vein and artery was visible. Tubes and wires protruded from her little body as she lay twitching in her tiny bed.

One of the nurses guided my hand through a port on the Plexiglas incubator. I touched her tiny left hand with my finger as tears rolled onto my pillowcase. It would be three days before I was able to touch her again, very briefly, and six long weeks before I could hold her.

A New Life Journey Begins

While Michelle was still in the recovery room, I (Jim Bob) called our family back home. I had called them after Michelle was taken into surgery, urging them to pray for Michelle and baby Josie. Grandma Duggar, Josh and Anna, the Querys, and many other family members and friends had been waiting on pins and needles to hear from us again.

"You have a new baby sister!" I told the family, including our seven youngest children, listening back home on the speakerphone. "The delivery went well, and Josie looks perfect. They're doing tests to see how she's doing. We think Mama's going to be okay. Just keep praying."

I had sent them pictures from my cell phone, and they were amazed to see how small Josie was.

"When's Mama coming home?" I heard a little voice ask.

It was a question I didn't know how to answer. "I don't know when

When doctors told us Josie would be born within thirty minutes, I hurriedly donned the disposable scrubs the hospital gave me and took a quick swallow of soda for my supper.

Mama's coming home, but we'll be together soon," I said. "We'll work it out somehow."

At the time, I had no idea how that would happen, but keeping our children near us was one of the guiding principles that governed our lives. It's why we chose to homeschool, why I had found a career that would let me work from home so that I could spend more time with Michelle and our children throughout the day. There were exceptions, of course, like the older children's current trip to El Salvador; but my goal was to keep us as close together as possible. Standing in the hospital hallway between the rooms where my wife was still battling a serious condition and my infant daughter was fighting for her life, knowing we had long, hard challenges ahead of us, I couldn't imagine how God would bring that about. I simply trusted that He would.

The news spread quickly. After several attempts, I finally connected with Jill in El Salvador around ten o'clock. Back home in northwest Arkansas, family and friends called other friends, and in a couple of hours the word had gone out on Twitter. The next morning, TLC posted an announcement on its website, and in a few hours, more than three thousand messages of encouragement and well wishes poured in.

About the same time, our *People* magazine contact, Alicia Dennis, was experiencing a health crisis within her own family. We called Alicia, not to tell her our own news but to offer her our prayers and support. We connected with her at a Texas children's hospital where her four-year-old daughter was taken after seizures due to a virus affecting her brain.

Alicia and I (Michelle) cried together as we talked, mom to mom, both in the hospital with our children, fearful about what our little ones were facing.

Alicia posted a brief note about us on People.com, and within another day or so we felt the love and support of thousands more people around the world. Of course some of the messages were filled with criticism and condemnation, but that was nothing new for us,

HONEY-BAKED OATMEAL

3 cups rolled oats
2 teaspoons baking powder
¾ teaspoon salt
1½ teaspoons cinnamon
2 eggs, beaten
½ cup butter, melted
½ cup honey
1 cup milk

Combine dry ingredients in a 1½-quart bowl. Combine liquid ingredients in a separate container. Add liquids to dry ingredients. Stir until evenly combined. Spread in a greased 8-inch baking dish or pie pan. Cover with foil. Bake at 375 degrees for 35–45 minutes. Stir. Bake uncovered 10–15 minutes more. This recipe can be assembled and kept, covered, overnight in the refrigerator before baking.

and they were far outweighed by messages of love, hope, prayers, and encouragement.

Other prayers came from strangers closer to home. One afternoon when I (Jim Bob) arrived at the hospital, a man waiting in the portico came striding toward me as soon as he saw me. "Mr. Duggar!" he said.

He told me he was the music minister at a Little Rock church where we have mutual friends. "I woke up this morning at seven o'clock, and God just seemed to put on my heart that I should come to the hospital and pray for you and your family and your baby. I just now got here and was praying about how to find you, and you walked in," he said.

I smiled and said thanks.

He told me a story about a time during his younger years when he hadn't instantly obeyed God's promptings, and terrible consequences had resulted. "So now, when I feel God telling me to do something, I do it," he said. "This morning I felt Him telling me to come here and pray for you—and here I am."

I thanked him again for coming—and led him upstairs to the NICU, where we joined in earnest prayer for Josie.

STRUNG OUT BY DISTANCE

For the first five or six days of Josie's life, the medical team's focus was simply on keeping her alive. Two ultrasounds showed no brain bleeds, a common problem for preemies. Her lungs were working, and her vital

*Josie was not allowed to be held
for her first forty days of life.*

signs were good. *Thank You, God!*

Michelle's condition didn't improve as quickly as we'd hoped, but every indication was that she *would* recover and regain her strength. The doctor told us that although the cure for preeclampsia is to deliver the baby, the condition is like a freight train that takes awhile to stop once it gets going.

One of the hardest things for both of us was being away from the rest of our family. We are both accustomed to being surrounded by children all the time; now we felt like our hearts were being stretched from one place to another, and from one continent to another.

We were concerned not only about Josie but also about little Jordyn, our baby back home in Springdale whose first birthday would be December 18, just a week and a day after Josie was born. Grandma Duggar, Josh and Anna, and our friend Debbie Query and her son, Peter, were doing a wonderful job caring for the seven youngest Duggars, but by Saturday, two days after Josie's birth, Jordyn had come down with a cough and other symptoms of a cold or sinus infection that was causing them some concern.

Still in the hospital because of my blood pressure, I (Michelle) kept in touch with the home base throughout that day, constantly asking about Jordyn. Since she'd had respiratory problems during the ice storm that required hospitalization, I wanted to make sure we stayed on top of the situation. I certainly didn't want my two youngest babies in hospitals that were a three-hour drive apart!

That evening, I asked Josh and Anna to take her to the pediatric after-hours clinic, where the doctor found that her right ear was infected and her lungs sounded a little crackly, which could be a sign of pneumonia. Josh called to let me know he had picked up some prescriptions and they were on their way home with Jordyn. I called the nurse at the after-hours clinic for more details—and thank goodness I did!

"Oh, no!" I said when the nurse told me what had been prescribed. "She's extremely allergic to amoxicillin!"

Several more phone calls were made, and Josh returned to the pharmacy to pick up a different prescription. I whispered a prayer of thankfulness that we'd dodged what could have been a second calamitous situation.

Two days later, on December 14, my heart got another boost when we got a call late in the afternoon from our older children, who had made it home safely from El Salvador. Now at least my family was secure within the same state. Twenty-four hours later, they were on their way to Little Rock along with Grandma Duggar, cousin Amy, and the Querys.

On December 15, 2009, the day after half of our family had returned from El Salvador, everyone drove to Little Rock to see their new baby sister, Josie Brooklyn Duggar.

I hadn't been released yet from UAMS, but the kind folks there understood how important it was for me to see all my children again—and for them to see Josie. After each child went through a quick health screening, the staff led our family to Josie's NICU room to see their minuscule sister in her incubator. Josie, still on a ventilator, was connected to what seemed like a dozen cords and tubes, and some of the older girls cried, seeing the tiny baby who seemed dwarfed by all the medical apparatus humming and beeping over her, keeping her alive. Her skin was still transparent, and she truly looked pitiful.

Jim Bob wheeled me in a wheelchair to another hospital room where the staff had gathered my family. Even though I would be released later that evening, we agreed it was a good idea to greet the children in a "controlled setting" so the younger ones wouldn't mob me or injure my sutured abdomen. Nothing worked better to raise my spirits than the gentle embraces of all those little (and big!) arms.

That evening I was released from the hospital, and our whole family (except Josie) gathered in a nearby hotel. It was wonderful to be together again.

Our family's favorite time together, without question, is nightly Bible time, when we gather at bedtime, usually in our pajamas, to listen to Daddy read a Bible passage and then discuss it with the children. It's also a time when we talk about our day—and maybe share what's planned for tomorrow.

Sharing Bible time in that hotel room was the best thing that had happened to us since Josie was born. How it blessed us all to be together again! We told our children all of the miracles surrounding Josie's birth, and they shared with us the wonderful adventures they'd had in El Salvador. We also loved hearing Jim Bob's voice reading the Bible to us, and everyone enjoyed talking together and asking God again to bless our family and give us strength for whatever lay ahead.

The Querys had to leave early the next morning to keep commitments back home, and they took Jessa with them so she could keep her appointment with an orthodontist. She would be our third child in braces!

The rest of the family returned home later that day, leaving Jim Bob and me alone in the hotel. Wiping away tears as I watched John-David drive our family bus away, I turned my focus back to the job at hand: helping Josie survive.

I'd been pumping breast milk since Josie's birth, but it wasn't given to her until her sixth day of life. The hospital's lab stored the breast milk until it was needed. On the same day she started receiving the breast milk through a feeding tube, she was taken off the ventilator and began breathing "room air" on her own.

Shortly after that, Josie cried a raspy little whimper, and we heard her voice for the first time.

What happy milestones those were! We rejoiced that our tiny little preemie seemed to be overcoming every challenge, and although we knew she still had a long way to go, we thanked God for giving her another day of life.

Then we learned the reality of what Josie's neonatologist would repeatedly stress to us: never trust a preemie.

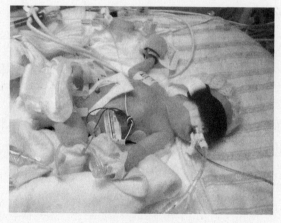

Josie's life was so fragile.

5

• Miracles and Milestones •

Be of good courage, and he shall strengthen your heart,
all ye that hope in the LORD.
—Psalm 31:24

Just as we were celebrating how well Josie was doing—breathing on her own and receiving her first few drops of breast milk through a feeding tube—we received an urgent phone call at 7:00 a.m. from one of Josie's UAMS doctors. He said a routine X-ray showed "free air" in her abdomen, which meant her intestines were leaking. He said she would probably need emergency surgery and since UAMS wasn't equipped for surgery on a "micro-preemie" like Josie, she was being transferred immediately to Arkansas Children's Hospital a couple of miles away.

We rushed to ACH, where a volunteer escorted us through the maze of long hallways and elevators to the NICU. When Josie's little incubator was rolled into the room, we were shocked to see the difference in her. She was back on the ventilator, and her abdomen, extended and tight, looked like a big, inflated balloon. Because of her obvious distress and the risk of infection, all feedings had been stopped.

Dr. Robert Arrington, known as Doc A, said they hadn't determined what had caused the perforation in Josie's bowel, but it was pretty common in preemies during the first seven to ten days of life.

Showing us the X-ray, Doc A explained the possible causes and their corresponding treatments.

We expected him to say Josie would be undergoing immediate surgery but, as we would quickly learn, Doc A thinks outside the box. Before they risked doing major abdominal surgery on tiny Josie, he wanted to insert a drain tube in her side to release as much trapped air as possible and then administer antibiotics. Maybe, he said, the perforation would heal on its own.

The situation reminded us of a sermon by the late Ron Dunn we'd heard years earlier. Pastor Dunn said most people think that one of these days they will get their "ducks in a row" and then only good things will happen to them. But the truth is, "Good and bad run on parallel tracks, and they arrive about the same time." As we were experiencing, on the same day something really good happens, something bad can happen too. But God promised in Romans 8:28, "All things work together for good to them that love God." We can trust Him to make even the bad things in our lives work for good. That's why we thank God for *everything*, even the challenges He allows to come our way.

A PRAYER ANSWERED

It was quickly becoming obvious that we might be at Children's for several weeks—possibly several months. We talked about how we were going to be able to take care of Josie in the Little Rock hospital and also stay close to the rest of our children, especially during the holidays. Christmas was the next week.

We prayerfully decided that we needed to move our whole family to Little Rock during Josie's hospital stay. So we needed a house, but how could we quickly find one with five bedrooms, the minimum size Michelle said we would need? How were we going to make it all work?

The morning after we had that conversation, we were at Josie's bedside in Children's when my (Jim Bob's) cell phone rang. I stepped out in the hallway to answer the call and was surprised to hear from Dr. Paul

Wendel, our friend who had directed Michelle's care back at UAMS. He said a friend of his had just called him, asking about us.

"She heard about Josie, Jim Bob," he said. "She lives near the hospital, and she and her family are leaving town for ten days over the holidays. She wants me to ask if you would like to stay in their house while they're away. She said she woke up early this morning feeling the Lord had laid it on her heart."

My own heart pounded in my chest, remembering my conversation with Michelle a few hours earlier.

Before I could say anything, Dr. Wendel continued with his message. "It's a nice house, Jim Bob, in a nice neighborhood," he said. "And it's big. It has five bedrooms."

Thank You, God!

I returned to Josie's room, knelt down in front of Michelle's chair, and said, "Do you want to hear some good news?"

Hearing about Dr. Wendel's call, Michelle melted into my arms, and we both cried.

The peace that came over us was indescribable. As we faced the toughest situation of our lives, God was telling us through someone we didn't even know, "I love you, and I'm going to take care of you. Trust Me!"

What an incredible gift, and what an amazing answer to prayer. Isn't God good?

We were blown away by the unknown woman's kind offer, but we were a little reluctant to borrow someone's house. I kept thinking, *Does she really understand that we have* seventeen children *living at home?*

About thirty minutes later, I stepped back into the hallway and was greeted by a friendly, smiling woman who said, "Hi, I'm Anne. I've brought you my house key and my alarm code. Here's the address."

Seeing the shocked look on my face, her smile widened. "The Lord laid this on my heart. You can move in Monday if you want. We'll be back after New Year's."

She told me that a few years earlier God had gotten her through a battle with cancer and also that one of her three children had been hospitalized for ten days. "I know how hard it is to go back and forth to the hospital when you live close, let alone when you live so far away. God bless you all," she said.

We were stunned by Anne's generosity and blessed by her thoughtfulness. We spent a couple more nights in the hotel we'd been staying in since Michelle's discharge; then, on Monday, we drove to the house to meet Anne's husband, Randy, and get a tour of the home.

It was breathtaking—the kind of home you see in home-decorating magazines. And it was beautifully decorated for Christmas, complete with a Christmas tree and all the things we would never have had time to bring together.

We were a little nervous about turning the kids loose in such an exquisite place, and Michelle gulped when she saw the *white* carpeting, picturing one of our little ones "redecorating" the beautiful canvas with finger-painted ketchup and peanut butter.

It was a wonderful gift, and when we told Anne about the very specific prayer we had prayed the night before she had called, we could tell that she was as blessed by the whole story as we were.

After we'd moved in for the holidays, some of Anne and Randy's friends brought us a delicious chicken-and-dumplings meal. He told us he'd known Anne for years. "A lot of us, when God puts something on our heart asking us to do something, we just think about it and don't do it," he said. "Anne isn't like that. When God tells her to do something, she does it."

Because Anne had a heart tuned to God's heart, our family would be able to spend Christmas together in a beautiful, comfortable home away from home. What a gracious blessing!

CHRISTMAS COUNTDOWN

Monday, December 21, was a good day for many reasons. Not only were Jim Bob and I (Michelle) moving into our "gift house," it was also our daughter Jinger's sixteenth birthday. It was a good day for Josie too—a "good day" being defined as one in which there were only minor issues and no major crises. In fact, Dr. Arrington told us the perforation in Josie's bowel had healed on its own, just as he had said—and we had prayed—might happen. Again we thanked God for His mercy.

We planned to celebrate Jinger and Jordyn's birthdays when the family arrived in Little Rock on December 23, a day we call "Christmas Adam" (because it's the day before Christmas Eve and God created Adam *before* Eve).

We both counted down the hours, so very eager to see all our children again. While I visited Josie during the morning, Jim Bob rushed out to a discount store for a whirlwind round of Christmas shopping. We try to keep our family's focus on Christmas being Jesus' birthday rather than letting it be a holiday focused on commercialism, but we still enjoy giving gifts, recognizing Jesus as the greatest gift the world has ever known. Our children draw names for a low-cost family gift exchange, and Jim Bob and I give each child gifts as well. That's how Jim Bob ended up at the discount store on "Christmas Adam," buying just about every Nerf gun the store had, plus a shopping cart full of other fun surprises.

Our fourth-oldest daughter, Jinger, loves to cook and has fun coming up with creative recipes!

The evening before, the children had participated in a Christmas music pageant at the Jones Center in Springdale. It saddened us to be unable to attend, and we admired and ached for the older children, who stayed up most of the night after the music pageant, packing up all the necessities for themselves and their siblings—seventeen people in all.

They came to Little Rock in two big vans, traveling through heavy rain the whole way. The windshield wipers went out on the van driven by poor Jana, already sleep deprived and exhausted. She said she stopped and Rain-Xed the windshield and basically tailgated the other van, which Grandma Duggar and Jill took turns driving through the rain.

We were ecstatic when they all arrived in Little Rock, so glad to have our arms full of children again. As the little ones came pouring through the door, the house erupted into a symphony of voices happily greeting us and telling exciting stories about things that had happened during the long, two-hundred-mile trip. Shoes had gotten lost and found and lost again, and songs had been sung, and games had been played—oh, my!

How wonderful to have our family together again. But then, shortly after everything had been carried inside and the younger kids had discovered the house's appealing playroom, Jana turned pale and started vomiting. Wiping her face with a cool cloth, I (Michelle) hoped it was simply a matter of stress and exhaustion that would be cured by resting. But then Justin started throwing up too, and I knew we were heading into another round of stomach virus, something Jim Bob and I could *not* carry into the NICU!

Sure enough, the bug ran its course through the whole family over the holidays, and there were days when Jim Bob and I couldn't

APPLE DUMPLINGS

2–3 cans crescent dinner rolls
2–3 apples, cored and cut into 8 slices per apple (Granny Smith or Fuji apples are best)
Butter or margarine
1½ cups granulated sugar
1 teaspoon cinnamon
1 12-ounce can Mountain Dew or Sprite

Spread out triangular dinner-roll dough. Put 2–3 apple slices in each one and then roll from the large end to the small end. Place dumplings in a 9 × 13-inch casserole dish.

In a small saucepan melt the butter. Stir in the sugar and cinnamon. Pour butter mixture over apple-filled rolls. Pour the can of Mountain Dew or Sprite over the rolls. Bake 45 minutes at 350 degrees or until golden brown.

visit Josie. The hospital didn't allow visits from children under age eighteen during flu season, but as things worked out, one or more of the older girls were healthy whenever Jim Bob or I was sick, so someone was always available to visit Josie each day. Whoever was there took daily pictures and videos to share with the little ones back home.

Christmas Eve arrived, and the house bustled with activity, but not all of it was holiday-related. I (Jim Bob) had been searching the newspaper for a large home to rent on a month-to-month basis. I found one that might have worked, except it

The Cornish House—
just five minutes from the hospital.

had a beautiful small lake right at the back door. Even though it was winter and the kids would be inside most of the time, I felt it would be too dangerous for the little ones.

Then, a few days later, I was in a Little Rock business office and mentioned to a woman working there that we were looking for a large house to rent. She called a Realtor friend, Jon Underhill, who made some calls and then contacted me and offered us, for a reasonable rent, a large historic home that was close to the hospital.

Grandma Duggar, John-David, Jinger, and I piled into a van to check out the house. It felt so good to be doing things again with a carful of loved ones!

The *five-bedroom* Cornish House had 8,150 square feet—more than our Springdale home!—and a fenced yard. It wasn't perfect (for example, despite having four bathrooms there was only *one* shower), but the rent was reasonable. It was empty, so we could move in right away, and it was about a five-minute drive from the hospital.

As always, we prayed about it before signing the rental agreement.

By that evening we had agreed it would be a good temporary home for the Duggar family in Little Rock. Knowing our family could be together again for the long haul made Christmas an even merrier time for all of us.

And there was something else that made us laugh that day: the plaque in front of the Cornish House describing the home's history. It said the house had been built in 1919 by a banker and his wife who had six children. Despite their own large family, the wife, Hilda Cornish, "was prominent in social and political issues of the day," the plaque says. "She was a leader in advocating birth control." We later learned she had been one of the founders of Planned Parenthood in Arkansas.

Life is full of ironies, isn't it? A historic house built by one of the biggest advocates of birth control was about to be occupied, many years later, by one of America's biggest families with a personal conviction *against* birth control!

Again and again during that time of trials and triumphs, we were amazed at how God worked all things for good. After Christmas, Grandma Duggar, Jessa, and Jana returned to our home in northwest Arkansas and filled a small box truck with several mattresses, Jill's harp, ironing boards, irons, laundry baskets, clothes, and what seemed like a million more necessities, and hauled it all to Little Rock, where we unloaded it in the Cornish House.

On Craigslist.com we found additional items needed for our second household. When Jessa and I took our box truck to inspect a used refrigerator, washer, dryer, couch and love seat, the seller told us he had recently changed girlfriends and his

We moved what seemed like a million necessities, including Jill's harp, to the Cornish House in Little Rock.

new girlfriend didn't want to use the old girlfriend's stuff. The items were in excellent condition, and the price was right, so they were soon installed in the Cornish House.

By December 30, we were able to move out of Anne and Randy's house directly into the house that would be our home for . . . well, we didn't know how long we'd be there. But we were comforted to know we could all be together.

We were relieved to see that the Duggar damage inflicted on Anne and Randy's beautiful home was minor: one broken bar stool and a slightly dented lamp. We gave the house a good cleaning and offered to pay for the damaged items, but Anne and Randy wouldn't hear of it. "We're in the furniture business," Randy said. "It's not a big deal."

CONCERN AND CELEBRATION

It would be impossible to recount here all the joyful ups and terrifying downs we endured with Josie's health during the seven-plus months we were in Little Rock with her. There were many days when her health was so fragile it seemed unlikely she would survive. Then Dr. Arrington and his medical team would try something new or something different, and by God's grace we would get through that difficulty and move on to the next challenge.

As the days rolled along, our faith and our steady belief that God was in control were both enhanced. Josie's health remained precarious, but amazing, everyday things happened in our family life that made us realize God was using our situation to show us His mighty power and His will for us. We believed He could instantly heal Josie of all her health issues, but instead He was showing us that He had a bigger plan for her life . . . and ours.

The news about Josie's premature birth and related health problems had spread quickly. Each time we were interviewed, whether it was by the *Today Show* team or *People* magazine or some other national media outlet, we had a new opportunity to publicly thank others for their prayers and to share our belief that each child is a blessing from God.

We certainly learned a lot about preemies through our long experience, and our daily schedule constantly changed to adapt to Josie's situation. When she was first born, we longed to hold and caress her but learned that preemies cannot tolerate any more than absolutely essential touching during their early days. Josie was due March 18 but was born December 10, so the natural progression would have been for her to still be inside Michelle for more than three more months. During those three additional months in the womb she would have developed the outer layer of skin that would have been very receptive to touching when she arrived on her due date. But without that layer, touching could induce distress, causing her heart rate to soar and her oxygen level to drop drastically.

So at first, while she was receiving nourishment through a feeding tube, she remained in an enclosed, temperature- and humidity-controlled Isolette with only the doctors or nurses touching her through flexible ports whenever essential attention was needed. For us, visiting her meant standing at her bedside, usually with our hands simply resting on top of the Isolette as we talked to her, prayed for her, or sang to her. As many times as she must have heard her mama sing "The Blessing Song," we expect her to burst forth singing it herself as soon as she learns how to talk! Sometimes we were allowed to put our clean hands through the ports and simply let them hover over her, without touching, but that was as close as we got for the first forty days—with a few exceptions.

I (Michelle) had gotten to touch her left hand with one finger as she was being wheeled from the delivery room to the NICU. Three days later, while we were still at UAMS, Jim Bob rolled me into Josie's NICU room in a wheelchair late one night. It was probably about the third time I'd seen her; I hadn't been able to visit the NICU more than that because I was still recovering from the C-section incision and because my blood pressure remained high and a constant headache all but incapacitated me.

But that night I managed to stand up and rest my hands on the incubator, praying over Josie and talking to her. In the early days of their lives, micro-preemies have one-on-one nurse staffing, and the nurse that night, so kind and thoughtful (as all of them were!), said, "Would you like to touch her?"

I was amazed; the "no-stimuli" order had been thoroughly explained to us. "Oh!" I exclaimed. "I can touch her?"

She said, "I'll let you. But you have to do it exactly as I tell you."

She said I couldn't stroke her. "Just lay your hand on her real lightly."

Josie was scrunched up in the fetal position, and I gently cupped one hand around her little diapered bottom and her feet and the other over her head. It was the sweetest moment, and I was grateful that the monitors showed that her heart rate did not go up and her oxygen level stayed level. Another blessing! Afterward I cried softly as I laid my hands on top of Josie's Isolette again and thanked God for her precious little life!

My own recovery was slower than we hoped. It took several weeks for my blood pressure to return to normal and I could stop taking the medication prescribed to control it. Likewise, Josie continued to have problems that refused to be resolved. We were very fortunate that she didn't have many of the vision, hearing, lung, brain, and heart problems that are common to preemies, but she continually suffered with constipation and other digestive issues that bloated her little tummy and caused obvious and serious distress. Almost all babies, especially preemies, suffer bouts of reflux, but Josie's symptoms went far beyond that problem.

Still, each problem in the digestive area that caused us concern seemed to come with progress somewhere else that gave us reason to celebrate.

FEEDING-TIME FEARS

At first, visiting Josie meant simply standing by her bedside and talking with Dr. Arrington and her nurses. As time passed, we were able to touch her more frequently, but all her care was done by the nurses. Initially she was fed through a feeding tube inserted directly into her intestines, bypassing her stomach. Then the tube was redirected to her stomach to see if it could function as it should.

Although the constipation, bloating, and similar issues continued to be a problem—and although most of the time we sensed that Josie simply didn't feel good—for the most part, she steadily gained weight. So her digestive system *was* working; it just wasn't working the way it should.

Gradually, Josie's third layer of skin developed, and her overall condition improved to the point that we got to hold her regularly. What a thrill it was the first time I (Michelle) got to hold her, skin to skin! Another fountain of tears flowed down my cheeks; I was so happy to get to do what I'd almost always gotten to do immediately after giving birth.

Then, more joy came when Doc A said one of Josie's scheduled tube feedings could be replaced by a bottle feeding. She would be given the same breast milk mixed with fortifiers that was being supplied through the feeding tube every three hours or so around the clock. We knew that was a big step toward the longed-for day when I could hold Josie in my arms and breast-feed her as I'd done with all our other children.

But we quickly learned that bottle-feeding a preemie is no

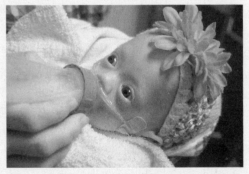

We rejoiced when Josie was well enough to be bottle-fed.

simple matter! The nurses handled that job while an occupational therapist began training me exactly how it had to be done—a process that went against some of my strongest mothering instincts.

Josie was too small and weak to cough effectively when even a drop of liquid ended up in her bronchial tubes, let alone if she choked on a big gulp of breast milk. During feedings she had to be held in the exact position necessary to keep the milk from going directly into the back of her throat, and the angle of the bottle had to be adjusted so that, at first, when she clamped down on the nipple and started hungrily sucking, she didn't get more than she could easily handle.

So instead of cradling her on her back in the crook of my left arm and holding the bottle with my right hand, as I might do when bottle-feeding a normal baby, Josie needed to lie out in front of me, turned perpendicular to my body so that I could ease her onto her side rather than her back. That would put the milk in her mouth rather than sending it immediately into her throat.

When you think about it, the occupational therapist said, the natural position for a baby to breast-feed isn't on her back but on her side, turned toward her mother's breast. But when most of us bottle-feed a baby, we end up holding the baby on its back and offering the bottle at whatever angle seems to work. Normal babies are usually able to cope with that position—although side lying would be easier for them, too, when they're being bottle-fed.

She taught me to bottle-feed Josie by positioning her perpendicular to my body on a "mom pillow," my left hand supporting her head and her neck. My right hand held the bottle, with my ring finger under her chin to help her keep it in the right position for nursing.

Another concern was Josie's epiglottis, the little flap at the back of the throat that normally seals off the bronchial tubes whenever we swallow. The tube that had been in Josie's throat for several weeks after she was born kept the epiglottis from doing its job—and also from developing as it should. Even after a preemie's feeding tube is removed, the epiglottis may fail to work; it just hasn't become strong enough to do its job. And the hard fact is, it may never get to that point.

Because of that problem, preemies need to lie on an incline—their heads elevated when they're being held or on a mattress-like wedge in their beds—so that the head is not lower than the feet.

Although it was a bit nerve-racking to remember all these instructions, the positioning of the baby wasn't hard to understand. The thing that *was* difficult for me, because it was such a contrast to what moms normally do, was holding the bottle at a lower angle so that when Josie first started sucking, *she got air instead of milk!*

When Cathy, the occupational therapist, showed me that position the first time, I blurted out, "Oh, that's going to cause her to have so much gas on her stomach!"

Cathy answered, "Yes, but that's okay because it's better for her to have gas on her tummy and be able to take food by mouth than to have to be fed through a tube."

So I started each bottle-feeding by watching carefully to make sure nothing was in the nipple, no milk at all, just air. When Josie would latch on to the nipple at the very beginning she was usually very anxious to eat, so if the nipple was full of milk she would suck too hard and get too much milk at once, a situation that could easily choke her.

She had to learn to pace herself, and she also had to learn the complicated process (for a preemie, at least) of sucking, swallowing, and breathing sequentially, not all at once. And I had to learn the pacing process as well, first giving her an empty nipple and then introducing a little bit of milk at a time until she'd developed her rhythm.

I saw how important the pacing could be when Doc A said I could try a session of "non-nutritive" breast-feeding to help Josie learn to adapt to nursing. I couldn't do all her feedings that way because when you're breast-feeding an infant, you can't regulate the flow of milk the baby's getting as I was learning to do through the pacing of the bottle-feedings. Also, the ACH lab had tested my breast milk and found it to contain twenty calories per ounce, but Josie would do best if she could get more calories than that. So throughout the day I delivered my pumped breast milk to the hospital lab, and they added the fortifiers that brought it up to twenty-six calories. That way, as Dr. Arrington said, we would "put a little meat on her bones" faster.

To begin the nonnutritive breast-feeding, I followed the nurses' directions and spent a long time in the hospital's "pumping room," emptying my supply of milk. Then I took little Josie in my arms and, wearing a nipple shield that mimicked what she was used to, I let her see what breast-feeding was all about.

She latched on immediately—what a smart little girl! But then, my body automatically "let down" in response to her sucking. And despite the time I'd spent in the pumping room, I still had enough milk to give Josie a huge mouthful!

She choked, and her mama panicked!

She didn't have the strength to cough, but she squirmed, struggled, gagged, and grimaced. Her heart rate dropped, and her oxygen level fell. Alarms went off on her monitors, and I was alarmed too!

However, with her trained eyes, the nurse on duty could see that, except for coughing, Josie was doing everything she was supposed to do to recover; she just needed a little help. The nurse provided a little suction and then listened to her lungs.

"It sounds like she still has just a bit in one lung, but it should be fine," she said. "It's natural for babies to get a drop or two of breast milk in their lungs once in a while, and since breast milk contains natural antibodies it usually doesn't cause a bacterial infection."

Once again I sent up a flare-prayer of gratitude, so thankful that Josie hadn't choked during a bottle-feeding when she would have gotten not only breast milk but the fortifiers in it that could have caused an infection.

There was another important requirement that added to the stress of feeding Josie: the bottle provided only part of the nourishment she needed in each feeding. The fifteen milliliters Doc A ordered for her to be fed by bottle had to be given successfully in fifteen minutes, because it would be immediately followed by the remainder of the feeding, given through the feeding tube. That way she got adequate round-the-clock nourishment with the fewest calories burned.

Feeding Josie was a wonderful experience—and also a stressful one. I rejoiced at getting to hold her in my arms, lift her onto my shoulder to burp her, and then cuddle her for a moment or two when we were finished. But it was also frightening. Thinking that I could cause her to have major problems if I made a mistake in how I held her, or in how I held the bottle, feeding time was a high-pressure situation for me. Usually by the time I diapered her and put her back in the Isolette, I was sweating and exhausted—but thankful that with each feeding we were one step closer to taking Josie home.

Riding the Roller Coaster

During the six long months Josie was a patient at Children's we learned firsthand what the doctors meant when they told us that the first few months of a preemie's life is a roller coaster of highs and lows. "You'll have days when everything's fine, and then something will happen and she'll go from stable to critical in the blink of an eye," one of them said. "That's just the way it is with a preemie."

In the faces of the other families we met on the elevator or elsewhere in the hospital, we saw the weariness that came from riding that emotional roller coaster. At first, we asked how other families' babies were doing, and many would say, "Oh, our daughter is doing great; the doctor said we might get to go home next week!"

But then we met parents who told us, "Our son isn't doing well. Now they're telling us there's nothing else they can do, and he has less than twenty-four hours to live."

After that, we were almost afraid to ask, but often we could tell by their faces whether their child was doing great—or not so great. The talented medical personnel at children's hospitals all around the world save thousands of babies every day. These hospitals are places where miracles seem to happen on a regular basis. But some babies simply don't make it. Three babies in Josie's six-infant micro-preemie "pod" in the NICU died during our stay there. We grieved with those parents—because we knew that almost any day could also be Josie's last.

6

• Difficult Priorities •

The LORD is my light and my salvation; whom shall I fear?
The LORD is the strength of my life; of whom shall I be afraid?
—Psalm 27:1

At first Josie got just one bottle feeding a day, but gradually, over the next few weeks, she progressed to having more and more bottle feedings that supplemented the every-three-hour tube feedings. Then she was weaned off the tube feedings one by one until she was fed totally by bottle. My (Michelle's) goal was to be there for every feeding possible, and when she progressed to being totally bottle fed, each feeding took from thirty to sixty minutes because it had to be done so carefully. In between feedings I spent time in the lactation room, pumping breast milk to hand off to the lab and also to store in our freezer back at the house so that when Josie came home, we would have plenty on hand.

During the last two months or so of Josie's hospital stay, I was spending most of my awake time at the hospital; I tried to get there for Josie's 9 a.m. feeding and often stayed to do the 11 p.m. feeding at night. My life revolved around Josie's schedule.

Jim Bob and our older girls managed the rest of our family back at the Little Rock house, and for most of them life went on as usual. Jim Bob was constantly finding new adventures for the kids to enjoy. Of course, he made many daily visits to the hospital. The older girls also came to help, but for the longest time I didn't trust Josie's feedings to anyone other than the nurses. Gradually, as they increased in volume, they also increased in time between feedings, following Doc A's orders, so I could slip back to the house for short visits during the day. I was thankful we lived so close to the hospital, but overall, it was a heartbreaking situation for me. Inevitably whenever I left the house during the day to go back to the hospital, a little one cried, seeing me go. I longed for the day our whole family could be together again under one roof.

Those were difficult days, exhausting physically and emotionally. Many nights I would leave the hospital after midnight to slip into our dark, still house. I would quietly climb the stairs to our bedroom, with each step asking God for strength to take the next one. All around me, my family slept peacefully, and I was grateful to know they were near and that they were being loved and cared for by Jim Bob and the older children while I was away. I was also thankful for dear friends, old and new, who stepped forward to help. They prepared and delivered meals, and shared fellowship, words of encouragement, and prayers for our family.

My being at the hospital most of the day, away from those precious little hearts and minds, was not ideal. But we agreed that my priority at that stage had to be Josie. So when daylight came, I would enjoy a little time with my family and then head off to the hospital again for Josie's morning feeding.

It was a thrill for us when Josie grew strong enough that we could hold her outside of the Isolette.

Many friends asked how I could maintain such a schedule, and I could only credit God's goodness and grace. My answer was always to cite 2 Corinthians 12:9, the scripture I had claimed long ago as my life verse: "My grace is sufficient for thee: for my strength is made perfect in weakness. Most gladly therefore will I rather glory in my infirmities, that the power of Christ may rest upon me."

Many times I seemed to get through the day not just hour by hour but minute by minute, constantly thanking God for the wonderful gift He had given us in our family and in our newest baby, and asking Him to hold us up when weakness threatened to pull us down in the face of otherwise overwhelming challenges.

One Step Forward, Two Steps Back

After all those long days and nights in the hospital, and all those trips back and forth to the hospital, April 6, 2010, was an extremely happy day for the Duggars. It was the day Josie, weighing a whopping four and a half pounds, left the hospital for home, nearly four months after her December 10 birthday. Watching us drive away with her, Dr. Arrington told a *People* magazine writer, "This is the first time Josie has seen sunlight."

The kids had decorated the Little Rock house to welcome Josie into her family, and we'd made careful preparations in our upstairs bedroom to create a special space for all the monitors and equipment that came with her, including a small oxygen tank. While Josie was well enough to come home, her health was still precarious. She continued to have digestive issues. We also knew that eventually, when she reached a certain weight, she would return to Children's for hernia-repair surgery; but for now, she was strong enough to go home, and we were thrilled to make that happen.

As we drove up to the Cornish House, an enthusiastic beehive of children came swarming out the door and down the driveway, eager to greet the little sister that many of them hadn't seen since the day shortly

LAYERED SALAD

Another great recipe from Michelle's sister, Pam Peters. (Big sisters can have such great influence on our lives!) This salad is not only delicious; it's also pretty.

First layer:
½ head lettuce, shredded
6 boiled eggs, chopped
½ pound cooked bacon, crumbled (we use turkey bacon)
Second layer:
½ head lettuce, shredded
1 (15-ounce) can peas, drained
1 small onion, chopped
Third layer:
2 cups real* mayonnaise
1 (16-ounce) container (2 cups) sour cream
2 cups shredded cheddar cheese

Spread layers in a 9 x 13 pan; top with the cheddar cheese. Chill in fridge at least 2 hours.

* Be sure to use real mayonnaise or you'll miss out on the amazing flavor!

after her birth, when they'd been allowed to walk by her incubator.

Everyone was given a chance to say hello before we took Josie upstairs, where Mama, Daddy, and Josie would be bunking in the same bedroom. We attached the monitors and oxygen and closed the bedroom door. Michelle would be staying with Josie at all times. We agreed that I (Jim Bob) and/or one or two of the older girls would always be home with her and Josie as well in case an emergency arose.

We expected to keep Josie in the Cornish House another two to three weeks, staying close to the hospital in case problems developed. Then, finally and joyfully, we would move out of our Little Rock house and take her home to Springdale.

As soon as Josie's nursery area was set up in our bedroom and she was sleeping peacefully after her first at-home bottle feeding, I had to load up nine of the middle kids and drive back to Springdale. The children were scheduled to complete some testing there with our homeschool group, and I was getting reports from Grandma Duggar and others that the grass was growing like crazy and other maintenance and repairs were needed. John-David and Joseph had spent quite a bit of time tending to things back in Springdale while we were in Little Rock, but there was simply more to do than they could keep up with.

Sometimes cleaning and decorating (or undecorating) our Tontitown house requires using the scissor lift to reach the highest cobwebs or to hang or retrieve the highest decorations.

So I left Michelle and Josie at the Cornish house with Jill, Jessa, and Jinger. Then Jana and I, along with the "middle" Duggar kids, headed back home to Springdale feeling confident that we had come through a fiery test and that soon we'd be making this same trip with all of our family together, heading home for good.

I was wrong.

EMERGENCY AT 2:00 A.M.

Josie made it through the first day and night in fairly good shape, but I (Michelle) could tell that as time passed she was suffering increasing discomfort. It was the constipation problem flaring up again. With each passing hour, Josie's tummy seemed to become more distended and tight, and although she would sometimes cry with hunger, she just didn't seem interested in her bottle.

When Jill and I got up for her 2 a.m. feeding, she was fussy but refused the bottle. I knew immediately that something was terribly wrong. I was watching the monitors when her heart rate slowed and her oxygen dropped low enough to make the alarms go off. And her temperature was falling. I hurriedly pressed her to me, skin to skin, and covered both of us with blankets, trying to warm her up, but her breathing was slow and shallow, and she was in obvious distress.

I honestly thought we might lose her. "Jill, call 911!" I said.

Jill's voice trembled as she relayed to the dispatcher the vital signs and other information I was giving her, and within moments, it seemed, the ambulance and paramedics were in front of our house. The gate across the driveway had to be unlocked—a complication of city living—and I carried Josie outside and climbed with her into the back of the ambulance.

A few minutes later we were back at our home away from home, Arkansas Children's Hospital. And there we would stay for nearly two more months.

AMAZING ANSWER TO AN AGONIZING MYSTERY

"Never trust a preemie," Dr. Arrington had told us, and that advice proved valid again and again during Josie's first six months. Back in the hospital, Josie was a miserable little girl for a while, and she had a frightened, worried mama. Finally, the latest round of constipation was resolved, but chronic digestive issues continued.

During the next six weeks, a wide array of tests were performed to determine why Josie's digestive system was working so poorly. Normally you can't keep a baby from pooping on her own. But Josie had to have regular enemas and rectal stimulation to have bowel movements.

As the tests continued, we held our breath, praying for a good outcome. Possibilities included cystic fibrosis and something called Hirschsprung's disease, a congenital condition that causes blockages in the lower intestine and requires surgical treatment. We thanked God, weak with relief, when both test results were negative. But still her problems persisted, and the team continued down the list of possibilities, working from most likely to least likely, trying to find what was making Josie so miserable. Her tummy was obviously hurting; she seemed to be constantly bloated despite having enemas every six hours, and she just wasn't thriving like a six-month-old baby should.

We knew, because the medical team had told us, that Josie's stomach and one part of her intestine were not "tacked down" as they should be, and those body parts had a tendency to shift around abnormally. Certainly that situation could cause problems but rarely as severe as those occurring in Josie.

The tests continued. When Josie was checked for allergies, all tests came back negative.

Finally, when all the obvious culprits had been ruled out—when the medical team had gone down the list, from the most likely to least likely possible causes of Josie's problems—the doctors decided to take Josie off breast milk temporarily and put her on a lactose-free predigested protein formula, a product called Pregestimil.

Overnight, Josie became a different baby.

Soon her belly shrank back to normal size, she smiled and gurgled and cooed, and she even produced a couple of dirty diapers on her own without the help of an enema.

All these months I had been vigorously expressing milk day and night, knowing that breast milk is the very best thing any newborn can have. The medical team was doing everything under the sun to enable Josie to take increasingly larger feedings so she could grow and thrive. All that time we earnestly worked our hearts out to feed her "mommy's milk," not realizing that the dairy products that were coming through my milk were causing her intestines to stay inflamed.

Finally—*finally!*—we all realized that Josie Duggar had a rare condition for someone her age: lactose intolerance—one of a handful of babies born each year who is unable to digest lactose in milk.

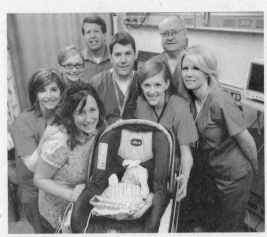

We are so grateful to Dr. Arrington and all of the other health-care professionals who worked to keep Josie alive!

PART 2

• Shaping Hearts and Minds •

But seek ye first the kingdom of God,
and his righteousness;
and all these things shall be added unto you.

—Matthew 6:33

7

• Living Under the Microscope •

Let your light so shine before men,
that they may see your good works,
and glorify your Father which is in heaven.
—Matthew 5:16

Josie was again released from the hospital June 3, 2010; her second homecoming was a much quieter event than her first. In fact, Michelle and her longtime friend Cindy Pascoe brought Josie home to an empty Little Rock house.

It was a good thing the rest of the family was on a trip when Josie was released—because several of them had chicken pox!

Jim Bob had taken everyone, including Josh, Anna, and Mackynzie, on a big trip out east. Their first stop was one of the annual home-school-related events we enjoy, the Nashville conference sponsored by the Advanced Training Institute (ATI).

During one of our family's trips out east, the children got to perform at Pigeon Forge.

Our big forty-five-foot-long bus (bought used a few years ago from a Port Huron, Michigan, hockey team) was just pulling into the Nashville conference's campground June 1 when five-year-old Johannah asked Jill to scratch her itchy back. Jill lifted Johannah's shirt to see what the itch was all about and said, "Uh-oh."

PERFECT TIMING

I (Michelle) was in the NICU with Josie and Dr. Arrington, preparing for Josie's planned release a couple of days later, when Jill's photo of Johannah's back came in to my cell phone. I showed Dr. A the photo and said, "Guess what this is!"

His eyes widened when he recognized what he was seeing. "Where are they?" he asked.

"Well, they're not here in Little Rock," I answered.

"That's good!" he said. "It's crucial that Josie *not* be exposed!"

Josie and I settled into the quiet Cornish House to be close to the hospital and also to wait out the chicken pox episode. The rest of the family continued their trip out east. By the time the bus arrived back home in Springdale two weeks later, eleven more Duggars, all of the youngest ones, had broken out.

The older children had already had the infection years earlier. Two weeks after baby Jinger was born in December 1993, when we had five other children all under the age of five—Josh, John-David, Jana, Jill, and Jessa—they all came down with chicken pox. In the years since then, the rest of them had not gotten it.

We were glad the infection swept the family when it did. It was better that everyone got it all at once rather than two now, three a week later, and on and on until the thing had run its course. That situation could have delayed Josie's arrival back home in Springdale a month or more. Although it was really hard for Jim Bob, Grandma Duggar, and the older children to cope with twelve young "patients" at once, especially while Mama was far away and unable to help, it all worked out in the end to be perfect timing.

Some other family events and commitments kept us scattered for another week or so after the chicken pox cleared up. But on June 21, 2010—just after Josie's six-month birthday—*all* the Duggars were together again in our Springdale house for the first time since our ordeal began on December 4, 2009.

What a wonderful day that was!

A FOUNDATION OF FAITH

The health-related challenges we've recently endured—my life-and-death struggle with preeclampsia, plus an agonizing gallbladder attack

> **WHAT'S IN *YOUR* KITCHEN?**
>
> Whatever you buy or have in your home to eat is what will be consumed! So be careful what you bring home. We try to have veggies and fruits for snacking. Little ones whose tummies are the size of their fists need to graze throughout the day. At times they will eat more than others, like during growth spurts. Our goal is to encourage eating veggies and fruits, low-fat proteins, and whole grains. Steamed instead of boiled and baked instead of fried.
>
> The mealtime rule is you have to try one bite, and then if possible another bite. When dishing out their portions, we remember the size of their tummies! One or two tablespoons is a start, and if they take a bite of each thing on their plate, then they may ask for seconds of their favorite dish.

leading to surgery in late summer 2010; our premature baby's fight for survival; the family chicken-pox epidemic—drew us closer to God and each other more than ever before. We fervently love God and are grateful to Him for getting us through these experiences. If it had been left up to us, we wouldn't have chosen some of the trials we've been through. But looking back, we can see how God worked "all things" for our good.

I (Michelle) certainly wouldn't have chosen to experience the agony and pain of preeclampsia, but on this side of the situation, I see how my own suffering helped me understand more personally the tremendous suffering Jesus went through when he died an agonizing death through crucifixion. He chose to endure that terrible death not as punishment for His own sin—He had none—but as punishment for *our* otherwise unforgivable mistakes.

And we could see how Josie's premature birth and health problems—again, things no one would have chosen—had worked for good, not only in making us rely more determinedly on our faith to bring our family through a fiery test but also in helping us become more compassionate and understanding, in a more personal way, of the problems other families are enduring.

For example, soon after Josie was born, a Christian friend in New Jersey, Hudson, called to remind us how God had worked his family's difficulty for good when one of their nine biological children, Nathaniel, was born with spina bifida.

Their experience, which began in the NICU and continued down through the years, opened their eyes to what it's like to grow up with a disability. Then they realized that, as hard as it is to have a disability in America, it's even worse in other parts of the world. After they learned how to take care of Nathaniel, Hudson and his wife, Patti, thought, *Maybe God allowed us to learn all these new skills so we could adopt other children with spina bifida.*

The younger children, including two-year-old Jennifer, loved creating artwork to show Mama while she was away from them tending to Josie.

To date, God has blessed their family with a total of twenty-one children, including twelve adopted from the United States, Ethiopia, Guatemala, and China. Many of their adopted children have special needs.

During his call after Josie was born, Hudson shared some inspiring words that had helped his family when Nathaniel was born. "God's will is what we would choose if we knew all the facts," he said. His family's decision has led to exhausting work, desperate prayers, financial challenges—and a more rewarding and fulfilled life than they ever dreamed possible.

When Josie was born prematurely, we could have thought God made a mistake. We could have become fearful, bitter, or angry. Instead we deliberately *chose* to allow that life storm to draw us closer to God, trusting His promise to bring good out of every situation.

Wisdom is looking at life from God's perspective. We know that God doesn't make mistakes. He created Josie, He loves her even more than we do, and He knows what He's doing. These facts are affirmed for us when we consider that little Josie has had a big impact on a lot of hearts and lives. We have had literally thousands of letters and e-mails from people all over the world who've said they are praying for Josie.

One even wrote to say,

> *Michelle, Jim Bob, and family,*
> *I have been watching your show the past few months and have really enjoyed getting to know your family. I am not a religious person at all and I do not attend any church. But I wanted you to know, when I saw tiny Josie be born so early, I got down on my knees in front of my TV and prayed for her.*

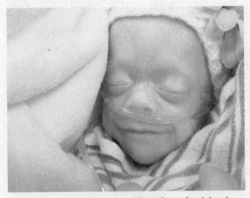

Josie was born at the outward boundary of viability, but her sweet personality was evident right from the beginning; she was obviously a little girl who loved to smile.

Josie was born at about the age of viability. If she had been much younger, she probably would not have made it. We were able to watch the end of her second trimester and her whole third trimester *outside* the womb. Our prayer is that the world will see that each baby, even the tiniest ones like Josie, are precious creations of God.

WHY NINETEEN CHILDREN?

Our faith is an essential part of our family's life; it's the foundation—the *why*—of everything we do. It's why we have a huge family. We spelled out the details in our first book, *The Duggars: 20 and Counting!* But here's the short version:

When we got married on July 21, 1984, we decided to plan our family size ourselves. We thought that eventually we might want one to three children. Michelle took birth control pills for three years before we decided we were ready to become parents. After our first child, Josh, was born in March 1988, we again used oral contraceptives, thinking we would decide the spacing of our children ourselves.

Despite being on the pill, Michelle got pregnant—and then suffered a miscarriage (we found out later that sometimes the pill will allow conception but then might cause a miscarriage).[1] We were devastated.

At that point we read in Scripture that children are a blessing from the Lord and a gift from Him. We asked God to forgive us for taking matters into our own hands and to give us a love for children like His love for them. We committed to letting Him decide how many children we would have and when they would be born. We stopped using birth control, not knowing after the miscarriage whether Michelle would be able to get pregnant again or if she could carry another child to term. God

After Michelle suffered a miscarriage in the late 1980s, we were blessed with twins: John-David and Jana, who turned twenty-one this year.

answered that question a couple of months later when she became pregnant—with twins!

Jana and John-David were born in January 1990, and a new baby Duggar has arrived, on average, about every eighteen months since then (our second set of twins, Jedediah and Jeremiah, were born in December 1998).

We had thought that having our first child, Joshua, was a big life change. When Jana and John-David were born, life *really* got exciting. Then came Jill, Jessa, Jinger, and Joseph. By that time we wondered if we could handle any more children. The seven we had were a great blessing, but our hands were full. We were way outnumbered!

Strangers would come up to us, see all the kids, and say, "Don't you know what causes this?" Friends and family members thought we were crazy to spend our lives having and taking care of all of those children. Maybe they thought they could save us from ourselves by making comments. We don't get upset or react to negative comments because we had that same mind-set ourselves before God changed our hearts about the value of children.

Admittedly, we often felt overwhelmed, but we had given this area of our life to God, and in faith we kept going. We are so thankful we didn't stop, because then we had Josiah and Joy-Anna. Then, after the birth of our tenth and eleventh children, twins Jedidiah and Jeremiah, some of the very people who had been so critical started complimenting and encouraging us as though we were having our first child. We didn't know if they gave up and decided they just weren't going to be able to change our minds, or if they finally understood that we consider each child a blessing from God and saw that our older children were turning out okay!

We dedicated ourselves to training our children to love God and serve others. Now, as we look into the precious faces of our children, we often think about how different our lives would have been if we didn't have each one of them. We are thankful for each child, and each one is grateful to be here.

STEPPING OUT IN FAITH

We happily welcomed each addition into our family and made changes in our lives that made it possible for us to support them and live debt free while also operating a home-based real estate business. That process is also explained in our first book, and we're still living and enjoying that family-focused lifestyle today.

As our family grew, so did our faith. As time passed, we would see again and again how God worked every setback into a blessing. Disappointments and challenges continue to happen in our lives, but we stopped asking God *Why?* several years ago, when one of the most vivid examples of Romans 8:28 unfolded for us.

In 1997, a totally unexpected, almost ridiculous idea occurred to me (Jim Bob): I felt God put on my heart the idea that I should run for a seat in the Arkansas legislature. It was a ridiculous idea because no one in my family had ever had any political aspirations or connections, and I was terrified by public speaking. Michelle was as surprised as I was when I told her about the idea.

Here's how it came about: We had a child who underwent minor corrective surgery at Arkansas Children's Hospital (our introduction to ACH several years before Josie's arrival). The day before a follow-up appointment in Little Rock, I heard on a Christian radio station that some Christians in the Arkansas legislature were planning a rally the next day to try to ban partial-birth abortion in our state. Michelle and I decided we would swing by the rally after the doctor's appointment.

More than two thousand people showed up in front of the capitol, begging the senators and representatives to pass this ban. Instead, they voted it down. I didn't hear any audible voices or see any lightning bolts from heaven that day, but I felt God speaking to my heart, telling me to run for state representative. My only credentials were that I could vote the right way on life-and-death issues, and I could probably encourage others to vote the right way.

By the time my campaign actually began, we had nine children and

Michelle became pregnant with twins. We worked hard, bringing our conservative Republican message to the voters and knocking on doors all over our area, almost always with a child or two accompanying us.

God confirmed His direction to me, and beginning in January 1999 I served two, two-year terms in the legislature. This experience took me completely out of my comfort zone, but repeatedly we saw God's leading as several important bills were passed and a lot of bad legislation was stopped. It was an honor to serve the people in our community by representing them at the capital.

During my (Jim Bob's) 2002 campaign for the US Senate,
we dressed all the children in red and traveled around the state in our motor home.

Then, just as God had put it in my heart to run for state representative, one Saturday morning He impressed on me to run for the US Senate. I have learned when God speaks to me with His still, small voice and impresses on my heart to do something, it's very important to obey first and understand why later.

I was running against an incumbent and had no party support, but we believed it was what God wanted me to do. Again the whole family campaigned together during the primary. We rode in parades, knocked on doors, and with many friends volunteering we had campaign rallies and barbecues all over the state.

We had just sold a piece of property, and Michelle and I felt led to spend $110,000 of it on the race, even though that was a drop in the bucket compared with the $2 million my opponent spent. By then we had thirteen children, and when Election Day rolled around, we took the whole family with us to vote, showing our kids the heart of what it means to live in a democracy. Trying to get all the kids in and out of the cramped voting area, we were barely aware of an AP photographer at the polling place who took our picture that day.

I received 22 percent of the votes and lost the primary, but we had peace. We had worked hard and been diligent in doing what God had asked us to do. We didn't understand *why* He'd asked this of us and then let us lose, but we knew we didn't have to understand. We had put our lives in His hands and we trusted His plan.

That night, we sat down as a family and talked about what had happened. We thanked God for all the miracles we had seen, all the special people we had met, and even for the outcome of the race, know- ing it was His will. Then we prayed, "God, we're ready for our next assignment!"

WHY WE DON'T ASK *WHY?*

The fact is, sometimes God asks us to do something we don't want to do. We try to teach our children this concept about life's choices from the time they are young. When we ask them to do something, they always have a choice. They can choose to obey and do what is right. Or they can choose not to obey and face the consequences.

As adults, we have the same choice when we feel God directing us. We can trust that God knows what is best and do what He's asking us to do. Or we can choose what *we* want to do—and face the consequences.

God will never ask us to do something that violates the principles found in His Word. But He will stretch our faith, and He will bring situations into our lives that test our relationship with Him. Following His guidance, I had run for the Senate—and lost. But soon we saw how obeying Him had led us to that position where we could share our faith from a much bigger platform—bigger, in fact, than we could ever have imagined.

The photograph taken on Election Day as we were walking into the polling place with our big family around us appeared the next day in *The New York Times* with a caption identifying me as the Arkansas father of thirteen who had run for US Senate and lost.

We didn't even know the picture had been published—we don't normally read *The New York Times*. A few days later, a New York–based freelance writer called, saying she'd seen the photo and wondered if we'd be willing to let her write our story for a national magazine.

We talked about it, prayed about it, sought counsel about it, and agreed. The story ran in *Parents* magazine, where it was noticed by Eileen O'Neill, CEO of the Discovery Health Channel. She asked Bill Hayes, with Advanced Medical Productions, a film-production company, to contact us. She wanted to know if we would be willing to do a documentary about our family to be broadcast on the Discovery Health Channel.

Because our family almost never watches broadcast TV, and we don't have cable, we'd never heard of Discovery Health. Again we prayed and sought counsel about this request, and we came to believe the documentary could be an opportunity to share with the world that children are a blessing from God. We agreed to the project as long as they agreed that our faith would not be edited out. Our faith is the core of our lives, we said. If you leave that out, you're not telling the whole story.

They agreed. When the documentary aired in 2004, it had the most viewers of any show the network had broadcast up to that point.

A few documentaries later, the channel's parent company asked us to do a weekly reality series (another thing we'd never heard of). That's the show that now airs regularly on TLC, attracting an average of one to one and a half million viewers on TLC each week.

Given the experience we've had, is there any doubt why we believe so fervently that God works *all* things for good? As we have obeyed and trusted Him, the Christian life has become an exciting adventure for us. Instead of focusing on the difficulties that sometimes happen and wondering *why* they've happened, we try to maintain a positive focus and a curious attitude, watching eagerly for the miraculous way God is going to use each temporary setback to do something wonderful.

Scott Enlow and Sean Overbeeke film a promo shoot for TLC.

8

Opportunities to Reach Out to Others

The fruit of the righteous is a tree of life,
and he that winneth souls is wise.
—Proverbs 11:30

Last year we were visiting the Bates family, our friends in Tennessee, and I (Michelle) had loaded several of the kids in our Suburban to pick up some take-out snacks from a fast food restaurant. I pulled up to the drive-through speaker and read off the items we wanted. The order taker repeated the list back to me and then asked, "Will that be all, Mrs. Duggar?"

I thought surely I'd misunderstood her, but when I pulled ahead to the pickup window I found a little crowd of curious faces peering out at us. "I *told* you it was her!" one of the uniformed girls squealed to her coworkers.

I was dumbfounded! It's one thing to be recognized when we go out in Springdale, but to have my *voice* recognized at a drive-through a thousand miles from home? Amazing! (Of course it could also have been the umpteen sandwiches I was ordering.)

YOU LOOK FAMILIAR

Our family's TV series, *19 Kids and Counting!* is now broadcast on the Learning Channel (TLC), and sometimes a series of our shows will be replayed over and over for several hours a day. That has landed our family in a new phase of life as far as public recognition.

It used to be that whenever we went out in public with our children, people would say things like, "You've sure got a lot of children. Are you a school group or something?"

In the next phase, which came after the initial documentaries about our family had aired on television, people would think they'd seen us somewhere before but just couldn't quite remember where. Maybe they would say, "Do you work at Dr. So-and-So's office, by chance? Or have I seen you at the post office?"

Now, it seems just about anywhere we go, people come up and speak to us, and usually they know our names. Some can recite all of our children's names in order. Many people say they know us so well they feel like part of our family. Several have said they take notes as they watch our show, gleaning ideas to apply to their own families.

It doesn't matter if it's at a fast food drive-through in Tennessee, driving down the interstate in Florida, stopped at a traffic light in Ohio, or standing on the sidewalk in New York City (where we were

In 2009, Gil and Kelly Bates and their seventeen children visited us during the Arkansas ice storm; then we traveled to Tennessee to help build an addition on their house.

astonished when a police van swooped over to the curb and an officer popped out and asked, "Hey, are you that big family from Arkansas?").

Sometimes people recognize us when there are just a couple of us. One day last year I (Michelle) made a quick trip to the grocery store and invited then-four-year-old Jackson to come along. Pushing the cart down one of the aisles we were stopped by a woman who said, "Oh! It's Michelle Duggar. I watch y'all on TV—and who's this? Why, it's Jackson. Hi, Jackson. How are you?"

We chatted a moment before the woman moved on down the aisle. Jackson, sitting in the seat of the grocery cart, leaned into me and whispered, "Mama, how did she know my name?"

I told him, "Honey, she sees you every week in her living room. She watches our family on television, and she feels like she knows us."

We think of these encounters as ministry opportunities—chances to

Members of the film crew for our TV series, 19 Kids and Counting, *have become like family to us.*

show God's love. Even if we're on a quick shopping trip to the store, we try to take time to visit with those who approach us and encourage them spiritually if possible. Many people have helped *us* along life's way; we're happy to pass on that encouragement. That's what it's all about, encouraging one another and building each other up.

SETTING LIMITS

Even though we love meeting others, we now have to limit our family's interaction with drop-by guests so we don't disrupt our family schedule too much. We've had viewers drop by our house as early as seven in the morning, wanting to meet us. Others have come as late as 10 p.m. wanting to stop in and say hi.

Setting limits has also become necessary because of some rather bizarre situations that have happened. One occurred a few years ago when we received an e-mail from a young lady who lived out of state. She wrote that she loved watching our show and wanted to meet our family. We thought maybe we could encourage her walk with the Lord, so we told her she could come visit us on July 4. She arrived in the morning, and we introduced her to our family, showed her around the house, and took her with us to the Springdale Fourth of July Rodeo parade. Then we returned to the house, where we visited until that evening; we took some pictures together and said good-bye.

A few weeks later we received an e-mail from a viewer who asked, "Did you know your daughter Jinger's diary is for sale on eBay for a hundred thousand dollars?"

I checked the site and asked Jinger, "Are you missing your diary?"

She felt sure it was in her dresser drawer, but when she looked, it was gone. When I showed her the eBay picture, she was shocked to realize someone had stolen it out of her drawer.

Who would have done such a thing?

The eBay listing showed that the diary was being sold from the same town where our recent guest lived. I contacted the young lady and confronted her about stealing Jinger's diary. I told her we still cared about her, and that we forgave her. But I also said that what she had done was wrong and that we would take further steps if the diary wasn't immediately returned.

She admitting stealing it. Then, maybe to ease her conscience, she said she didn't read the diary and that it was the first thing she had ever stolen. We received it back overnight.

The experience provided good lessons to teach the children: first, that we can't trust everybody, and second, that we need to forgive others even before they ask.

TRUTH, DISTORTIONS, AND BELIEFS

One evening I (Jim Bob) invited Michelle to go out on a date. We left the oldest children in charge, and twenty minutes after we'd left, one of them called and said a woman had rung our doorbell, saying she was a writer and wanted to ask a few questions. One of the little ones had answered the door and allowed her to step into the house.

Then she said, "You don't mind if I take a few photos, do you?" as she snapped pictures left and right.

Our oldest daughter, Jana, politely spoke with her and told the woman she would have to talk to her dad. She gave her my cell phone number, and the woman gave Jana her number. By the time the kids called me, the "writer" had already left.

I immediately called the woman. It took several tries to make contact, but I finally reached her. She said she was a reporter for *Star* magazine, and she was in town to do a story about our family.

I told her firmly that I did not appreciate her coming into our house as a reporter without an appointment when Michelle and I weren't there and that she did not have permission to take pictures inside our home.

She said, "We'll see about that." She said she would be in town several days to interview people, including some of our former high school classmates.

Sure enough, the next week one of the top *Star* stories was headlined, "The Great Cover-Up! Exclusive Duggar Family Pictures and Interview." The woman had gone around town talking to people we had gone to high school with as well as others who know us. Then she sensationalized the story. She also

Because of security issues, we've had to install a fence and gate in front of our Tontitown home.

took excerpts from our first book, including a story describing Michelle's teenage years, before she was a Christian, when she would wear a bikini to mow the grass at her family's house. Then, the article said, after Michelle got saved, she started dressing modestly. *That* was "The Great Cover-Up!"

After this incident, we installed a gate at our driveway entrance.

Another tabloid, the *National Enquirer*, also did a Duggar story, but at least that reporter didn't just show up at the door unannounced. She called to tell us the *Enquirer* was doing a story about our family—with or without our input. We decided to talk with her and spent about an hour on the phone with her. The next week we were surprised when the *National Enquirer* printed an excellent article. Maybe our family's story is so unusual just as it is, the *Enquirer* didn't feel the need to change anything!

We find it amusing how many reporters copy and paste information they find about us that someone else has copied and pasted without checking the facts. For instance, even though Wikipedia and some Internet blogs report that we are part of a QuiverFull movement, we are not. We are simply Bible-believing Christians who desire to follow God's Word and apply it to our lives. God says children are a gift and a blessing, and we believe it.

We believe God made women and men with unique qualities, strengths, and weaknesses. Men are not superior to women. As a matter of fact, we believe women are the most special of all of God's creations, and men should treat them like queens. We teach our sons to open doors for ladies and, when possible, to lend a hand when they see a woman carrying something heavy. We teach them to treat women with respect, just as they want others to treat their mom or sisters respectfully.

Sometimes our beliefs get distorted so it seems we're against a lot of things. For example, we're not *against* women getting college degrees, starting their own businesses, or having good-paying jobs. The Proverbs 31 passage in the Bible describes the virtuous woman as one whose number-one priority was to provide excellent care for her family physically and spiritually; she made products that she retailed and she bought real estate on the side. We appreciate the women who serve in wonderful and vital ways. We're grateful for the women doctors and nurses who have helped deliver and care for our children. We are thankful for the conservative women who have served in public office.

Likewise, we're not *against* TV. We simply choose something else for our family. Yes, it *is* kind of ironic that we have a weekly TV show but don't watch broadcast television ourselves. We do turn it on and pull out the rabbit-ears antenna when there's a presidential speech or some other good, history-making event we want our children to see.

This attitude began before we were married, when a doctor friend, Ed Wheat, challenged us not to have a TV our first year of marriage. He sold us on the benefits of concentrating on each other without the TV's distraction. That first year of our marriage in our little nine-hundred-square-foot, fixer-upper house was wonderful; we were living on love.

I (Michelle) fell in love with Jim Bob in part because of his fun-loving sense of humor.

Then, after we fulfilled our pledge, someone gave us a television, and in 1985 we excitedly got cable service. But soon we realized we were both addicted to it, even though we were shocked to see how bad the broadcasting content had gotten in a single year! Gradually we realized that as we sat there staring at whatever show happened to be on, our communication dropped off.

After three weeks, we decided as a couple that television was detrimental to our marriage. We shut off the cable service and got rid of the TV. Looking back, we consider that decision one of the best things we've done for our family—not only because there is so much portrayed on TV we're not comfortable with, but also because it robs us of our most precious resource: *time.*

Now we occasionally gather everyone to watch a rough-edit version of our show on our computer. Or we might watch a live broadcast of the show with my brave sister and brother-in-law, Deanna and Terry, who welcome the whole Duggar clan into their home. But usually by the time the segment is over, the youngest ones have fallen asleep or wandered off to play. It's just not all that interesting to them to see their family relive an ordinary day.

To our children, the best thing about having a television series is "playing" with the film-crew guys, Sean, Scott, Jim, Frank, Bill, and John, who have become like family members to all of us. The little kids love it when they get to carry one of the cameras or ride on sound technician Jim Goodwin's shoulders while he follows someone around with the microphone boom. They especially love getting to record the "teasers" to be used before commercial breaks: "Coming up next on *19 Kids and Counting.*"

The older children have a better grasp of what's going on, and they understand that we consider the show a family ministry. Josh and Anna welcomed the crew to film their engagement and wedding in 2008 because they wanted to encourage other young people to wait for the one God has for them. The cameras were rolling when they had their first kiss, which was also part of the wedding ceremony.

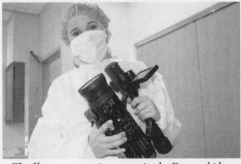

The film crew sometimes recruits the Duggar kids as part of the videography team. Here, Jessa prepares to shoot footage of Jordyn's C-section delivery.

INTERNATIONAL INTERVIEWS

We get broadcast and print inquiries from international reporters who want to know how a couple could raise nineteen kids in today's world. We forward most of the inquiries to our publicist, Shannon Martin, at the Discovery Channel (parent company of TLC) for consideration. Then we prayerfully consider her recommendations, believing that God has opened up this short window of time in our lives when we can share God's love and Bible principles on a wider scale than we could without the media attention.

Not all the things we agree to do are news- or documentary-style stories. One Japanese broadcaster sent several people to our home to film for five full days for a twenty-minute segment on a popular Japanese TV game show! Contestants watched various film clips that depicted a mysterious problem in the Duggar household; then they had to guess what the problem was. As the clips continued, they told the story of our family but also continued to report the problem we were dealing with.

And what was the problem? We sometimes run out of hot water!

We enjoy meeting these international teams, and for the most part, we've been pleased with how they report our family's lifestyle and our beliefs. One positive outcome of Josie's premature birth being announced internationally was the flood of heartwarming prayers and encouragement that poured in from around the world. Hundreds of parents wrote and e-mailed to share their own experiences as NICU veterans. We especially loved the messages that told us about preemies who had overcome severe problems and were now rambunctious toddlers or rugged football players or busy college students.

Those letters inspired a mental picture for me (Jim Bob), a future hope and dream I shared with *People* magazine: Josie, as a future bride being escorted down the aisle on the arm of her daddy, who tells her she's a beautiful miracle. We continue to pray that Daddy's dream someday comes true, and we know that many others share that hope.

SHARING WITH THE MULTITUDES

Matthew 9:36 says Jesus saw the multitudes and had compassion on them. He looked beyond others' outward appearance and social status to discern the hearts and spiritual needs of those around Him. He guided His spiritual truths around their mental roadblocks and taught principles through stories and analogies. Through His three and a half years of public ministry, He impacted the world.

We want to follow Jesus' model for ministry. He went around meeting others' physical and spiritual needs. He washed His own disciples' feet and fed the poor. At the end, He gave His sinless life as the sacrifice to pay for the things *we* have done wrong. He offers an abundant life to those who seek Him and eternal life to those who ask. Jesus is the ultimate example of the servant-leader spirit, and that's the spirit we desire for each one in our family. We train our children to look around and see others' physical and spiritual needs and be motivated by love to reach into their lives.

That's why we want our programs and interviews to be not about us but about helping other families and individuals. We hope to show them how to develop a relationship with Jesus and find true meaning in life. Just as others have encouraged us over the years, we pray that our shows help strengthen other marriages and relationships between parents and their children.

We have another hope, as well. From the beginning, when we did the first media interview with a local TV station long ago, we've said that the challenges of being in the spotlight would be worth it if someday we hear that one girl who was considering an abortion heard us say that children are a blessing from God—and decided to keep her baby.

How blessed we've been, over the years, to receive letters and e-mails telling us that prayer was answered. Here's an example:

> *I want to personally thank your entire family for the inspiration they have given me. I grew up actively practicing my Christian*

*faith, but somewhere in the transition to adulthood I lost my way.
I found a man and we "dated" for about four years, and then I
found out I was pregnant and I was scared. On the night before my
scheduled abortion I was flipping through the TV stations looking
for something to watch, and came across* 17 Kids and Counting!, *and somewhere through the course of the show it came to me—if
you can handle seventeen children, I can surely do it with just one.*

*I now have the most precious gift from God. I never imagined
how wonderful children could really be until I had one. I ended up
marrying that boyfriend a couple of months before I gave birth, and
we are still married today. I have found my way back to the Lord,
and although my husband has not, I pray each and every day that
God will give me the strength, patience, and perseverance to lead
him to God.*

*All marriages are tough, but I feel as though this dynamic defi-
nitely creates new challenges for both of us. It was through Josh and
Anna's website that I learned about the movie* Fireproof *and the
"Love Dare." I am not quite finished with the dares, but I hope that
upon my completion my husband and I will have fireproofed our
marriage and journeyed closer to God together and can live much
happier lives.*

*I know that you, Jim Bob and Michelle, agreed to do the show
hoping to inspire others and to share your faith. I hope that your
show never gets canceled and that you never want to stop taping. I
cannot imagine what all you have done for people when I look at
how God has used you to work in my life. You have protected my
unborn child, brought me back to the Lord, and helped in repairing
my unstable marriage. Once again, I thank you. Never forget that
you are tools for God to use and you are allowing him to use you
very well!*

THE POWER OF AN ENTHUSIASTIC GREETING

One of the first things we try to teach our children when we're out in public or having guests in our home is the power of an enthusiastic greeting. We tell them that genuinely expressing Christ's love to each person you meet through a joyful countenance and caring words opens the door to share further with him or her about our faith.

If we're successful in these lessons, then those people who stop us in the grocery store or on the sidewalk somewhere are greeted by a host of bright, friendly smiles. We tell our family that people want to know you care about them, and a child's bright, sincere smile can be a powerful encouragement to anyone. It can lift weary spirits and warm broken hearts. That's the first step in how we teach our children to serve others and begin developing a ministry mind-set. The Bible says it's "more blessed to give than to receive" (Acts 20:35), and we emphasize that lesson to our children by reminding them always to give others a smile.

We teach them to overcome shyness by constantly reminding them of another foundation of our faith: Jesus' instruction to treat others the way you would want to be treated (Matthew 7:12). To us, it's not cute when our little ones turn away when someone speaks to them, or hide their faces in Mama's skirt, or stare back, wide-eyed and wordless; we believe that behavior is disrespectful of the other person. In contrast, eye contact shows respect; it tells the other person, *You're important; you're special.*

THE BLESSING OF HOSPITALITY

One of the character qualities we teach our children is hospitality: "cheerfully sharing food, shelter, and spiritual refreshment with those whom God brings into our lives." It's related to fellowship: "the oneness of spirit enjoyed by those on the same side of a struggle."

There's something special about sharing fellowship and food with those you love. Some of my (Michelle's) fondest childhood memories are of the wonderful aromas wafting from our family's kitchen and then gathering with family and friends to enjoy rich fellowship around the table.

Our prayer is that you too will enjoy many memory-making recipes with your loved ones—perhaps some of the recipes we share here!

Turning away means the child fails to acknowledge the other person, and it also nurtures in the child a self-centered focus, something we want each one to learn to overcome as he or she matures. "How would you feel," we ask, "if you smiled and said hello to someone and that person turned away or refused to answer you? Is that how you want to be treated?"

It is vital to us as Christians that we express God's love to everyone we meet. So we practice introductions and shaking hands. We role-play ways to return a friendly person's greeting, beginning with a smile and a hello. And then we head out to the store—or to New York City—and get some real-life practice.

Yes, we also teach our children about the possible dangers awaiting them and we teach the talkative ones (five-year-old Jackson comes to mind) to be friendly with everyone, but if anyone talks about bad things or says, "Don't tell your mom or dad," you instantly go tell!

Like other parents, we've established guidelines to keep our family safe. We stress that when we're out in public, they're never to go *anywhere* alone. When we're away from home, we use our system of buddy groups, partnering our young adult children with younger ones and going out two by two to keep everyone accounted for.

HAVE A SERVANT'S HEART

Our faith teaches us to follow Jesus' words and example, and one of His strongest examples was putting others first by serving and helping. He said whoever wants to be great must be the servant of all. We try to teach that principle to our children on a daily, and sometimes an hourly, basis. In our family these training moments come quite often.

For example, our family's rule is that older kids get first pick of seats in our van, both because we want the younger ones to learn respect for the older ones and also because it's much harder for the bigger ones to climb over seats or squeeze through narrow openings to get to the back.

Like all rules, this one occasionally gets challenged. In fact, while I (Jim Bob) was writing this chapter, I heard a report about two of our boys who had ridden with Mama to drop off some items at our nearby thrift store. When the older one got out to unload the items, the younger one climbed into his brother's seat. (Yes, we have car-seat disputes in our family too!) When the big brother returned and asked his brother to move over so he could have his seat back, the younger one said it was now *his* seat.

We all are born selfish, wanting the best for ourselves. Of course the younger one should have graciously moved over, but what would Jesus have done had He been the older brother? When we sat both boys down and talked to them, they realized they both had been self-centered, and they both apologized, following another lesson we've taught them—that apologies need to be made quickly with a humble spirit: "I was wrong for being selfish and not moving over. Will you please forgive me?"

MODESTY MATTERS

Another part of our life in the public eye that's linked to our faith is the way we dress. Actually, we prayed about this area of our lives and established standards long before the world showed up on our doorstep.

The styles we choose for ourselves aren't specified in the Bible, but the Bible does encourage modesty. In Exodus 28, which includes God's instructions for making garments to be worn by Aaron's sons, verse 42 describes "linen breeches to cover their nakedness; from the loins even unto the thighs they shall reach." And Isaiah 47:2–3 mentions the thigh as being "nakedness." From these passages we drew an understanding that God defined an exposed thigh as nakedness, and we agreed that in our family we would wear clothing that covers the thighs. That usually means the boys wear pants or sometimes long shorts that are at least knee-length.

The girls have a personal conviction about wearing dresses based on Deuteronomy 22:5: "The woman shall not wear that which pertaineth unto a man, neither shall a man put on a woman's garment." Our girls choose skirts and dresses that are about midcalf when they are standing so their knees will be covered when they're sitting.

We believe that a man's physical drives are excited by what he sees, and it is *defrauding* for a woman to wear clothing that accents her body, instead of bringing attention to her countenance. *Defrauding* means "stirring up sensual desires that cannot be righteously fulfilled." We know that certain desires are a normal part of adolescence and adulthood, but as much as possible, we want to help our children to learn to

Modesty is important! Our goal is to dress to draw attention to our countenance.

have self-control over those desires. And we don't want to defraud others. The Bible tells us not to be a "stumbling block" (Romans 14:13). So we choose to dress modestly.

That includes when we're swimming. The girls order swimwear from www.wholesomewear.com, and the boys usually wear a surf suit. These swim garments cover all the body parts we don't want to expose but still allow us to enjoy swimming—or playing on Daddy's hillbilly waterslide.

We're realists. We know the world is full of sensual images at every turn. So while we try to avoid those images whenever practical, we also teach our children self-control, morality, and common sense. If we meet a scantily clad person while we're out in public, you might hear one of us softly say, "Nike!" That's our code word to our boys that it's probably best to drop their eyes to the sidewalk for a few steps.

We're not rigid about our dress code, but we do teach principles of modesty to our children, and as they grow older they make their own choices. Our older girls buy most of the clothes for our whole family now. Like many teenage girls, they enjoy shopping and love finding bargains. (You probably already know that most of our purchases come from thrift stores and consignment shops because frugality, something we'll talk about in a later chapter, is a very important part of the Duggar family life.)

We don't dress one way at home and another when we're out in public or in front of the cameras. Our faith and modesty are part of our everyday life, not just an image we put on for others.

One afternoon, while we were living in Little Rock, we went on a tour of the USS Razorback *submarine.*

9

Developing a Servant Heart

The Son of man came not to be ministered unto,
but to minister.
—Matthew 20:28

Our goal is to teach our children to have a ministry mind-set, always looking for ways to serve others.

This gift of serving doesn't have to be a major production. We sometimes get e-mails from viewers who've seen our family on TV serving a meal at a soup kitchen or helping rebuild a home in El Salvador or doing some other seemingly elaborate ministry project. Often these parents say they want to develop a ministry mind-set in their children too, but then they add something like, "I'm a mom with young children, and we're barely making ends meet. What can I do to help my children learn how to have a servant's heart?"

I (Michelle) have a special place in my heart for those exhausted mothers with young children. Been there, done that! And I'm still doing it! A few years ago I was a mom raising five children under five, and even fewer years ago I was a mom tending ten children under age ten! I know what it's like to have a tight budget, limited time, and quickly evaporating energy.

Here are some of the ideas I share with these fellow moms.

If there's enough money in your budget, perhaps you and your children can bake some bread and mix up some fresh honey butter or make a batch of cookies or muffins for someone who needs a little encouragement. Take your gift to an elderly neighbor, another tired mom with sick children down the street, or to the fire station or police department in your town.

Your visits don't have to be long; in fact, it's probably best if they're short—thirty minutes or less. You may not have time to do anything but hand over the cookies and offer a cheery message: "We were just thinking of you today, and we made this for you. We hope you enjoy it. God bless you!" Know that even these brief encounters and little gifts can be a blessing to others. Most important, your children will learn to invest in the lives of others.

When we take cookies to our local firefighters, they graciously pose for a picture with the kids.

Another way to include the little ones is to have your toddlers draw (or scribble) a simple picture as a gift for the person and then add your own note or Scripture verse to their artwork. It can also be a gift to someone just to have the children sing a little song (along with you) or quote a Scripture verse to share encouragement.

Mingling Generations

We love singing and playing instruments as a family at our local nursing homes. Sometimes our piano teacher even schedules her piano recitals at a nursing home. The students learn to play in front of others and get to encourage and show love to the seniors at the same time. It also helps the piano students relax, knowing some members of the nursing home crowd probably won't notice if they make mistakes. These performances help them focus not on themselves but on others, playing "as unto the Lord," as the Bible would say. The elderly people also love to sit and talk with the kids after listening to them play.

Nurturing a love of ministering to others also builds up the love within your own family. On the way to our visit, we coach our kids, saying, "This person could be your grandma or grandpa, or this could even be you someday. How would you want somebody to treat you if you couldn't walk or talk or if your legs hurt? Wouldn't it be nice if someone came and told you a funny little story or sang a song for you? Or you could ask them about when they were little—what things were like back then. Ask them if they have ever served in the military or ask what kind of work they've done over the years."

We tell them, "You're blessing people with your smiles, and you give them a smile of their own. You watch and see: when you smile, they're probably going to smile back."

It's so cute to see these little guys start out feeling timid and afraid, obviously thinking, *I don't know these people.* But then, even though they're afraid, they start singing and smiling—and suddenly someone claps or says, "That was nice!" Then we can see the understanding dawn on those little faces: *I've blessed that person!*

We talk about it again on the way home. One might say, "Did you see that lady? She had tears in her eyes, she was so happy."

Sure, some of the little ones might also say, "Mama, why was that one lady talking out loud while we were singing?" or, "Why was that man in the wheelchair making those strange noises?"

I (Michelle) explain, "You know how baby Jordyn or baby Jennifer chatters and talk-talk-talks sometime while you all are doing your schoolwork? It's the same thing. Sometimes when people get older they kind of become like babies again in their minds. They just chatter away. It doesn't mean they aren't having fun; they're probably really enjoying it. I think they really liked having you visit."

We believe these little visits teach our children to come out of themselves and not be shy and learn how to have a friendly conversation with others. This is an important part of growing up, to be thoughtful, respectful, caring adults.

Of course, it's true that not everyone is able to carry on a full-blown conversation. But we find that it's totally possible for elderly people and toddlers to communicate beautifully, even though they don't hear or understand each other completely. I tell our little ones, "Did you see how that lady clapped her hands when you sang the 'Blessing Song'? Did you see how that man smiled when you gave him your picture?"

The children learn, *I may not be able to do much, but I can sing and make someone smile. Even though I'm tiny, I can give something. I'm blessing someone else—and I feel blessed myself.*

Nursing homes are usually quite receptive to visits like these, except during flu season, when little ones can carry in some uninvited germs. It's always best to call and ask the activities director when the best time for a visit would be.

If you're new in your community or don't know any elderly or lonely neighbors who would appreciate a visit, ask for ideas at your church. Pay attention to prayer requests and think of ways you might encourage someone who's going through a rough time.

You may not know this side of heaven the impact you have had on others.

These visits also provide another benefit. Through our family's outreach activities and field trips, the children learn how to interact not only with those their own age but also with people of all ages—another bounce-back blessing.

Tangible Thank-Yous

Another simple and inexpensive way to help children develop a ministry mind-set and a servant's heart is to show them ways to demonstrate an attitude of gratitude. Sometimes as a homeschool writing project, and other times just out of the blue, we ask our children to write notes of thanks or appreciation to someone outside the family who has done something good. It might be a thank-you to someone at the nursing home who told them a story, or it could be addressed to firefighters and police officers in our area who serve our community with such dedication and courage.

A thank-you note creates something the recipients can hold in their hands and read again and again. And writing the note helps the kids practice not only speaking but communicating through writing.

Years ago our oldest child, Joshua, wrote a letter to Fayetteville mayor Fred Hanna expressing gratefulness to him for his stands on several issues and thanking him for making a difference in our community. A few days later Josh received a handwritten letter from the mayor saying how much Josh's letter had meant to him. Mayor Hanna said he had shown the letter to several others and had displayed it in his office. He said many times people will write or e-mail to complain about something, but few take the time to say thank you.

We like sharing little unexpected acts of kindness—like surprising our TV series producer, Sean Overbeeke, with a cake and candles on his birthday.

It doesn't take much to make a difference for good in someone's situation. Once you and your children start looking, you're sure to find plenty of ministry opportunities all around you. If your experience is anything like ours, you'll soon find yourself blessed beyond measure as you and your family work together to bless others.

TAKING A STAND

We not only want to help and encourage others one on one, we also want our children to see us standing up for those who can't speak for themselves—and joining us in that stand when it's appropriate. That's

CORN DIP

Many of our favorite recipes originate from my (Michelle's) home state of Ohio. My sister Pam Peters, the eldest of seven in my family, has shared many recipes with us, including Corn Dip, an appetizer or snack that fits right in with any tortilla-chip-dipping party!

(And if you need a corn-related activity for your party, try Cornhole, a great game that we highly recommend for family fun. You can make your own Cornhole boards and bags as a fun family project. Find patterns at www.cornhole-game.org.)

Soften in microwave:
¾ stick of butter (6 tablespoons)
8 ounces cream cheese

Mix together butter and cream cheese, and then stir in:
16 ounces frozen shoe peg white corn, cooked (Green Giant is a good brand to use.)
1 teaspoon to 1 tablespoon jalapeños, chopped or pureed (We go the mild route and puree ours so we can't see them.)

Serve with corn tortilla chips. Very unique, yummy flavor!

why we've taken our children to right-to-life rallies on the steps of the Arkansas capitol building.

To support children's homes, homeless shelters, and pregnancy counseling centers, we've also participated in fund-raisers such as banquets, service projects, and walking or running events. We usually opt for *walking* the 1K portion, although Jim Bob and some of our kids picked up enough speed to take the top places in one of those events.

Last summer we took the family all the way from Arkansas to Michigan to present some Duggar-family musical performances at an outdoor tent revival. We also visited Michelle's family in Ohio, and we accepted an invitation to speak at a church in Canton. During our program the church took up an offering to benefit the Ohio Children's Home.

That kind of speaking engagement is a relatively new thing for us. We're still not comfortable as public speakers, but again we want our children to see us overcoming our natural fears to reach out and encourage others, stressing our belief that children are a gift from God and sharing some of the ideas that have worked for us in our big family. We try to make it clear that we don't claim to be experts and that we're still learning ourselves.

Michelle usually introduces her message by saying she's much more accustomed to sharing one-on-one (or one-on-nineteen) than with a large audience. We may not be polished speakers, but our hope is that a message from our heart will reach another heart and make a difference in someone's life.

Michelle has always had a learning spirit, and over the years she has read many child-training books and learned from other families who are raising godly children. She is quick to glean ideas that we then discuss, considering whether those ideas would be effective for our family and planning how we might implement them.

SPEAKING UP FOR OUR COMMUNITY

Sometimes serving others means taking a stand that's not popular with everyone. Shortly after Josie was born and Michelle had been discharged from the hospital, a friend, Arkansas state representative John Woods, called and said, "I thought you would want to know about a meeting this afternoon of the state's Alcoholic Beverage Control Board."

He said the board, known as ABC, would be considering whether to allow alcohol to be sold in a Springdale convenience store, something that has been prohibited for years. In our town, prepackaged alcoholic beverages can be sold only in dedicated liquor stores. Now the board would decide if that rule would continue.

We knew that if one convenience store was allowed to sell alcohol, soon all would be. We believed that decision would change the character of our town, and we were adamantly opposed to it. Plus, this convenience store was close to a junior high school.

Springdale has been named one of the top places to raise a family, and we've been blessed to have grown up here and raised our family here. We know many people drink, and that is their choice, but this discussion was about the children in our community being exposed to alcohol at every turn.

I (Jim Bob) asked Michelle if she felt up to attending the board meeting. The truth was, she probably didn't feel like it, but we both agreed it was important. We knew that those who stood to profit from a yes vote would be there, so we told our friend we would go.

The hearing was being held across the street from Arkansas Children's Hospital, just down the street from UAMS, and we arrived at the 1:30 p.m. start time—and then sat through two and a half hours of other discussion before the Springdale permit was finally brought up for consideration. This application had already been vetoed by the director of the board, but the determined folks representing the convenience store had appealed for a vote of the entire board.

We decided Michelle would be the one to speak, and when her turn came, she spoke from her heart as a mother. I was so proud of her and had tears welling up in my eyes. She spoke for eighteen minutes, explaining why she didn't think a yes vote by the board would be good for our community. It would give minors greater access to alcohol, she said, and she predicted it would change the civic landscape of Springdale.

Attorneys representing the convenience store asked her if she was against cigarettes, and she could enthusiastically say yes. She told the board that her mother, who died in 1990 at age sixty-four, had smoked most of her life, and Michelle had seen the health consequences she suffered. And then she pointed out an important difference between alcohol and cigarettes.

"We all know cigarettes are bad for us, but people don't go home, smoke a pack of cigarettes, and then beat their wife and kids," she said.

The fact was, we had owned a convenience store ourselves at

Michelle and her mother, Ethel Ruark.

one time, and because of our beliefs chose not to sell cigarettes, even though the decision dropped our profits considerably. The principles that governed our decision were, first, that a good name is better than riches and, second, that we did not want to profit from another person's loss—in this case, the loss of health due to smoking.

Michelle told the ABC board she didn't believe much good comes from alcohol. "People who want it know where to get it," she said. "Don't put it out there in front of our children at the convenience stores they ride their bikes to for candy bars and snacks. I don't want that for our community."

Michelle wasn't the only one who spoke against the permit; there were four or five others, including a state representative, a pastor, and some parents who were raising their family near that convenience store.

At the end of the meeting, we were gratified that the board ended up denying the permit but shocked to see a television news report that night saying something like, "Michelle Duggar stages ABC protest hours after getting out of the hospital following the premature birth of her nineteenth child."

Oh, well, I (Michelle) thought. *That's not the way it really was, but the Lord knows the truth, and that's what's important.*

COPING WITH CRITICISM

Anytime you stand up for what you believe is right, you open yourself to criticism. That's just the way the world operates. We've certainly received our share of it.

They might say, "When I first heard on the news that you had your nineteenth child, I thought you were crazy; but then I watched your show and I love the happiness I see in your family."

Some viewers can't stand our convictions or how we do things, but they admit to being fascinated. They might say, "I don't even know why I watch your show. You've gone completely overboard on your conservative beliefs, and the way you dress is old-fashioned. I really have nothing in common with you at all." And then maybe they'll add, "By the way, I love your kids. They're awesome!"

The vast majority of the one hundred to two hundred e-mails we get through our website every day are positive—or at least ambivalent. But inevitably each day there also will be one or two that say things like, "You people are disgusting. You ought to have yourselves neutered."

That line may have been inspired by news reports surrounding a billboard campaign that was proposed by PETA—People for the Ethical Treatment of Animals. The group was ready to pay an outdoor billboard company to put up signs around the area saying, "Doggies Multiply Faster than the Duggars!"

When the billboard company contacted us about using our name on the billboards, we thanked them for doing what was right, seeking our permission, but we said a definite "No!"

Like everyone else, we don't enjoy being ridiculed. But we recognize that everyone has a right to his or her opinion. Long ago, when we felt God calling us to get involved in politics, we got on our knees and gave our reputation to God. We knew He wanted us to stand for truth and we knew that would not be well received from everyone.

We learned to obey what God puts in our heart to do, and we don't worry about what others think. When I (Jim Bob) was running for state representative the first time, we had nine children. That made us different from a lot of families, and some folks simply don't like people who are different.

As we went around town handing out campaign cards, we could see that some people were shocked by our family picture on the front and information about what we stood for on the back. Some had never seen such a big family, and they were repulsed by the whole idea. At one house, a woman opened the door, and I introduced myself. She said, "I know who you are, and I'm not going to vote for you until you get a vasectomy!" Then she slammed the door in my face.

On the other hand, most people have been very nice. Several have told us that their grandparents had ten-plus children, and they share their fond memories of getting together with their cousins.

When Michelle got pregnant with twins in the middle of the campaign, it was a surprise for us, but I think it stunned most people in town. Everyone seemed to develop an opinion about us pretty quickly (people either loved us or thought we were crazy), but amazingly, when the election results came in, we had won 56 percent of the vote compared with the opponent's 44 percent.

When we're targeted for criticism or condescension, we remember Jesus' words in the Sermon on the Mount. He said we should feel blessed when people "say all manner of evil against you falsely, for my sake" and that we should "bless them that curse you, do good to them that hate you, and pray for them which despitefully use you" (Matthew 5:11, 44).

The value of Jesus' instructions has been proven to us repeatedly. For example, a few years ago, a columnist in San Francisco wrote a short but vile piece about us. It was one of the most well-read articles about us up to that time. It created a lot of controversy in the area where it appeared, and many people wrote to the publication either defending us or criticizing the writer for excessive harshness.

We did not react or respond at all. Actually, the media blitz caused by the article was funny to us. Because it mentioned www.duggarfamily.com, it became the number-one referral link to our website during that month.

Another negative article appeared when I (Jim Bob) was running for the state legislature. Because I didn't have a Republican opponent, I didn't think I had to file a pre-primary report. I was wrong, and by the time I realized my error the deadline had passed, and I filed my report late. As a result, the agency that oversees such things, the Arkansas Ethics Commission, fined me fifty dollars for the late filing. (Later the law was changed to exempt primary candidates from filing if they're running unopposed.) Our local newspaper ran a front-page news story about another candidate and me, sensationally reporting, THOUSANDS IN ETHICS FINES.

The article was critical of me and, to my mind, at least, totally unfair; my first reaction was to call the reporter and set him straight. But then those words from the Sermon on the Mount floated through my mind, Jesus' instructions to bless our enemies. So I didn't call the reporter, and whenever I came in contact with him, which happened pretty frequently because he covered politics, I made a point of being nice to him and showing respect for him.

After I won the legislative seat in the general election, I maintained my conservative philosophy as I began my work in Little Rock. I agreed to interviews whenever the reporter called, and I showed him kindness. Gradually, the articles he wrote about me or quoting me became more favorable and balanced. But even when his old attitude reappeared from time to time, I maintained my pleasant demeanor toward him. By following that biblical directive, over time my "enemy" became my friend. The reporter actually sent me a Christmas card a couple of years later, and he signed his name under the words, "your friend."

Our children have heard these stories again and again as examples of how important it is to have the right response to criticism or injustice. Anger and ugliness never accomplish the best outcome, but kindness can work wonders, and forgiveness is a cornerstone of the Christian faith. I show our kids how these modern-day Duggar experiences prove the truth of something Joseph, an Old Testament hero, said to his brothers long, long ago after they had sold him into slavery: "Ye thought evil against me; but God meant it unto good" (Genesis 50:20).

I teach our children that because we live in the public eye and under the microscope, we're going to incur criticism—justified or not. "We can learn from our critics," I tell them, "either because what they're saying is true—or because of the way we respond when it isn't."

When we follow God's guidelines, we can trust Him to make something good out of the hard thing that's happened to us. Sometimes criticism becomes acclaim.

10

• Making Faith Fun •

O come, let us sing unto the LORD:
let us make a joyful noise to the rock of our salvation.
—Psalm 95:1

If you ask our children what their favorite part of being a Duggar is, a lot of them would probably tell you it's Bible time. It's when we wind down together at the end of the day, talk as a family, and share a Bible reading.

Because we call it *Bible* time, you might think this is a serious, "churchy" family tradition where fun is hard to find. Not at all. We've worked to create this as a delightful close of the day for our children. At Bible time, we gather comfortably in our pajamas in the boys' room, the boys on their beds and the rest of us sprawling over the floor, to hear stories, from the Bible and from each other, and do fun family things—like decide names for the next baby! We might also talk about what each person has accomplished that day or maybe tell a funny story about something someone saw. Usually we thank whoever helped fix our meals that day or helped out with the laundry. Then we may sing a song together as a family or pray about a request.

I (Jim Bob) love to sit in the midst of my children and tell them, "Tomorrow, I've got something really special planned." Sometimes I tell them what's in store, and sometimes I keep them guessing. Every night, I try to make Bible time new and exciting—or at least interesting enough to keep everybody awake.

We also read the Bible. The Old Testament book of Proverbs has thirty-one chapters, and it's full of wise and practical verses, so sometimes during Bible time we read the proverb that corresponds with the day of the month. On October 1, for instance, we might read Proverbs chapter 1. Other times we spend a month or so reading a book in the Bible verse by verse. Sometimes I just open the Bible and read wherever it opens. It's amazing the insights we've found "by accident."

Sometimes I take a little one's special request to read an exciting story, like the one about Daniel in the lions' den.

I like to keep everyone guessing and make them eager to know what's going to happen next, so I read right up

I (Jim Bob) like to keep our kids guessing what fun activity I'll have for them next. Who knows? They might even get to ride a camel, like Justin (left) and Joseph did when we went to a wildlife park.

to the most exciting part—Daniel is thrown in with the lions and the king says, in effect, "Let your God save you now!"

Then I close the Bible and say, "Well, that's all for now. Good night, everybody."

Inevitably there are loud groans and protests: "Daddy, you have to tell us what happens next!"

But my answer is usually, "You'll have to wait until tomorrow night to find out what happens—unless you want to read it yourself."

BRINGING BIBLICAL LESSONS TO LIFE

Most nights, I try to think of life illustrations as I read to help the children understand how Scripture applies to everyday life. Michelle and I also tell stories about ourselves to reinforce the biblical lessons.

For example, I tell them about my family's financial struggles during my boyhood and how those experiences motivated me to become the best dad I could to them. One of their favorite stories is about the time there was no food in our house except a jar of rice my mom had displayed as decoration. That morning, Mom cooked that rice for my sister Deanna and me. One way or another, I say, the Lord made sure we had *something* to eat.

Or I may tell them how, when I was in junior high, our family got behind on our house payments and the bank foreclosed. My parents lost thousands of dollars in equity, and we didn't know what we were going to do. We ended up moving into a rental house that was out in the country but close to a new highway the state had just built. The landlord wanted to sell the house to us, and my mom prayed that she and Dad could buy it, but they just didn't have enough money, and someone else bought it.

A year later, my parents' finances changed and Mom's prayer was answered, and they ended up buying the rental house from the new owner. Then they heard that a developer wanted to put in a large hotel and convention center in our area. Dad

JILL'S MINESTRONE

Our daughter Jill loves to cook, and soup is one of her specialties. It's amazing to see how she (and all our girls) can throw together ingredients from whatever we have on hand to make a gourmet meal. Improvising with different ingredients is easy to do with soup recipes.

6 cups water
3 tablespoons chicken base
1 cup onion, diced into ½-inch pieces
½ teaspoon (1 clove) garlic, minced
1¼ cups (2 whole) carrots cut into
    ½-inch slices
1½ cups (1 squash) zucchini cut into
    ¼-inch half-circle slices
1 (14-ounce) can diced tomatoes
1 (15-ounce) can kidney beans, rinsed
½ cup (2 ounces) uncooked macaroni
½ teaspoon salt
½ teaspoon oregano, dried
5 ounces frozen spinach, broken apart

Heat water in saucepan. Add chicken base and whisk to dissolve. Add onion and garlic to broth. Bring to a boil. Reduce heat to low and simmer 10 minutes. Add carrots, zucchini, tomatoes, kidney beans, macaroni, and salt. Bring to a boil again, and then reduce heat and simmer 20 minutes. Add oregano and spinach and bring to a boil. Remove from heat. Let stand 10–15 minutes before serving.

went to Springfield, Missouri, to talk with the developer, and he and Mom ended up putting together the real estate deal for the project. As real estate brokers, they sold the developer many acres of land between the rental house and the new highway. Then they wisely used their commission to purchase two additional properties next door, which became income-producing commercial properties.

I tell my children, if Grandma and Grandpa had not suffered that foreclosure, they would not have had the opportunity to complete that large real estate transaction, which was a great financial blessing for them. God does bring good out of bad!

I tell them that my childhood family

Jim Bob's mother, Mary Duggar (shown here with our daughter Jana), always encouraged her children to trust the Lord, no matter what challenges they faced.

went through some awfully hard times, but through them all, their grandma repeatedly told my sister, Deanna, and me, "Praise the Lord in all things! We can trust the Lord. He will get us through this!" And she was right. We never slept on the street and we never went hungry. Praise God!

These stories teach our children a lot about trusting God during tough times. They can understand how, with each setback, I grew more determined to become a good provider for my own family in the future so that they won't face the worries and hardships I experienced.

Everyone loves a good story with a happy ending. I'm not at the end yet, but I'm certainly happy. When I sit down at Bible time with my big, joyful family around me, I see again how God used the hard stuff of my childhood to instill faith in me. My faith truly grew from watching my mom's faith during the tough times.

Another story I tell our children is how beneficial Bible time has been to *me*. I wasn't a strong student when I was in school. When it came time to take a test, others might finish in five minutes and they would get an A. In contrast, I might sit through the whole class period and barely have time to finish, struggling to think of the answers, and I would get a C. I was also afraid to get up in front of my class to do book reports or give other presentations. For one thing, I wasn't that great of a reader.

Looking back over our twenty-plus years of Bible time, I can see that it's really helped me become a better reader and a leader. Now I'm able to read something and explain it to my children in a way I really struggled to do in school. I'm better at articulating the lessons I want to share with them. So it's been a great benefit to all of us.

It's so easy to get busy with life's responsibilities and think you don't have thirty minutes to an hour to do Bible time every evening, but if that is your situation, I would encourage you to rethink your priorities. As I look back through the years, I agree with my children: Bible time has been some of the best moments we have had together.

Duggars on Parade

We try to make our faith not only meaningful but also fun for our family, so we're always looking for new and different ways to share and celebrate the Gospel message. A couple of years ago, we decided to enter a living nativity as a float in our town's annual Christmas parade.

The kids had done living nativities at our home in earlier years. For a decade the big church next door to our Johnson Road house put on a "living Christmas tree" musical performance with about two thousand people attending each night for four nights. The Duggar kids loved dressing up in robes and headdresses and arranging themselves in a live manger scene in our front yard just as the big church's performance was ending. They considered it a gift to give the passersby a little something extra to enjoy as they were waiting in traffic while heading home.

Our nativity may not have looked as "professional" as the church's, but the kids always had a blast standing in front of a spotlight portraying a Middle Eastern husband and wife along with angels, shepherds, and others dressed in animal costumes. Joshua used his preaching skills to narrate the Christmas story right out of the King James Version of the Bible.

The kids doing a living nativity scene at the Johnson Road house.

The year we decided to participate in the Christmas parade, we decorated our forty-five-foot-long bus with hundreds of Christmas lights powered by the bus's generator. Behind the bus we pulled a sixteen-foot trailer that was also outlined with lights and outfitted with the manger scene to become our parade float. The cast included Mary and Joseph, portrayed by Josh and Anna, plus other Duggar children and friends portraying angels, shepherds, and wise men; a doll played the role of baby Jesus. We asked our friends at Wilderness Drive-Thru Safari to supply some live animals to add authenticity, and they showed up with a miniature donkey, a baby goat, a monkey, and a camel. Perfect!

We connected the trailer to the bus (after overcoming the problem of a towing-hitch ball on the back of the bus being a different size than the hitch on the front of the trailer) and loaded the cast of characters onto the float. By the time we'd added the crowd of extras who would walk alongside the float handing out candy, plus the camel-and-donkey caravan behind it, we could have been a whole parade, all by ourselves!

I (Jim Bob) had planned to ride the camel, regally bringing up the rear as one of the wise men who brought gifts to the baby Jesus, but the beast growled at me when it was time to mount up, so I opted instead to be a pedestrian wise man. The growling camel didn't bother our son Joseph, so with our safari friends' help, he confidently climbed into the riding seat and bobbed calmly down the street, waving to the crowd. We had so much fun.

I (Michelle), eight months pregnant at the time, rode inside the bus with the littlest Duggars, watching the faces of the bystanders as they spotted the different elements of the float. Riding inside, safe and warm, and thinking about the Christmas scene we were depicting, I had a powerfully poignant appreciation for the Virgin Mary, Jesus' mother, who had ridden to Bethlehem on a donkey when she was nine months pregnant. What a brave and strong young woman she was.

NOAH AND THE DUGGARS

Starting at young ages, our children take piano and violin lessons so they can learn to express themselves through music. Jackson, five, and Johannah, four, already enjoy beginner piano lessons.

Music is a big part of our family's lifestyle. If you come to our home almost any time of the day or evening, you'll probably hear someone practicing the piano, violin, harp, or some other instrument. And much of the time the kids aren't just practicing, they're playing for enjoyment. This is true especially for the older girls, who play simply for the joy of playing—but also as a way to relieve stress or anxiety. Which means we heard a lot of beautiful music last year in the days before Jana and Jill had their wisdom teeth surgically removed!

Most of the music our children play is classical or Christian hymns. We teach them that their music, both instrumental and vocal, is another way they can praise God and share their love for Him. We do lots of recitals and musical programs in our area—and elsewhere too.

One of our most memorable appearances was in Branson, Missouri, less than a two-hour drive from our home in northwest Arkansas. Branson is an entertainment mecca, home of dozens of live music shows, the *Shepherd of the Hills* outdoor drama, and the Silver Dollar City amusement park, among other things. One of our favorites is the spectacular stage play *Noah, the Musical*.

During Bible time one night, I (Jim Bob) asked the children, "Did you know Noah and his family lived in a time when everyone else in the world turned away from following God?" We read the story of how Noah followed God's instructions to build an ark—in the middle of the desert—to prepare for a prophesied flood that would wipe out everything on earth except the family members and animals Noah gathered into the ark.

I pointed out to the kids how Noah's story shows the contrast between a devoutly believing family, unified in their love for God, and the people around them who did not share their faith—and even ridiculed them for following what God told Noah to do.

Then came the exciting news: "Tomorrow morning we're going to wake up at about seven o'clock. We're going to get on the bus and go to Branson and see the play *Noah, the Musical*," I said. "And who knows? Some of you might even get to be *in* the play!"

Of course, some of the little ones had no idea what a *play* was. All they knew was that another Duggar family adventure lay ahead.

When we arrived at Sight and Sound Theatre in Branson, we were warmly greeted by the show's director, who surprised us by saying *all* of us could be in the play that evening if we wanted to!

First, we all got fitted for our costumes, similar to the robes and headdresses we had worn in our living nativity during the Christmas parade. Then we settled down to watch the matinee so we would have a better idea of what we were expected to do. Later that evening, we got outfitted with our final costumes and makeup, plus a beard for me (I would probably be as old as Noah before I could grow a decent one on my own!). I looked so different with all that hair sprouting from my face that two-year-old Jennifer refused to have anything to do with me (besides bearded daddies, she's also afraid of horses and sports team mascots—a very serious little girl).

Then we waited backstage and moved out on cue, following the person in front of us as some of us played the parts of Noah's family members working on the ark. We all were so grateful to get to participate in this incredible experience of retelling Noah's story onstage.

LAUGHTER AND JOY

We have welcomed selected film crews from around the world into our home. This crew came from Japan.

Another way we keep our faith fun is that we live life with joy. These stories exemplify how the joy of our faith overflows into the everyday. There's a lot of laughter in the Duggar house, and that's the way we like it. We have a good time together. One thing that made us laugh recently was a DVD we received in the mail from a foreign film crew that visited us earlier to tape a segment about our family. The DVD was the finished program about the Duggars that would be broadcast in another country.

We popped the DVD in a computer and laughed uncontrollably as we heard ourselves speaking fluent Korean. The producers had dubbed the Duggar voices so we magically became multilingual. Few things make us laugh harder than seeing and hearing Mama, Daddy, or one of the kids suddenly speaking a language we don't know!

Playing, Preaching, and Pranks

Another thing that makes us laugh is watching movies together, but not the Hollywood kind. Our kids love watching old home videos of themselves or their siblings in their early years. To them, the *real* Duggar reality series is just as entertaining as the one on television.

They especially love the old movies of Josh playing church. He was probably eleven or twelve at the time, and Jim Bob was running for the legislature. Josh has always been an outgoing leader who can talk to anybody about anything. In the old home movie, he has gathered up a flock of his younger siblings on the bunk beds, and he's delivering an impassioned message combining the Gospel message and political commentary. "They that be with us are more than they that be against us!" he shouts as part of his loud, earnest speech. His words are accompanied by dramatic hand gestures, wild facial expressions, and a domineering stage presence that had his little congregation falling over with laughter.

Our children love to play—and they also like to play good-natured pranks on each other and sometimes our houseguests. You may have seen the episode on our TV series when a young professional photographer was sent to our house by *People* magazine for a Duggar-family portrait after the birth of our eighteenth child, Jordyn-Grace Makiya.

The young man was concentrating on arranging us perfectly, getting the lighting just right, and then pulling off the near impossible job of getting all twenty-one of us (including Josh's wife, Anna) looking at the camera at the same time. During a brief break while he swapped out some of his equipment, Josiah, one of our biggest pranksters, walked up to the photographer carrying the newborn baby wrapped in a blanket.

"Would you like to take her picture?" he asked innocently, extending the bundle toward the photographer—just in time to trip over a light-stand cord (or pretend to). As he stumbled, he dropped the baby on the hard tile floor right at the photographer's feet, nearly causing the poor guy to faint! But it wasn't really the baby; it was one of the little girls' life-sized baby dolls.

It took the photographer a moment to recover, and when he did he took some great pictures. But we're guessing if *People* wants him to photograph the Duggar family again, he's gonna want more money!

With ten boys in our family, there are always good-natured pranks and jokes going on. Josiah is one of the most clever pranksters. (He's also a talented musician.)

The Duggar kids do like to play pranks, especially the boys. When Josh and Anna came hurrying out of the reception hall following their wedding, planning to make a fast getaway in Josh's car, they found it not only decorated with shoe polish but also completely encased in a thick shroud of plastic wrap that was almost impossible to get off. (You know how hard it is to find the end of the roll once it's stuck down—and no one in the crowd seemed to have a pocketknife.)

Maybe that's why, when they finally made it to Myrtle Beach, Josh told the film crew he and Anna had to keep their honeymoon location a secret "because there are lots of pranksters in my family."

WHO *IS* THAT CHILD?

We also have friends who enjoy playing little pranks on us. One of them is Mike Huckabee, former Arkansas governor and now Fox News talk show host. He invited us to bring our family to New York City and appear on his show a couple of years ago. As our segment on the live show began, he brought the two of us onto the set and explained that he thought it would be fun to give us a little test.

GOLDEN WHOLE WHEAT BREAD

Jinger (and our fellas too!) enjoys making delicious homemade whole wheat bread with our Bosch mixer. In a matter of two hours we have a wonderful hot, healthy meal on the serving line. We bought some industrial mini-loaf pans at a used-restaurant-supply store that can make eighteen small loaves—like the kind you get at a fancy restaurant. Hot, fresh homemade bread served with hearty soup (like Jill's Minestrone, page 117), a big green salad, and fresh or frozen fruit for dessert—now that makes for a delicious meal!

3 cups warm water (110–115 degrees)
6 tablespoons oil
2 tablespoons honey
1½ tablespoons active dry yeast
8 cups (2⅔ pounds) whole wheat flour (hard white wheat flour is our preference)
2¼ teaspoons salt

Combine water, oil, honey, and yeast in a 4–5-quart mixer bowl with a dough hook. Use wire whisk to dissolve yeast. Let sit until foamy, 5–10 minutes.

Combine flour and salt and add to liquid mixture while mixer is running. Mix until almost all ingredients are fully incorporated. Increase to medium speed and mix for 7–8 minutes or until gluten is developed (a small piece of dough can be stretched paper-thin without tearing). (Note: Dough should pull away from the bowl halfway through the kneading time. If it doesn't, add more flour, 1 tablespoon at a time.) Cover with plastic or a clean dish towel and let dough rise in a warm place for one hour. Divide for desired use (see suggestions below). Cover and let dough rest for 20 minutes. Shape, let rise, and bake accordingly.

VARIATIONS
—Replace ¾ cup whole wheat flour with all-purpose flour.
—Substitute hard white wheat flour with hard red.
—Raisin Bread: Add 1 cup raisins and 2¼ teaspoons cinnamon (¼ cup chopped nuts, optional) to dough along with flour.

SHAPING THE BREAD
For loaf bread........................ 6 balls (1½ pounds).........8½ × 4½ loaf pans
For rolls .... 8 balls (12 per ball)..........6 rows of 4 rolls on cookie sheets
For 12-inch pizza crusts........ 11 balls (13 ounces).........12-inch pizza pans

LOAF BREAD
Press each ball out flat into a ½-inch-thick rectangle. Roll up tightly, pressing dough into roll with each turn. Pinch the ends together. Place dough, seam side down, in greased pan. Let rise for 1½ hours or until doubled in size. Bake at 350 degrees for 30–35 minutes or

GOLDEN WHOLE WHEAT BREAD (CONTINUED)

until lightly browned on bottom and sides (200-degree internal temperature). Remove from pans and cool on wire rack.

ROLLS

Roll each ball into a 12½-inch log. Cut into twelve 1-inch slices. Roll each piece into a smooth ball. Place on greased cookie sheets, six rows of four (sides can be touching). Let rise for 1½ hours or until doubled in size. Bake at 350 degrees for 15 minutes or until lightly browned on bottom.

PIZZA CRUSTS

Roll out dough on lightly oiled surface. Place on greased pizza pan. Prick in center and along crust's inside edge to prevent bubbling. Let rise until desired thickness is reached, 15–30 minutes. Par-bake at 375 degrees for 6–7 minutes or until starting to brown.

Probably thinking of how some of us parents, especially when we're concentrating on something else, want to call the nearest child to come help us with whatever we're doing but end up going through the names of every *other* child first, and sometimes the dog and cat as well, before we can finally get the right name to come out, Governor Huckabee asked our children to come out one by one, or with an older child carrying a younger one, to see if we could instantly name each one.

Well, the pressure was on! We confidently named each Duggar child as he or she stepped onto the set. And then Jessa came out carrying . . . well, instead of instantly naming the infant she was carrying, we were instantly confused. Who *was* that child?

It turned out she wasn't ours! The governor had "borrowed" a baby from a staff member for Jessa to carry out to us. Everyone had a good laugh.

NAILING IT DOWN

I (Jim Bob) was born on a Sunday in 1965, and the next Sunday I was in church. When I was seven, I went to my mom after a revival service at Calvary Baptist Church in Fayetteville and told her I wanted to become a Christian. She took me to talk with the pastor, who explained the simple Gospel message.

At the end of our talk, the preacher asked if he could lead me in a prayer, and I agreed. At the end of the prayer, he looked up and said, "How do you feel?"

I told him I didn't feel any different. Then he led me in a second prayer, asking again for God to forgive me, take control of my life, and take me to heaven when I die. Then he said, "Now how do you feel?"

I was embarrassed that I didn't feel anything, so I said I thought I might feel different this time. Well, that was my first lie, and it came right after getting saved! *Now* I understand that salvation is not a feeling; it is a relationship with God.

Years later, in my early teen years, I started having doubts about my salvation. Then I heard a man teach that sometimes those who commit their life to God at an early age have doubt that they understood what they were doing during that childhood experience. He said, in effect, "Don't let your doubt keep you from being sure of your salvation. Don't worry if you did everything way back then with the proper procedures. Nail it down *right now*."

So I prayed, asking God to forgive me, and committed my life to him—and I haven't had a doubt since!

Michelle became a Christian at fifteen after a friend told her about how we can be forgiven for everything we have done wrong. Although her beliefs didn't come as early as mine did, they've been just as strong as mine. We are two people who love the Lord, and we want to give our family the same strong foundation of faith that we value so dearly. We all want to live for Jesus, to thank Him for what He has done for us.

WORSHIPING TOGETHER

We took our children to church from their earliest days of infancy. Our roots are in the Baptist church, and we still feel a close connection to that denomination. But as our family grew and reached Sunday school age, we did not want to find ourselves scattering in different directions when we arrived at the church door as each one headed off to his or her Sunday school class, which is usually determined by age. We wanted to stick together as a family during church worship and Bible study time.

Our pastor at Temple Baptist Church, Don Elmore, taught a class called the Oasis that was intended for senior citizens. We asked him if we could come as a family to the class, and he said sure. It worked out great. Our kids loved being among friends who reminded them of their grandparents, and the older members of the class seemed to enjoy having a group of well-behaved youngsters in their midst. When the class had social gatherings and activities, we all joined in.

Pastor Elmore is an excellent teacher who has a gift for telling stories and presenting lessons so they are memorable and appealing to everyone, no matter what age. We would all listen to his colorful lessons and then talk about them on the ride home or later during that week. It was rewarding for all of us.

Some teachers think they have to talk to children on a juvenile level in order for them to understand biblical concepts, but we've decided that's not always the case. Children are smart and eager to learn, especially when surrounded by older siblings and parents who love them and want the best for their lives.

It's why we homeschool the way we do—with all the children gathered around our long table for some of the lessons, hearing the same instruction before working on related assignments that are geared for their ages and abilities.

The youngest ones may not understand the ideas the moment they hear them, but we believe the information goes into their brains and accumulates like a big pile of snow. The snowdrift gets bigger and bigger and bigger as the children hear new information, especially when it's presented appealingly. Then, gradually, as these children mature, the ideas they have heard start melting and soaking into their hearts and minds, and they begin comprehending.

The Bible says God's Word won't return void (see Isaiah 55:11), and we strongly believe we see that principle played out as we read to them during Bible time and discuss what the stories and passages mean. We see how these lessons, presented repeatedly and interestingly, make a difference in their lives when they see them applied and watch how they work in real life.

An example of this occurred when we watched a video of a gifted pastor preaching about being a giver or a taker. He gave funny examples from current-day life, describing the zany things people say and do that identify them as givers or takers. Then he linked those examples to scriptural passages, including one from the story of Daniel.

Hearing that, our son Jed's eyes grew as big as saucers. "That's exactly what Daddy was talking about last night in Bible time!" he said.

Another snowflake lands with the others. . . .

As time went on and our family grew, we almost outnumbered the senior citizens in our Sunday school class! Around that time, we met Clark and Denise Wilson, who had moved from Mississippi to northwest Arkansas to do church planting. They started a little Baptist church that was meeting in an office trailer. We decided to join them.

Their focus was on encouraging families to worship together—the

We got to know Clark and Denise Wilson and their family when we started attending a church they planted in Springdale. Later, Clark helped us build our 7,000-square-foot house.

way *we* loved to worship. Several other likeminded families joined that church fellowship, and through the messages and teaching, we grew into a close-knit group, all desiring to train our families to impact the world for Christ. Some got involved in politics, ran and got elected, while others developed family music outreaches. We all have a heart for widows and the fatherless, knowing that God says caring for and serving them is true religion and ministry.

Our church services included each family's prayer requests and praise reports to share what God had done in our lives that week. It was truly a time of revival in our hearts, and we saw God open many doors. We loved worshiping together as families—although, as you can imagine, with so many small children from infants on up, there was quite a bit of noise. The preacher would press on through the dull roar of children wiggling and babies crying.

We eventually outgrew the office trailer and started taking turns meeting in the different families' homes where there was more space. The Sunday morning services then expanded to include a fellowship dinner afterward; we call it a pot-faith dinner—because we don't believe in *luck*. Everyone brought food to share, and the families stayed for several hours after church and had a great time of fellowship together. The girls would talk or play games while the boys usually played football in the yard. The adults would visit while keeping an eye on the children.

After a few years, Pastor Wilson and his family moved back to Mississippi to be near their family and assist his mother, who was ill. At that point the men in the church took turns sharing each week, or we would watch excellent teaching videos by gifted preachers like Pastor S. M. Davis and then discuss how we could apply the lessons to our lives. We were like iron sharpening iron.

We have been fellowshiping and worshiping together in this family-integrated church setting since 1999, and it has worked well for our family.

Our experience confirms that a church is not a building or a list of rules or traditions. It is a group of believers getting together to have fellowship, Bible study, worshiping God together, and challenging each other to fulfill Christ's commands.

Friendly Chapel

One night shortly after Josie's birth, I (Jim Bob) was going from Michelle's UAMS hospital room to Josie's NICU pod and noticed a man in the labor-and-delivery waiting room leading his family in prayer. I thought to myself, *That is a godly man!*

Later, as I was walking back to Michelle's room, the man and his granddaughter stopped me and asked if I was the father of the family with nineteen children. The granddaughter said she loved watching our show, and the man introduced himself as Paul Holderfield and told me one of his daughters was in labor.

We continued visiting, and he told me a fascinating story. He said his dad, Paul Holderfield Sr., had grown up near Little Rock during a time of tense racial prejudice. Paul Sr. was a Golden Gloves champion boxer in his younger days; then he became a fireman. He was a tough guy who developed a serious alcohol addiction, probably following in his own father's footsteps. Even though his widowed mother prayed for him daily, he didn't want anything to do with God.

One day in 1957, he and several other white firemen were standing out in front of the fire station when a black man who had been his neighbor years before came walking down the street. The neighbor had given him rides several times to boxing matches.

Paul Sr. tried to turn away so the man wouldn't recognize him, but as he got closer he came straight up to him, stuck out his hand, and said, "Mr. Paul." With all of his white friends watching, Paul just stuck his hands in his back pockets and pretended not even to have seen the man's hand. He was concerned about what his fellow firemen would think of him if they found out he was friends with a black man.

Totally rejected, the man walked away.

Afterward Paul felt horrible, consumed with guilt. Years later, God used that shameful situation for good. Paul's godly mother, who had continued praying for her son through the years, became very ill, and her declining condition had a strong impact on Paul Sr. When she seemed at death's door, Paul told God if He would allow his mom to live until Sunday, he would give Him his heart.

When that happened, Paul got alone and cried, asking God to forgive him for the awful things he had done. He asked Jesus to take control of his life. He told his wife and his three kids they were going to start going to church, and he threw away his alcohol and cigars and instantly stopped his filthy language. God made him a new person!

He had never forgotten the shameful incident when he had refused to shake his black friend's hand. Now he resolved to make amends for his former bigotry by reaching out to some of the poor African-American boys at the North Little Rock Boys Club. He invited some of them to attend his church, but the church did not receive them well. He couldn't believe the discrimination shown by people claiming to be Christians.

Paul got permission from the Boys Club to start a regular Bible study there, and through that effort, several boys turned their lives around. One of them, a boy named Nate, went on to become a firefighter himself; he was the first African-American fire captain in North Little Rock.

Eventually Paul Sr. had a vision to build a church in the North Little Rock community that once had the highest crime rate in the whole state of Arkansas. The church Paul started reached out to those who needed help the most; it became a church where people of all races and colors could worship God together. Under his leadership, the church started a soup kitchen to feed the poor and homeless and opened a thrift store to provide clothing and basic necessities.

Paul's little church flourished and is known today as the Friendly Chapel Church of the Nazarene in North Little Rock. The man I met in the UAMS hallway was Paul's son, Paul Holderfield Jr. He told me that twelve years earlier, after his father's death, he had gone from driving a bread route to becoming the pastor of the church his dad had started forty years ago.

Today about five hundred people attend services in Friendly Chapel each Sunday, he said. About two-thirds of the congregation are black, and the rest are a mix of other nationalities and races. Some are homeless, some come from middle-class families, and some are professionals and business executives. It is a diverse and ministry-minded congregation.

The church's soup kitchen serves meals to one hundred to as many as five hundred homeless and poor people each weekday. In its thrift store, nothing costs more than two dollars. It also operates a temporary shelter for those needing vocational or spiritual assistance.

Nate, the boy who was inspired by Paul Sr. to become a firefighter, has led the music at Friendly Chapel for more than thirty years.

As Paul Holderfield Jr. was telling me (Jim Bob) about his dad and their church, I thought it might be a place where our family could worship while we were living in Little Rock. It sounded like a church where we could be a part of the mighty work the Lord was doing in that community.

I grew up attending a large conservative Baptist church in Springdale that was almost totally Caucasian. With the explosive growth of several large corporations since my growing-up years, the mix of nationalities and races in northwest Arkansas has changed. Despite the multicultural makeup of our community now, Michelle and I and our children had never attended a church reflecting that diversity. To be honest, we just hadn't thought about it.

In Little Rock, the more we learned about Friendly Chapel, the more we wanted our family to share its true heart for doing God's work. It is one of the most ministry-minded congregations we've ever known, reaching out to the poor, providing basic needs for people who don't have clean clothes or a place to sleep and who have nothing to give in return for the kindness shown them. Friendly Chapel's Christians love the poor like Jesus loves them. We were amazed to see how the church's focus on selfless service impacted that whole community.

We attended Friendly Chapel regularly during our six months in Little Rock, and we made lifelong friends there. The girls got to spend a day in the soup kitchen and were able to help a little with the thrift store.

In June 2010, when all the Duggars back home in Springdale had recovered from the chicken pox and it was safe for Josie to join her family, our Friendly Chapel family and some other friends helped us move out of the Cornish house. Many of them were the same friends who had brought our huge family meals during our difficult time in Little Rock and helped us in countless other ways. What a gift their friendship has been to us as they joined us in making our faith not only meaningful and fun but also taught us how to meet the needs of others practically.

Here is a poem that Paul Holderfield Sr. adapted for the church's ministry:

SOAP, SOUP, AND SALVATION

Soap, soup, and salvation may cause you to smile
But this combination is really worthwhile.
These three great essentials in everyday life
Were always put into practice by Brother Paul and his
*   wife. . . .*

When one is filthy without and hungry within
They're in no condition to repent of their sins.
But soap in the shower and soup in the bowl
Put them in a condition to think of their soul.

Soap, soup, and salvation—when these you apply—
Gets them fit to live and ready to die.
Down at the Friendly Chapel, this wonderful three,
Soap, soup, and salvation, are all three free.

Original poet unknown; adapted by Paul Holderfield Sr.

PART 3

Big Hope for Our Children's Future

Be ye doers of the word,
and not hearers only.

—James 1:22

11

• Homeschool, Duggar Style •

*And these words, which I command thee this day, shall be in thine heart:
And thou shalt teach them diligently unto thy children.*
—Deuteronomy 6:6–7

We have homeschooled our children because we want to spend time with them and train them to become mature Christians who love God. We want to instill in them qualities of Christlike character, and we hope to shape them into responsible leaders who can make a positive impact on their families and the world around them.

And as we're working toward those goals, we want to make homeschool fun and fascinating too.

We shared our homeschool routine in *The Duggars: 20 and Counting!* so we won't repeat the overall structure here. Instead we'll share a closer look at how we teach some of the lessons and subjects we consider priorities.

One of the advantages of homeschooling is that we can incorporate our faith into the curriculum. When I (Michelle) first began my role as a homeschool teacher almost eighteen years ago, I

During one long-distance field trip, we took our homeschoolers to Petersburg, Kentucky, to meet Ken Ham and tour the incredible Creation Museum, which he founded there.

felt the Lord impressing upon me the importance of getting His Word into my children's hearts and minds. Not just teaching them to *know* His Word but to hunger and thirst for it as an essential part of their lives.

SALT THE OATS!

But how could I do that? Everyone knows the old adage that says you can lead a horse to water but you can't make it drink. How could I make my children *thirst* for God's Word? The answer came in a message I heard somewhere that said simply, Salt the oats! Show your children how interesting God's Word can be. Once they get a taste of that "saltiness," they'll thirst for more.

To bring out that saltiness, as we're seated together around the table during our family homeschool time, we memorize passages of Scripture that are especially meaningful to us. And we create hand motions to do together that help us seal the memorized passage in place.

In the past we've memorized passages depending on what was happening in our family. For example, we learned Matthew 18 when the children seemed to be going through a stage of bickering and I wanted them to learn the biblical model of conflict resolution. I didn't want them to argue.

We learned that passage, and when one of them would come to me, tattling, I would say, "There's an answer for this in Matthew 18, remember? What do you do?" (We'll go into a little more depth about how we teach our children to use Matthew 18 in a later chapter.)

Other passages we've memorized include Romans 6, which talks about overcoming sin by God's grace, and Psalm 1, which expresses who we should spend time with and what we should be busy learning if we want to be a man or woman seeking God.

Last year, after Josie was discharged from the hospital, I spent three weeks with her alone in the Little Rock house waiting for the kids back home in Springdale to get over the chicken pox. During that time I committed myself to memorizing another favorite passage, Matthew 5, which includes Jesus' Sermon on the Mount, so that I could teach it to our family as soon as homeschool lessons resumed. I don't always memorize the passage ahead of time, but because of my solitary schedule during chicken pox season, I was able to do so. The more of the chapter I committed to memory, the more eager I became to share Jesus' profound teaching with my children. I longed to get those words embedded in their little hearts and minds, hoping they will meditate on them and incorporate them into their daily lives.

THE DUGGAR METHOD OF MEMORIZATION

Come to our home as we begin memorizing Matthew 5, and here's what you might hear:

"'And seeing the multitudes, he went up into a mountain.'

"Now say it with me: 'And seeing the multitudes, he went up into a mountain.'

"Again: 'And seeing the multitudes . . .'"

We'll say the first verse over and over again. Then I'll say, "Okay, what motions do you think we should put with that verse?" Suggestions will be made, and we'll agree on motions to accompany the verse. Maybe we will put our hand to our eyes for "seeing the multitudes," and perhaps we'll put the fingertips of both hands together in a pointy shape while we say, "He went up into a mountain."

Verse by verse we'll memorize the chapter and add the motions. Sometimes we get through two or three verses a day. Each day we start over at the beginning of the chapter, reviewing what we've already memorized, complete with motions, and then we memorize the next few verses.

We're all sitting at the table together facing each other, which makes it much easier to help each other. Each sibling sees someone else make the motion and is helped to remember what to say. (Everyone likes to watch Jeremiah, because he never seems to forget anything.)

The motions work with the mouth, the eyes, and the memory—a multisensory experience that helps us all learn faster and remember longer.

In the afternoon we do wisdom book lessons around the dining room table.

We always review the entire passage we've learned from the beginning and then add the new verses. The day we completed memorizing Matthew 18, we repeated the whole thing, plus the last few verses up to verse 32! What a wonderful feeling of accomplishment that was for all of us.

We talk about each verse as we're memorizing it, and I explain what it means. Some of the younger ones might not understand what the concepts are behind the words we're memorizing, but gradually, as we review our memorized texts and discuss them, it begins to make sense and sink in.

We occasionally quote together the passages we have memorized to keep them current in our hearts and minds. Also, we encourage our children to quote the scripture they have memorized and think about each verse as they are falling asleep at night. We've learned that by meditating on God's Word this way and by thinking pure thoughts, we shift our focus off the busyness of that day and prepare for the next one.

MEMORY LANE

During the part of our homeschool day called Memory Lane we review the Bible passages we've memorized, as well as other memorized lessons such as the operational definitions of character qualities (from the Advanced Training Institute; see the Resources section). It's just about everybody's favorite part of the school day—because that's when I hand out treats as rewards! It may just be a single Skittle or one M&M, but it's a reward and everyone who can recite a memorized tidbit—a character-quality definition or a memorized verse—gets one.

Sometimes we'll recite "popcorn style," which means I call a name and that child pops up and quotes something we've memorized—anything he or she wants from our Memory Lane folder. For instance, I'll say, "Jedidiah! It's your turn." And he'll pop up and quote a quick portion of Romans 6. I'll hand him a Skittle or an M&M and say, "Johannah, you're next!" And Johannah will pop up and quote the definition of self-control: "Instant [she claps her hands, our motion for the word *instant*] obedience to the initial prompting of God's spirit" (or as much of the definition as she can remember; she's only four).

Another way we do Memory Lane is to recite together the operational definitions of three or four of the character qualities we've learned over the past months. We also memorize—and then recite during Memory Lane—quotes by famous Christian leaders and founding fathers.

Often my older children, those who've already graduated, will join us for Memory Lane, in part because it's fun and also to help coach some of the younger ones.

Usually Memory Lane is something we do in the afternoon, around naptime. When my children were all really young, I *had* to take a break and put everyone down for a nap—sometimes Mama took one too! Now that our family has spread out over a wider age range, from preschool to high school, Memory Lane is something we do while one or two of the youngest children nap in a playpen next to the dining table where we do our schoolwork.

But, seeing how much fun we're having, the little ones often fight those heavy eyelids as long as they possibly can. They want to be part of the fun. So, many times, I'll let the little ones sit at the table with us for the first few minutes of Memory Lane, watching, absorbing—and learning.

Recently little Jordyn, who then was about eighteen months old, sat buckled in her little high chair at the table as we started quoting

Matthew 18 during a Memory Lane review. She started mimicking our motions—learning just from watching. And when we finished, she held out her little hand for a Skittle too, of course. Then we had a popcorn round, and Jordyn got to go first. She wasn't really quoting anything, but following Mama's lead, she echoed the first five words of the first verse—and got a wild round of applause from her brothers and sisters, as well as another Skittle.

We continued on with the popcorn round, and Jordyn quickly fell asleep with her head resting on the table. We shifted her into the play-pen beside my chair, and she snoozed away. What a wonderful way to fall asleep (except that we didn't get to brush her teeth)—surrounded by your loved ones as they quote Bible verses and wise definitions.

Before a visit to George Washington's home in Mount Vernon, Virginia, our children learned about our first president during homeschool.

LINKING CHARACTER QUALITIES TO WISDOM

Another big part of our homeschool curriculum is learning to identify bad character and replace it with Christlike character. Knowing precise definitions of character qualities gives us the basis for building and praising the character of God in others. We memorize and study them, and then look for them in other areas such as science, math, medicine, or law, which we study in the Wisdom Booklets from the Advanced Training Institute (see the Resources section). We also look for the positive character qualities in one another.

For example, maybe our character quality for the month is *kindness*, defined as "seeing needs in the lives of others as opportunities to demonstrate my love for Christ." We want to incorporate these qualities into our lives constantly, but while we're focusing on a specific one, we pay extra attention to it: for example, noticing when someone shows special kindness to his or her siblings.

That child might make a little thank-you card, noting that he or she saw someone showing kindness to someone else. Maybe the card says, "I saw Josiah show kindness when he helped Jedidiah carry out a heavy bag of trash without being asked." It wasn't really the second brother's job, but he saw someone who needed help, so he helped him. Maybe that night at dinner or Bible time we might ask if anyone wants to share a praise report. Someone might say something like, "I saw Jinger cleaning the kitchen and dining room without even being asked!" Then we all clap for her.

We're teaching them to notice, and praise the good character qualities of Jesus as they see them demonstrated in others' lives.

We also encourage our children to do kindness in secret, as well as when it's noticeable; that's another biblical concept. Jesus said when we do kindness in secret, "thy Father which seeth in secret himself shall reward thee openly" (Matthew 6:4).

Then, as we continue our Wisdom Booklet work, we might look for kindness as we study science, history, law, or medicine. You would be amazed at the insights and correlations we find. For example, in science and history the Wisdom Booklets might introduce the story of George Washington Carver and the amazing research he did, focusing on the peanut, and the discoveries he made. We learn that he was an incredibly humble man and showed kindness to many people. He turned down the wealth of the world to continue working in his little laboratory at the college where he felt God calling him to work. He called it "God's little laboratory."

Then we look at a map to understand more about George Washington Carver, and we find—what do you know!—his birthplace is less than a hundred miles from us at George Washington Carver National Monument in Diamond, Missouri. Everybody on the bus! (It usually doesn't happen quite that fast, but we do love making things at least *seem* spontaneous sometimes. And we do love family field trips.)

The Wisdom Booklets offer innumerable ways for homeschoolers to focus on different parts of a subject at increasingly advanced levels. They suggest such a wide variety of projects you could never exhaust all the choices provided. And we firmly believe that curiosity is the best way to learn. Arousing curiosity is another way we "salt the oats."

INDEPENDENT STUDY

Our homeschool assignments, music practice, and chores keep the kids busy throughout the day. We do Wisdom Booklets and memorization together, usually in the afternoons. In the morning, after everyone's up, dressed, and fed, and when morning chores are completed, those in grades three and up typically settle in for self-paced work on the computers. For about three years now we've used the Switched on Schoolhouse (SOS) software from Alpha Omega Publications (see Resources section); it works very well, describing each subject in text, pictures, diagrams, and video tutors.

Working at his or her own pace, the student has three opportunities to answer the questions or problems presented. Each answer is graded, and after three tries, the answer is revealed. If the student misses too many questions on the quiz at the end of each section, it is reassigned to him or her. Right now our older daughter Jessa is in charge of checking all the computer grades and watching for those who are having trouble with something. And of course all the children know they can come and ask us questions anytime they don't understand something. Youngsters in third grade and younger complete their assignments in Accelerated Christian Education (ACE) workbooks while seated at the dining table with Mama or in the schoolroom with Mama or one of the older girls.

Starting around age five we use Typing Tutor software to teach the children computer-typing skills. Piano, violin, and harp lessons also help them develop hand-eye-brain coordination while also giving them a beautiful means of expressing themselves.

WHEN AND HOW?

We homeschool year-round but take breaks from the computer work when we're traveling. We enjoy practicing Memory Lane while we're riding on the bus. When we moved temporarily to Little Rock after Josie's birth, we took the computers, and the older girls and Jim Bob made sure schoolwork continued as usual—or as close to "usual" as we could manage.

Other homeschool parents sometimes ask how our schedule changes after the birth of a new baby. I answer that it depends on the delivery. Usually after two weeks I'm able to get back into a somewhat normal schedule, even though I don't do any heavy lifting. During those early weeks I also might take a nap while the youngest ones are napping. Jim Bob or one of my older girls is always so sweet to help hold down the fort if I need a nap. They make sure the children finish their schoolwork and music and complete their checklists.

Usually my newborn babies just sleep and eat, so most of our days continue pretty much as usual, except that we have a precious little new addition snoozing or gurgling through our homeschool days with us. I usually have the baby in a bouncy seat and move him or her wherever I'm working. While nursing the baby, two great items I recommend are the My Brest Friend nursing pillow and a good nursing cover or cape. These aids let me nurse the baby discreetly while simultaneously leading Memory Lane exercises, teaching things like ABCs or phonics flashcards, helping younger ones with their reading, or leading multiplication drills.

These are the methods and ideas we use in our homeschool now (or at least we were using them when we wrote this book), but we're always open to new ideas, software, and other materials.

The resources we've found at www.titus2.com also have helped us tremendously in getting our lives more organized.

PAN-FRIED BEAN-AND-CHEESE QUESADILLAS

8 cups cooked pinto beans
3 tablespoons taco seasoning
2–3 cups cooked rice (optional)
2 cups shredded cheddar cheese
Olive oil
30 tortillas
Optional toppings: lettuce, tomatoes, sour cream, salsa, taco sauce

Mash or blend beans. Add taco seasoning and stir in rice and cheese. Heat a tablespoon of olive oil in a frying pan. Place one open-face tortilla with mixture spread on half of it in pan. Cook till golden brown on bottom. Fold top over. Add whatever toppings you like, and it's ready to eat. Makes 30 quesadillas.

READING ABOUT THE DUGGARS

We've enjoyed presenting several musical programs at both public and Christian schools, and we've also participated in reading events and other programs we've been invited to help with.

Sometimes these appearances lead to some insightful conversations later around our dining table, and sometimes things happen that make us laugh. Last year, when we (Jim Bob and Michelle, not the whole family) were invited to be interviewed by a public relations class at the nearby University of Arkansas, I (Jim Bob) dropped off Michelle at the front of the classroom building so she could hurry on ahead, and then I parked the car (we were running on Duggar time, as usual). We wanted to give the students in the class a copy of our first book as a little gift, so when Jim Bob came into the building, he was carrying an armload of them.

Another student riding the same elevator glanced at Jim Bob, noticing the stack of books he was carrying, and said, "I tell you what, I'm glad I'm not in a class that has to read about the Duggars."

Jim Bob smiled and said, "Yeah, that'd be awful."

12

Vocations, Goals, and Roles

Whatsoever ye do, do all to the glory of God.
—1 Corinthians 10:31

We pray daily for our children, that God would protect them and that they won't be led into temptation, and we are excited to see what God is going to do through them. Our goals for them are that:

1. They keep a close relationship with God.

2. They learn to listen to God's still, small voice and follow His plan for their lives.

3. When they make mistakes they humbly confess those things to God and to whomever they have wronged and maintain a clear conscience.

4. They would look for ways to serve others and express gratefulness for what others have done for them.

If we meet our goals and teach our children those things, they will be a success in life.

As they get older, we encourage our children to pursue the direction they feel God leading them to a future occupation, whether it is being a missionary to Asia or ministering to others as a nurse or starting their own businesses. There is no safer place than being in the center of God's will.

In our travels through the years, I (Jim Bob) have heard many young people say they would love to be in full-time Christian work. I respond that God does call some to devote themselves totally to full-time church and mission work, but even the apostle Paul, who wrote several books of the New Testament, also had a "secular" career to support himself. He was a part-time tent maker while he was busy sharing the Gospel with others every day.

We teach our children that they can have a great impact working side by side with others in the workplace, interacting with them daily. Once others know you are a Christian, we say, they're going to watch your every move to see if you act like one. With God's help, you can point them to the One who has the answers for life's challenges—not by preaching to them every chance you get, but by living out your faith and waiting for God to create a time that will open an opportunity to share your faith. A good question to ask non-Christians in order to direct a conversation to a spiritual level is, "How would you like to be forgiven for everything you have ever done wrong?" Most people are interested in having God's redemption plan explained to them.

We talk frequently with our young-adult children about the importance of pursuing training for a job that they would enjoy and that would allow them to support themselves and their future families. Recently we shared the story of a woman we met who said when she'd had the choice of going to architecture school or majoring in accounting, she had chosen accounting because she could graduate quicker. Once she got her degree and got a good-paying job, however, she realized she hated accounting. She ended up quitting the career she had trained for and now wishes she would have pursued something she enjoys. She even pays someone else to do her taxes for her, she said, because she can't stand doing them herself!

Spending time with those who work in the field the young people are interested in can help them decide if it's the right career for them

Josh and Anna enjoy running their own business selling pre-owned vehicles.

before they spend thousands of dollars and years of their lives preparing for that line of work. We suggest as they're considering a specific career that they ask themselves, Is this a job that I would enjoy doing for years to come? Is travel going to be involved? Will it take me away from my future family, or will I have to relocate to do this job? Will the job require me to work nights, weekends, or holidays? Will it require me to do anything that would violate my convictions or conscience? How much will this job pay? Do I want to get advanced training now while I'm young to get better pay throughout my career? Is there a creative business I could start that would provide a sufficient income while allowing me to serve others (either trying my own idea or adapting someone else's successful business model)?

There are many questions to consider. If you make the wrong decision, we tell our kids, you could waste years of your life. If you make a wise decision, you could reap many benefits.

When I was getting out of high school in 1983, I thought I wanted to go to a computer school in Little Rock and learn how to work on computers. I figured before long everyone would have one, and they would have to be repaired from time to time.

The Bible says, "A man's heart deviseth his way: but the Lord directeth his steps" (Proverbs 16:9). I planned to get computer training in Little Rock, but the Lord directed my steps to Michelle, and I fell in love with her. She had one more year of high school, and I wasn't about to leave her to go to Little Rock. So I kept my high school job, working at a grocery store and praying about what to do.

One day a thought came to me, *What do most people spend their money on?* The answer was food, houses, cars, insurance . . . My parents were third-generation Realtors, so I already knew how that business worked. I signed up for a real estate class and got a real estate license. Since then I have ended up making more money working part-time— buying, selling, and renting real estate—than all of the other work I've done combined. It's been a career that has let me work from home and spend most of each day with my family.

After Michelle and I got married, we both got life insurance licenses. We made a little money with that, but selling insurance was primarily a great learning experience for us. Next we opened a small used-car lot; then we added a towing service, and this com-bination of businesses became our primary in-come through the years until the rental proper-ties started making a big enough return for us to live on.

During the early years of our marriage, Jim Bob worked such long, hard hours in our car-sales and towing businesses that he was often exhausted during the few hours he was home.

Our first book de-tails our trials during our "last and least" busi-ness experience: a convenience store that I did not pray about before purchasing. I overrode Michelle's cautions, and as a result we endured two and a half years of headaches and hard work that generated less than minimum wage. Now we know what we're talking about when we urge our children to pray about each decision; get wise, godly counsel; and compare everything they do to God's Word and His principles of finances. We know from experience the severe consequences that can occur when those principles aren't followed.

We were six years into marriage before our Sunday school teacher showed us the Jim Sammons Financial Freedom Seminar (www.iblp .org), which literarily changed our whole view of finances and family principles. We encourage others to go through the seminar, follow its biblical principles, and watch how God uses its teachings to strengthen their marriages and show them a clear life direction. I tell others the twenty-session seminar will be worth a thousand dollars for every hour they watch if they will apply the principles it teaches. I urge them not to make any major financial decision without watching it.

DREAMS FOR OUR DAUGHTERS

As our older twins, John-David and Jana, were talking one day about John-David's work with our community's Tontitown Area Volunteer Fire Department, Jana listened carefully as John-David described the various tests and challenges involved with the training. He's served with the department for about a year and a half, and he's had some interesting experiences.

"I might like to join the fire department too," Jana said.

Now twenty-one years old, Jana is one of our family's biggest daredevils. She's nearly fearless—except maybe when it comes to public speaking. Like the rest of the family, her twin brother admires her

John-David started Duggar Towing. He stays busy towing cars and fixing vehicles.

tremendously. A couple of years ago when Josh, Jana, and Jim Bob went skydiving, John-David wanted nothing to do with it—except for saying he would love to be a pilot so he could fly the plane. While Jana's personality may be as a risk taker who dares to do anything, John-David has always loved to *drive* anything, from back-hoes and tow trucks to our forty-five-foot-long bus. He's mechanical and can fix about anything that breaks.

Our next-oldest daughter, Jill, has expressed interest in becoming a nurse, even though she has a fear of pain and needles. It's amazing where encouragement can come from when you have a dream. Jill was encouraged last year when she overheard a nurse at the hospital describing the start of her own career. The nurse said, "When I started nurses' training, I freaked out every time anyone came near me with a needle. Thankfully, you do get over it!"

While spending a lot of time at the hospital with Josie last year, Jill was able to see the joys of nursing, and she could talk with nurses who answered questions and provided encouragement. Both Jana and Jill have attended several births and have taken some doula childbirth-assistant training.

With this background in mind, it probably won't surprise you to read that when John-David decided to take a first-responder course last year to supplement his firefighter training, Jana and Jill decided to join the volunteer fire department and take the course too. They knew they could probably apply what they learned in the course to help their family as well as helping others in our community and those they encounter in their mission work.

We're so grateful for our oldest children at home: Jana, Jill, and John-David completed first-responder training with our local volunteer fire department.

During the training, each firefighter, wearing full gear,

had to crawl through a dark structure with a fifty-pound air tank on his or her back. The girls completed the task, although they came home completely exhausted afterward. "They're trying to kill me!" Jana joked.

Becoming volunteer firefighters and first responders has been a real learning experience for the girls, one that has stretched their capabilities. Now, with their first-responder training completed and their firefighter training continuing, Jana and Jill are responding with John-David to car crashes and assisting at medical calls. Just yesterday they worked a major brushfire in our area.

It has been a joy to see our older children expand their knowledge and experience and find ways to make a difference with their lives. We're eager to see how the Lord leads them during the next few years.

Our older girls, including Jessa, Jinger, and Joy-Anna, our "older daughter in training," have also developed many other skills. They know how to cook and bake for an army! If they chose to, they could develop a catering-style baking or meal-preparation service. They also are capable of teaching music lessons and working as paid musical performers, especially with the harp, violin, and piano. They have already had jobs providing background or featured music at weddings and other events. They can design and sew clothes for themselves and others. They can cut, perm, and style hair and might want to become licensed to provide those services to others.

We are totally supportive of our daughters deciding to become firefighters—or just about anything else they feel the Lord is leading them to do. Our goal is to provide all of our children with a solid scholastic education so they're prepared to pursue whatever additional training or education they feel led to do. Ideally, all of our children will have the skills and knowledge necessary to support themselves as adults.

Proverbs 31:10–31 says the virtuous woman is not a lazy person who sits around the house eating bonbons but a wise woman who is diligent in everything she puts her hand to. The virtuous woman not only manages her household well but also is very savvy at making business decisions and buying and reselling merchandise.

Early in our marriage we decided that if I (Michelle) worked, we would not become dependent on the money I earned. We both agreed that when we started having children, I needed to be home with them.

I had real estate and insurance licenses and I did substitute teaching at our local public schools. Jim Bob and I also worked together in our different businesses before Josh was born. Any income I earned went into savings or was used for extras.

I've kept my real estate license for more than twenty years now, and I still help Jim Bob in our commercial real estate business, visiting prospective properties with him and helping him evaluate their potential.

We are helping our daughters prepare for life. Once they're married and having babies, though, we hope they will make their families their number-one priority and will stay home to nurture their children. (Note: We personally know some single moms whom we highly respect, who have sacrificed financially by choosing a job that allows them to spend more time with their children. It hasn't been easy, but these women have raised godly children.)

BUTTERSCOTCH BROWNIES

One of Mama's favorites when made with Sucanat, a whole-cane sugar that can be used in place of either brown or white sugar.

1 cup brown sugar, or Sucanat (If using Sucanat, add 2 teaspoons water.)
¼ cup vegetable oil (or 3 tablespoons olive oil)
1 egg
1 teaspoon vanilla
¾ cup flour
1 teaspoon baking powder
½ teaspoon salt
½ cup nuts, chopped (optional)

Mix together the first four ingredients. Then add remaining ingredients and mix well. Spread into a greased 8 × 8-inch baking dish. Bake at 350 degrees for approximately 20 minutes. Do not overbake. Enjoy!

PREPARING OUR SONS FOR FAMILY AND COMMUNITY LEADERSHIP

We have raised our sons a little differently from our daughters. We provide more financial support for our maturing daughters than we do our sons. For example, we have provided our older daughters with cars when they get old enough to drive.

Our sons have to work to earn the money to buy their own cars. We want them to feel the pressure of needing to support themselves financially so that someday they'll be ready to support their families. (And, of course, given our frugality principles, none of the Duggars has ever owned a *new* car.)

Josh and John-David already own their own businesses: Josh and Anna have a pre-owned auto sales lot, and John-David owns a towing business. The two brothers work together, and they are often assisted by their younger brothers, especially Joseph and Josiah, who are watching and learning as they help clean, repair, and mark the cars offered for sale.

Our boys (and our girls as well) learned a lot of carpentry and construction skills while we were building our house. Every child eight and older had his or her own used cordless drill! The older boys have continued to develop those skills since our house was completed. In fact, as we were starting this book, John-David and Joseph were in Tennessee helping our friends the Bates family complete a remodeling project.

We enjoy watching our children consider all the possibilities for their future.

What About College?

As we were completing this book, several of our older children were beginning the process of earning a college degree through CollegePlus! This program lets students earn a bachelor's degree in a fraction of the time and for much less money than enrolling in a traditional brick-and-mortar college.

Students learn and study from home and then transfer a large bulk of their credit to an accredited college to complete their degree in the major of their choice. For example, our girls who want to pursue degrees to become registered nurses can complete their prerequisites online and then attend the local community college or the nearby University of Arkansas while living at home.

The beauty of a program like CollegePlus! is that the family does not have to be fragmented for the sake of college. Another advantage is that it lets our children earn a degree without being exposed to teaching that is opposed to a conservative Christian worldview. CollegePlus! fits our values and allows our children to keep moving forward in the special ministry God has entrusted us with. The program helps students understand and fulfill the unique calling and purpose God has placed on their life.

Through CollegePlus!, high school students can be dually enrolled in college and high school courses so that, through College Level Examination Program (CLEP) testing, they can graduate early from both.

I (Jim Bob) recently heard an alarming statistic that cited government figures indicating student-loan debt has surpassed consumer credit-card debt in the United States. Years ago we learned about the pitfalls of debt, so when it came to college for our children, using student loans was not a part of the equation. Recently a family friend from Ohio completed the CollegePlus! program and graduated from college with a bachelor's degree in business in two years; he graduated 100 percent debt-free.

CollegePlus! is helping students in all fifty states earn degrees that cost more than 70 percent less yet hold the exact same form of accreditation.

You can learn more about CollegePlus! by going to www.college plus.org/duggars.

PREPARING OUR KIDS TO DO GOD'S WORK

We heard someone say that the sign of good parenting is not what you do for your children but what you teach them to do for themselves. We are devoting our lives to giving our children a spiritual, practical, and academic education that prepares them to do God's work in their future homes and in the world.

It's fun to hear our children talk about what they want to be in the future, especially the youngest and middle children. Right now, for instance, five-year-old Jackson says he wants to be a policeman so he can "shoot guns and help people." James wants to fly military jets with the Blue Angels. Jeremiah wants to be an artist while his twin brother, Jedidiah, dreams of being a missionary. Four-year-old Johannah says she wants to "play outside and eat yogurt."

Our son James wants to fly military jets with the Navy's Blue Angels when he grows up.

Eating yogurt is a good thing to do, both now and in the future. But like all parents, we want our children to know how to do much more than eat. We want them to know how to feed their own children someday. The more skills and knowledge we can help them acquire while they're growing up, the more capable they'll be someday of supporting their own families—and then teaching their own children to support themselves.

We love seeing the spark in a little one's eyes when he or she learns a new letter of the alphabet. We were thrilled to hear the excitement in Joseph's voice when he came home from the Bateses' Tennessee remodeling project and said, "I put all the siding on the south wall by myself." Our hearts are blessed when a child calls home from a poor village in El Salvador or a Christian outreach program in Indonesia and says, "I feel God telling me this is what He wants me to do with my life."

JOSH, THE ENTREPRENEUR

Our goal is to encourage and teach our children in a godly, love-filled, and fun way. When you bring them alongside you and mentor them to learn the same skills you possess, they're likely to feel inspired to accomplish remarkable things. We saw that happen in our oldest child, Josh.

He spent his first few years growing up in the house that served as both our home and the office for our used-car business. When Jim Bob expanded into a towing service, we got Josh a little pair of coveralls, and he often rode along with Dad to pick up disabled or impounded cars. Jim Bob taught him the names of the streets as they were driving around town, and before long little Josh had become our own little human GPS.

We talked to our kids a lot about the benefits of having their own businesses when they grew up, but Josh didn't wait. When he was about seven years old, he started his own business: selling rocks on our front porch. With his enthusiastic brother John-David assisting him, he collected some choice specimens from our back yard, cleaned them off, and lined them up on the porch railing with a sign proclaiming, ROCKS FOR SALE!

When Michelle's sister, the boys' Aunt Freda, became their first customer, the boys were thrilled. She carefully selected five rocks for ten cents each and asked the boys to calculate how much she owed. When the purchase was complete, she told them, "I'm buying these rocks, but I'd appreciate it if you would keep them here for me. You can store them in your backyard, and I'll go look at them whenever I'm here."

The boys didn't quite understand why she didn't want to take her new rocks home with her but happily agreed to her request.

Sales fell off after that, but Josh was already on to something bigger. By that time we had accumulated several bicycles that we had bought used for the kids at different stages. They were always breaking down, so I was always fixing them—usually with Josh, John-David, and their sisters sitting in the little garage beside me, watching and handing me tools, and eventually using the tools themselves, especially Josh and John-David.

Josh saved up a little money and bought a broken bike at a yard sale. He fixed it with John-David's help and then parked it in the front yard with a FOR SALE sign hanging from the handlebars. J & J (Josh & John-David) Bike Sales bought, repaired, and sold many bikes that year. Some days we would have as many as three bicycles parked in our front yard for sale at one time. As the business expanded Josh learned how to do more complicated repairs, sometimes necessitating a trip to the local bike store for parts.

We knew we were probably spending more money on gasoline driving Josh back and forth to the shop than he would make when he sold the bike, but the lessons he was learning were far more valuable.

I (Jim Bob) heard Josh tell someone recently, "My dad always had us boys under the hood of a car." It's true; I loved fixing things, especially tinkering with cars, and it was just natural that I would pass that knowledge on to my children. When you own a used-car business, you spend a lot of time working on cars, so almost every day our kids had an opportunity to stand beside a car or crawl under a car with Dad and talk about why something wasn't working and what needed to be done to make it run.

Josh's entrepreneurial creativity got a boost from something I had heard about the previous year. Another dad had offered his children a hundred dollars if they would give up drinking soda pop for one full year. I thought that was a creative idea that would probably pay for itself by saving dental expenses. Josh eagerly signed up for the "program," and by February 2000, he had completed the challenge and was ready to collect.

I told him, "Okay, you've earned your money, and I'm ready to give it to you. Or . . ." I paused like the best television game-show host, ". . . instead of that hundred dollars, I'll give you a car."

I showed him the 1974 260 Datsun-Z I'd ended up with on some kind of trade a year or so earlier. The car didn't run, but that hardly mattered; Josh was only twelve. It was probably worth about five hundred dollars, primarily for parts. I thought it would be a good project car for Josh to tinker with. I told him, "This deal is only good *today*. Take it or leave it."

He took the deal, and for the next year or so, he, my dad, and I worked together on the car frequently while Josh continued his used-bike business. A year later, when he'd built up some savings with his bike sales, he was browsing through the classified ads (a skill Grandpa Duggar and I taught him) and saw a 1984 Mazda pickup advertised for two hundred dollars. He asked me about it, and I said, "Let's go look at it."

Before he was even old enough to drive, Josh (right), with the help of his dad, and John-David (left) restored a 1984 pickup he bought for $150.

On the way, I coached him a little on how to negotiate the price if he decided to buy it. He ended up buying it for $150, and we hauled it home on a trailer (it was another vehicle that wouldn't run). We worked on it and finally got it running, and Josh ended up driving it for two or three years after he got his learner's permit at age fourteen and then his license.

Soon he would be buying, repairing, and selling old cars the same way he had sold bikes. He had grown up riding around town in his family's cars with shoe-polish FOR SALE signs painted on the windows. Before long, he was driving his own SALE cars. But first he expanded into a sideline business: selling singing fish.

BIGMOUTH BILLY BASS

You surely remember those ridiculous head-bobbing, tail-flapping plastic fish so popular a few years ago. Each one was mounted on a wall plaque and embedded with a motion sensor so that when you walked by it, the fish, Bigmouth Billy Bass, would sing, "Take me to the river. Drop me in the water." (We would just like to add, if you *don't* remember those silly gag-gift items, count yourself fortunate. For a while they seemed to be everywhere, especially for the Duggars, as you'll soon see.)

One day Josh was in a big-box store with Michelle and, having the inherent Duggar radar for bargains, he found a clerk marking down a big stack of Bigmouth Billys in the clearance section; the new price was one dollar each after starting out at an original twenty dollars. Josh's entrepreneurial thoughts started spinning. He called me (Jim Bob) on Michelle's cell phone to discuss his idea.

I've taught our children that, in the world of buying and selling, you make your money when you buy an item at a good price rather than when you sell it. When we purchase something intending to resell it later, we always want to buy it under wholesale so that we can resell it at a bargain price later and still make a profit.

That day Josh called me, excited about the prospects of this new business venture. "I think I can sell them for at least five dollars each," he said.

He had saved up another $120 from his bike business, and that day he spent everything he had on his new investment, buying all but five of the store's Bigmouth Billys. John-David was along, and he chipped in five bucks to buy the remainder.

For quite a while after that, it seemed that "Take me to the river. Drop me in the water" was *always* playing somewhere in our home. The boys lined up ten of the singing and flapping Bigmouths, and the rest of the kids delighted in walking down the row of them and setting them off, one by one, until "Take me to the river" was ringing in everyone's ears.

Incredibly, Josh sold more than thirty-five of the singing fish for ten dollars each. Then he and Grandpa Duggar took a load of them to the local flea market, where he sold twenty more at five dollars each.

He still had eighty left. One day Grandpa took him to a convenience store, where he made a pitch too good for the chain's district manager to refuse. "Look, I've got these great items that retailed for twenty dollars, and you can buy them for three dollars each."

Josh made a nice profit off his Billy Bigmouth sales (although he may have inflicted some mental anguish on his family members, who had to listen to "Take me to the river" almost constantly for more than a month). His success in sales continued as he expanded into buying and selling cars from home, which eventually led to his opening the car lot.

Learning by Doing

John-David's story is similar to Josh's, except that John-David's interests lean more toward repairing and driving vehicles. As soon as he got his driver's license, he was driving our family's large bus around the country, and he now operates the towing business as well as occasionally helping Josh with the car lot. Anytime we need something fixed, we call on John-David.

It's so rewarding for us as parents to see our children using the skills we've helped them learn. We love being the ones who help prepare them for the future, and we can hardly wait to see what that future holds for them.

13

Daily Training, Tips, and Practicalities

Train up a child in the way he should go:
and when he is old, he will not depart from it.
—Proverbs 22:6

Each day is different in the Duggar home. There's almost always a planned schedule, but as I (Michelle) always say, there's the plan . . . and then there's reality. Our home is usually abuzz with what I call serene chaos. You have to be flexible to have a family of nineteen children!

We're often asked how we train our children and keep our family running smoothly through ordinary days. But the truth is, we don't really know what an *ordinary* day is, and things rarely run smoothly according to plan at our house. Most days do pass happily, busily, and, if all goes well, productively. If those are your parenting goals rather than perfectionism, we hope the ideas, tips, and principles we share here will be helpful to you. As always, we don't claim to be experts in parenting, but we're happy to share what we've learned along the way.

KITCHEN HELPERS

Children learn by doing, and they love helping their parents and older siblings *do* just about everything. That's how we've taught our children practical skills ranging from tire changing to cooking. We almost never do anything alone; we've almost always got at least one and often more of our children alongside us. And we try hard to make working together fun.

Having a huge family means spending a lot of time in the kitchen. I (Michelle) certainly couldn't spend much time in there alone, not with a tribe of creative youngsters scattered around the rest of the house getting into mischief! So I taught the children to work with me.

Then, as now, when there are cans to be opened or potatoes to be scrubbed or bread slices to be spread out for sandwiches, our little guys are right there with me. Actually, they're usually in there with the older girls, who spent so much time in the kitchen learning to cook that now, they enjoy doing almost *all* of the cooking for our family, as well as most of the kitchen instruction for the little ones.

I have been amazed at what they have the younger kids doing—and the little ones love to be in the middle of everything, knowing they're helping. They love to put on their aprons and wash the lids of the cans before they're opened or scrub those potatoes. (Important tip: Spread a couple of towels on the counter beneath a plastic, flat-bottomed tub with a little water in it. *Don't* give them access to the faucet, and especially not the sprayer!)

The older girls have even found ways for the younger kids to do "dangerous" jobs (which are oh-so-exciting). Standing beside an older sister, the younger ones are sometimes given a small pair of kitchen shears and allowed to cut things like green onions or celery for a recipe. I never would have thought of doing that ten years ago, but it's such a joy now to see the children enjoying working together. The young ones feel needed and an important part of whatever is going on.

Of course there *are* times when, instead of helping, they need to sit at the kitchen counter watching and chatting with the big sisters as they work.

In our family everyone works together to keep our home running. Even the toddlers have little jobs to do (usually with a lot of coach-

Older children help, encourage, and mentor their younger siblings—or sometimes their younger niece, as Joy-Anna enjoys doing with our granddaughter, Mackynzie.

ing), such as putting their dirty clothes in the laundry bin. In our first book we described how we've grouped different ages of children, older with younger, into buddy teams that look out for each other, with the older ones making sure everyone's accounted for whenever

we're traveling. Throughout the day the older ones help their younger team members with daily tasks such as toothbrushing, hair combing, music practice, and helping them pick out their clothes for the next day.

Everyone who's old enough has a "jurisdiction" he or she is responsible for—an area of the house to be cleaned or a chore to be done.

MENTORING AND EXPECTATIONS

Working alongside our children is a means of mentoring them. We show them how something's done. Then we watch them do the job, sometimes repeatedly, until we're satisfied they know how to do it safely and effectively. Then we turn them loose to do it on their own (maybe while secretly watching from around the corner or through the window the first few times). That's the way I (Jim Bob) taught our children how to do simple construction jobs when we were building our house (after our carpenter friend Clark Wilson taught me).

It's also how I've taught them to check the oil, fix a flat tire, and restock our big pantry after a trip to the market (a system based on what I learned during my years of working in a grocery store as a teenager and early in our marriage).

Yes, there are times when Michelle cringes as she watches one of them take off on the lawn mower for the first time, but so far we've all survived those first-time experiences.

We told you earlier how Josh and John-David picked up on a host of life and career skills by spending lots of time under the hood of the car with their daddy. We've continued that same principle with the rest of our children, of almost always having at least one of them beside us whenever we're working.

Mentoring a child isn't the fastest way to get a job done. It's almost always easier to do it ourselves, but that doesn't provide the valuable teaching we want our children to experience. It comes back to that perfectionist mind-set. Parents need to realize that it's almost always more important for the child to learn something than it is for that task to be completed perfectly. It's a little hard for some parents to get past that attitude, but if all your child does is watch *you* do something, he or she is probably not going to learn how to do it successfully.

On the other hand, when children know their parents have high expectations of them as well as confidence that they can do what is expected of them, they can accomplish amazing things. Confidence is contagious! Knowing that their parents believe in them, children look forward to learning new things and conquering new challenges. Children love pleasing their parents.

An example of that occurred about five years ago, when Josh had just turned seventeen. We headed out in our older-model motor home on a month-long vacation to California. We made it almost twenty miles and then realized the twenty-foot-long camper trailer we were pulling behind the motor home was just too heavy to tow.

We called my (Jim Bob's) parents, and they brought over our fifteen-passenger van. We connected the camper trailer to the van and put Josh in the driver's seat. Following the motor home, he drove the van and pulled the trailer all the way to California, up and down the Golden State, and then all the way home to Arkansas. Quite an accomplishment for a seventeen-year-old! A lot of parents wouldn't allow their teenage son to drive a fifteen-passenger van pulling a twenty-foot trailer

We take our job as parents seriously—but that doesn't mean we can't be silly sometimes too, as we were with the Chicken Blessing Lady at a visit to Dollywood in Tennessee.

to California and back. But we had thoroughly taught Josh the responsibilities of being a careful driver, we expected him to take his job seriously, and we had confidence that he would succeed—which he did.

Another example is the commercial sewer-auguring machine we bought several years ago at a pawnshop. It seemed like once a month we had to rent an auger to clean out a drain at one of our rental buildings or we had to hire someone to do it for us. We negotiated with the pawnbroker and bought our own auger for a good price, and within a few months it paid for itself. I taught our older boys how to use the machine, sometimes lifting the auger up on a roof and running the snake down a roof vent, and other times running the snake through the main drainpipe after pulling an overflowing toilet.

It can be very nasty work with "stuff" splattering around, but we typically save a hundred dollars or more, and usually the clean-out job takes only thirty to sixty minutes. Now the older boys who have worked beside me are teaching the younger boys to help with this job.

CHORE CHECKING

We don't stress over a messy house. That's quickly obvious to all who visit us. I tell friends, "If you're coming to see *us*, come anytime. If you're coming to see the *house*, please give us two weeks' notice." Someone gave us a little sign that says, MY HOUSE WAS CLEAN LAST WEEK. SORRY YOU MISSED IT. Jana commented recently that we need two of those signs so we can put one by the front door and one by the side door.

We have no hope of having a perfectly clean house 24/7. But we do expect our children to work hard and do their best at their chores and the jobs we ask them to do. We try not to ask them to do something and then forget about it. When we give them a job, we expect them to check in with us when they're finished—or keep working until we see that they've completed the job satisfactorily.

Recently six of our older children were away at recitals or practices for recitals, and I (Michelle) gave our three youngest boys some jobs our bigger kids usually do. The boys had only rarely been asked to sweep the tile floor in our living room and our two kitchens (the one we call the "pretty" kitchen and the industrial kitchen where the serious cooking is done). I described what I wanted them to do and showed them some of the dirt or crumbs that needed to be cleaned up. Then I told them where to empty the dustpans and reminded them to call me for an inspection before they put away their brooms.

Each boy was assigned an area, and James drew the job of sweeping the industrial kitchen. The girls and I had done a lot of baking that day, and that floor was especially dirty, littered with flour and crumbs.

Although I knew James *wanted* to do a good job, I also knew he's a boy who is very easily distracted. When I didn't hear the sound of sweeping in the industrial kitchen, I called, "James, where are you?"

Sure enough, he had swept something interesting out from under one of the counters and paused momentarily to go get a brother or sister to admire his "find." Along the way, he stopped to see what Justin had swept up in the living room, and then he heard the sounds of another sibling doing something interesting in the playroom. After that, all thoughts of sweeping the kitchen evaporated.

I sent him back to his task, and in a few moments he came out with a big smile. "All done, Mama. Come and look," he said.

I stepped through the swinging door and smiled at him, standing there so sweetly with his broom. But as I looked around . . .

"Oops! I forgot to sweep that side," James said, scurrying over with the broom.

I left, and a little later, he called me to inspect his work again. The same thing happened. I didn't have to say anything. His eyes followed mine as I looked over the floor, and before I said a word, he spotted the areas he had missed. It was after many inspections that we finally agreed the floor was swept clean. Then he got a hug, thanks, and lots of praise for sticking with a difficult job.

We expect our children to do their best when we give them a job, and we check their work, both to make sure they're learning to do the job right and also so we can acknowledge and praise them for helping.

OBEDIENCE AND SELF-CONTROL

It's normal for everyone, especially children, to get distracted occasionally. But the older a child gets, the more we expect him or her to have the self-control to stay focused for longer periods. James was nine that evening he swept the industrial kitchen for the first time. It was a big job, and he is a high-energy boy. He's the one who is constantly losing his chore pack, losing his workbook, or losing whatever the thing was that he had in his hand just a second ago—and then losing track of what he was looking for when he sets out to find whatever he lost!

Still, he's learning that we expect him to work harder and focus more intently, and we're seeing steady improvement.

We start teaching our children

GROUND TURKEY SEASONING MIX

We use ground turkey instead of hamburger; it's cheaper and lower in fat. We add this seasoning mix and then use the ground turkey in recipes that call for ground beef. Delicious and healthy.

2 tablespoons nutmeg
2 tablespoons thyme leaves
2 tablespoons garlic powder
2 tablespoons sage

Put ingredients in a tightly covered container and shake until well blended. Label with these instructions:
½ teaspoon per 1 pound ground turkey
    seasoning mix
2 tablespoons ketchup
1 tablespoon soy sauce

In a skillet brown the turkey with the seasoning mix, ketchup, and soy sauce. Drain and serve, or use in other recipes calling for ground meat.

self-control at a very early age—often as early as eighteen months, when we start blanket training. It's a wonderful idea another mother shared with us years ago that trains little guys to entertain themselves and stay put for up to an hour or so. Usually this training begins with a blanket on the floor, but once the concept is understood it can be adapted to other places. For the Duggars, it means toddlers learn to sit quietly on a chair, entertaining themselves or listening to their siblings during family homeschool time. Or it might mean sitting at the kitchen counter watching Mama or the big girls cook dinner.

We described details of how to blanket train your children in our first book. In the time since that book has been published, we've heard from hundreds of parents who say it has not only helped bring peace and harmony to their busy homes, it's also taught their children to have self-control and self-discipline, to entertain themselves, and to be pleasant in almost any setting.

The important thing about blanket training is making it a *fun* experience for the child. While they're learning to stay in one spot and play quietly with a favorite toy reserved specifically for blanket time, it's crucial that they be praised for the good work they're doing. When our toddlers are sitting quietly at the table during school time, I (Michelle) often point out their accomplishment to their older siblings: "Look at Jennifer! Look how quietly she's playing with her toy while we do school. She's practicing such good self-control and obedience. Thank you, Jennifer."

And Jennifer beams as the praise falls upon her.

Once children gain self-control through blanket training, then activities such as attending church, eating out in restaurants, and visiting with guests become pure pleasure. They might be sitting on someone's lap, sitting in a high chair at the restaurant, or playing quietly beside Mama on the couch while she visits with guests; a blanket isn't necessary for blanket training!

This isn't to say we expect our children to sit silently like statues all the time. All of our children have been wigglers from time to time, and we Duggars do love to talk and ask questions. But gradually, over time, the child learns to sit relatively still and maintain self-discipline while either listening to what's going on around him or her or quietly playing with that special toy or reading a favorite book.

Remember that the concept of blanket training hinges on the child learning that it is fun. That might include not only a special toy or book but also a little song to help the child "play" self-control. Four-year-old Johannah's favorite song right now describes a child who's sitting quietly when—oh no!—a wiggle worm comes crawling across her shoe! The silly song suggests that the child will "squash the wiggle worm" when she "feels the urge to squirm."

We also teach self-control as a part of potty-training. I remind the little potty-trainees that the operational definition of self-control is "*instant* [I clap my hands] obedience to the initial prompting of God's spirit."

In the same way, I tell them, they need to respond *instantly* (clapping my hands again) to that initial prompting of their little bodies telling them they need to head for the bathroom.

Even though they might not understand the big words at first, I say it so many times, always with the hand-clapping and other motions, that they soon catch on. I tell them, "My prayer is that when you're learning to instantly obey Mommy and Daddy that you'll also learn to instantly obey God when you feel His prompting in your spirit."

The wonderful thing is seeing the joy that comes over their little faces when they are successful at self-control.

We believe the joy that comes from succeeding at self-control leads to an understanding of the real meaning of obedience, which is defined on our character-qualities chart as "Freedom to be creative under the protection of divinely appointed authority." We don't force our children to sit still by making angry threats. Granted, there is a place for correction and reproof but never in an angry, condescending way. We want to lovingly teach our kids to sit still by praising and rewarding them for choosing to practice self-control; that makes for lots less correction all the way around.

TRAINING AND FORGIVENESS

We praise our children's character in front of the family, a practice that multiplies the praise. But if a child has done something wrong, we talk to him or her privately, if possible. We don't believe humiliation is a beneficial part of the training process. Once we talk to wrongdoers privately and establish what consequences are necessary to learn this lesson, we have them go back and apologize to the one they wronged or the one who witnessed the situation. This step of humbling ourselves before others is a life lesson all of us must learn as part of having healthy relationships.

As parents, we've learned that if we are consistent in training our children during their toddler and preschool years, they will have learned basic self-control by the time they're school age. There are exceptions, but our experience has shown us the importance of being consistent. We've also learned that a lot of times it is the parent who is being trained to be consistent!

I (Michelle) am far from perfect. Like our children, I don't always have the behavior I know I should have as a godly mother. But my goal is to discipline consistently, correct lovingly, and then assure the child that everything is forgiven so he or she doesn't have to carry around guilt for that disobedience.

I urge parents not to use "rejection for correction"; don't use words or actions that put your children down, thinking that will train them to obey you. If we as parents respond wrongly by raising our voices, yelling, or exploding in anger, we train our children to act the same way; that reaction builds a wall between us, and it pushes the child away. Instead, humble yourself and ask forgiveness if you have responded the wrong way in correcting your kids, and tell them that by God's grace you are working to become the parent He wants you to be.

When I deal with our children with a loving response, even though they have misbehaved, I'm strengthening my relationship with them while also strengthening their relationship with God, whose Word lays out the concepts of self-control, discipline, correction, and forgiveness.

Here's an example of how it plays out for the Duggars: Let's say one of the little guys is disobeying and I'm busy fixing breakfast and don't deal with that disobedience right when it occurs. Ten or fifteen minutes later, that boy will probably do something else he knows he shouldn't. Then, a little later, he'll try to get by with something else, and by that time I'm irritated and find myself snipping and snapping, not just at the culprit but also at the ones who aren't misbehaving.

Finally I realize what's happening, and I take that child aside. When I'm correcting our children, I get down on their level and say, "Look in Mommy's eyes." When the boy has done that, I tell him, "You know what? God never intended for Mommy to feel this way toward you. It's my fault we got to this point because I didn't do what I should have done earlier. Remember earlier when I was cooking eggs and you did such-and-such and you knew you shouldn't have done that? Remember right after that, you did that other thing, and then a little later you did yet another thing? I should have stopped and corrected you right then! Because I didn't, I built up frustration and wasn't talking sweet. I'm sorry for getting frustrated and angry with you; I should have taken care of the first situation when it happened. Will you please forgive me for that?"

When they do, I ask, "What did you do that was wrong?" (appealing to their mind and conscience).

The little boy in our example might have a long list to confess if Mommy hasn't been consistent in her child training! Or, if it's a single incident, one of the little girls might say, "I hit my brother on the head and ran off with the toy—but I had it first!"

I ask, "Would you want someone to treat you that way?" (appealing to the child's heart).

"Noooo," the culprit replies.

"What should you have done?"

"Well, I should have . . . asked him to . . . please give my toy back?"

Sometimes I need to help them with the proper response to "What should you have done?" This is a teaching / training moment. It's so important for children to know not only that they did something wrong, but also how to make it right. We want them to learn how to handle themselves when they're in a similar situation in the future; we want them to know how to use the right approach to ask for something and to take turns.

Next I may ask, "Now what do you need to tell Mommy?"

Then I hear this sweet voice say, "Mommy, I was wrong for . . . Will you please forgive me?"

Next I decide on the appropriate consequences. If two children were arguing or fighting over a toy, for instance, often I'll say that neither of them gets to play with the toy for a few hours, or sometimes for the rest of that day. Then the little one is probably sent to find the toy-theft, head-bonked victim to offer an apology—and not just a quick, "Sorry." Duggar-style apologies include looking the wronged person in the eye and giving a description of the wrongful deed: "I was wrong for being selfish and for taking your toy and hitting you on the head. Will you please forgive me?"

Because all the children have been in the apologizer's shoes at one time or another, it's very common then for the "victim" to hug and encourage the brother or sister, accepting the apology; if they don't hug on their own, we ask them to do so. A few seconds later they're playing happily together again.

After everything is resolved and the apologies are made, there are lots of hugs and kisses with Mommy so they know no matter what they do, I still love them. At that point, the situation has been dealt with, and our relationship is restored. In contrast, if you don't come to the point of making things right with each other, then those offenses can build a wall and cause many future relationship problems.

Yes, this rather elaborate process can be tiring when it's required again and again, but the more the children are consistently trained in the right response, the more natural it will become for them to do right in the midst of those weak or selfish moments, especially when they know without a doubt there *will* be a consequence for their wrong behavior. I believe that many times children don't respond right (outside of selfish and willful disobedience) because we as parents haven't lovingly trained, explained, modeled, corrected, or expected it from them.

In Part 4 of this book, I'll share more about how I strive to correct my children with patience and a soft voice.

CONFLICT RESOLUTION

With eighteen children living in our home, occasional bickering, tattling, and arguments are inevitable. But we've learned to resolve or even prevent a lot of those problems by following and teaching our kids the biblical method of conflict resolution.

Everyone probably knows an adult who's been estranged from his or her family for years because of some major or minor dispute that happened long ago—sometimes so long ago that the people involved no longer remember exactly how the estrangement started. We never want that to happen to any of our loved ones, especially our children. So it's important to us that they grow up knowing how to settle disputes in a way that nurtures their relationships with their siblings.

We stress to our children that their responses to any situation have consequences, either positive or negative. The Bible offers strong guidance on how we should communicate with each other and how we should respond when something is said or done that has the potential to upset us. The psalmist wrote, "Let the words of my mouth . . . be acceptable in thy sight, O LORD" (19:14). Our goal is always to speak to each other in a way that is pleasing to God. We're not perfect, so we don't always meet that goal. But we try to use our own and our children's lapses as teachable moments.

One of those moments happened recently when several of the children went into the woods near our home to play in their clubhouse.

Nine-year-old Jason rode his bike, and the rest of them walked. After they'd played there awhile, eleven-year-old Jeremiah hopped on Jason's bike and took off toward the house. Understandably, Jason wasn't very happy about his brother stealing his bike. He tore off after Jeremiah, yelling at the top of his lungs as he chased him all the way back to the house.

Before long, both boys were standing in front of me (Jim Bob), on the verge of tears. Jason said Jeremiah had taken his bike without permission. Jeremiah said, "Daddy, all of a sudden I realized I needed to go to the bathroom really bad." He insisted that as he jumped on the bike, he told Jason, "I have to borrow your bike. I'll be right back."

But Jason didn't hear Jeremiah. All he knew was that Jeremiah had taken his bike. Once I got both sides of the story, I asked the boys what needed to happen next. They looked at each other, realizing they'd both reacted wrongly so both of them needed to apologize. Jeremiah apologized for not communicating clearly and loudly enough to Jason about why he needed to borrow the bike. Jason apologized for reacting so harshly.

The incident taught the boys how important good, clear communication is, and how much damage a harsh reaction can cause. If that relatively minor in-

An argument between Jeremiah (shown here) and Jason over a borrowed bicycle created an opportunity for learning about apologies and forgiveness.

cident hadn't been resolved quickly, they could have stayed mad at each other all day (or longer), urging their siblings to align with them on one side of the argument or another. Instead, the two apologies cleared the air and wiped the slate clean.

Incidents like this one also give us opportunities, either at the time they occur or later during Bible time, to talk to our children about biblical principles of love, forgiveness, and conflict resolution. For instance, in the case of the borrowed bicycle, we talked later about Jesus' example of forgiving others even before they ask for forgiveness. Jesus said we are to forgive others for their mistakes just as God forgives us for ours.

We also remind our children that Jesus said we need to do something good for the person who has been mean to us, which is usually just the opposite of what we naturally want to do! But, we tell them, as you invest in your adversary's life, any bitterness you have toward him or her is removed.

ATTITUDE CHECKS

We try to stay vigilant about monitoring the mood and tone of communication going on in our home. If I (Michelle) hear one of the kids say something harsh or hurtful to a brother or sister, I try to quickly pull that child aside and say, "It's not like you to say something like that. Are you okay? Is there something on your heart that you need to talk with me about?"

Sometimes it seems half the family, especially that middle group of kids, can backslide into whining, arguing, and bickering, and it may continue awhile before we realize it's happening.

Some of that happened recently, with bad attitudes flashing back and forth and different kids saying things like, "You did so-and-so," and the other one answering, "I did not!" Somebody had apparently done something wrong or hadn't given a brother or sister a turn, or one had moved something that another sibling had meant to come back for later. Nitpicky things. One of them would come to me and report the situation, and I would say, "Go tell them I said to . . ."

Then someone else would come along and complain about someone else, and I would send another message back to the culprit. The bickering and tattling seemed to go on and on and on, and finally, it occurred to me: *Michelle, what are you doing? These aren't the little ones who don't know how to fix arguments. These are kids you have trained for years to handle this kind of fussing peacefully among themselves. They know this is unacceptable. As the mom, you shouldn't be using your own energy handling a problem they know how to fix.*

By the time our children are eight to ten years old or older, they know they're not supposed to tattle about petty little issues to Mama or Daddy. When it's a three- and four-year-old, we'll take the time and spend the energy dealing with it, teaching and training them to resolve their own minor disagreements. But the bigger kids supposedly grew out of that stage long ago. They *know* how biblical conflict resolution works.

That day, we'd just gotten home from a long trip somewhere, and we were out of our normal routine. The house was in an upheaval because we were unpacking the bus, and a lot of the middle children were getting cranky and starting to nitpick at each other. Then came the tattling and complaining.

So here's what I had to do. I called the middle group of children together, the ones who were doing the arguing and not responding right to one another. Realistically, I could see that the situation was arising from our momentarily upside-down day as we tried to get back into our routine. But that didn't excuse their response. I knew I needed to help them get back on target.

I told them, "You know how to resolve disputes. I have trained you from the time you were little. I know it's crazy right now. I know our schedules aren't flowing right now as they should be. We're trying to finish unpacking. But I'm *not* going to allow you to revert back to those negative attitudes of arguing, complaining, and tattling on each other. The little ones are watching you to see how you handle feeling frustrated when things aren't going the way you want. So now, you tell me how you're supposed to handle the problem."

I replayed one of the incidents: somebody wasn't holding the dustpan as she was supposed to do to help the one who was sweeping the playroom. What *should* have happened? I asked.

"I should have talked politely to my sister and encouraged her to hold the dustpan like she was supposed to do before I came to Mama," the instigator said.

"That's right," I answered.

They know this because they've memorized Matthew 18 and it provides a biblical guideline for handling disagreements. It tells us when there's a disagreement, you go to your brother (or your sister) *alone*, and try to lovingly encourage him or her to do what's right. In kind, levelheaded words, point out the transgression with the goal of restoring your relationship. In other words, the victim is to ask the offender to do what is right, as God teaches us, and to turn his or her heart toward God. Matthew 18:15 says when that happens, "If he listens to you, you have won back your brother" (AMP).

That's how God says we work at conflict resolution. "If he'll hear you, you've gained your brother or sister," I tell our children. "If your brother or sister won't hear you, *then* you get someone to go with you—that's Mama or Daddy. One of us will come in at that point," I say.

"But if you come to me first with a grumbling, complaining attitude, tattling on your sibling—*That person is irritating me and I want to get him or her in trouble, so I'm gonna tell Mama*—and you haven't done step number one and tried to encourage your sibling to turn his or her heart toward God and do what is right, then *you're* not doing what is right and *you* will receive correction too."

We remind our children that they love one another. "And when you love someone, your heart's attitude is not that you want to get him or her in trouble; it's that you love that person so much, you don't want him or her to act wrongly. So first go to your brother or sister and try to work out your differences calmly and in a sweet voice. If that doesn't work, *then* come and get Mama or Daddy."

In a family this size we can't be dealing with multiple petty little disagreements all the time. After I (Michelle) had this talk with the middle kids, they knew that if they had a disagreement with one another they needed first to try to work it out agreeably themselves. They also knew that if one of them came to me before that crucial first step was done, then both children were likely to be corrected—one for doing the wrong thing to begin with, the other for failing to try to resolve the issue peacefully before tattling.

After the talk that day, there was no more bickering. That middle group of children had been reminded that there would be praise and rewards for them as they show maturity and responsibility, but on the swing side of that, there would be consequences for those who knew the right thing to do but didn't do it.

By now, our children know that a peaceful, harmonious home is much better than one filled with acrimony and bitterness. Sometimes all it takes is a reminder that we are a family who loves one another and we enjoy being together and working together. They're learning that yes, they may end up being assigned to a job they don't really like and they got a tough job the last time chores were handed out. But when they do their job as though they're doing it for God (which they are!), without a complaining or murmuring spirit, they learn to feel the joy that comes as they accomplish difficult tasks.

They're also learning that it's much more fun to work as a team than alone. But being part of a team means they have to resolve petty differences quickly and kindly before the situation escalates and gets both of them in trouble.

To understand the importance of peaceful conflict resolution, children have to learn that their responses bring consequences: praise and rewards for the right response and temporarily unpleasant consequences for the wrong response. Teaching this lesson takes patience and consistency, and we admit to falling short occasionally on both counts. But we know that one of our God-given responsibilities is to train our children how to deal with struggles and challenges. When we succeed in doing that, we see the immediate payoff in a calmer, more pleasant home when we follow the biblical principle of conflict resolution.

SING A HAPPY SONG

During one of those "mommy moments" when I was tempted to let myself feel exhausted and overwhelmed by the job of being a good, consistent parent to all my children, I determinedly pushed myself in another direction. Instead of feeling discouraged, I reminded myself of the importance of speaking life and encouragement to my children and myself.

At that moment, a little song formed in my mind, a heartfelt offering of praise and worship that pulled my heart toward God and away from the pressures and challenges of being a busy parent to our many children. Thus the "Duggar Happy Family Song" was born:

> *We are a family, a happy, happy family.*
> *We serve each other every day.*
> *We are a family, a happy, happy family;*
> *We're building character God's way.*
> *God designed the family;*
> *He's given us His principles to follow faithfully.*
> *If we do as He commands,*
> *Our family will honor God and stand!*

Our children enjoy singing and playing together.

14

• Life Is a Classroom •

Those things, which ye have both learned, and received, and heard,
and seen in me, do: and the God of peace shall be with you.
—Philippians 4:9

Some of our young-adult children have already graduated, but we tell them they will never be finished learning. As a homeschooling family, we believe that life is a classroom and that a child's education continues 24/7 year-round.

For example, ever since we built our house, the boys and I (Jim Bob) are always examining how things are built and appreciating the creativity of different designs. One year we went through the Chesapeake Bay Bridge and Tunnel, and as we were driving, I was asking the kids how such a huge underwater tunnel could be built. Discussing the possibilities, we came up with a lot of clever speculations. Then we stopped at the visitors' center and found a book that described the amazing way they built it. (I don't want to ruin the surprise, so you and your family will have to look it up for yourselves.)

We encourage our children to be on the lookout for interesting puzzles and discoveries throughout each day. Sharing what they find with their family creates excitement and curiosity—and great learning opportunities. (That may be why little James got so excited about whatever it was he found under the counter that evening when he was assigned the job of sweeping the industrial kitchen. He just had to go share the thrilling news . . . and thus, the sweeping was temporarily forgotten.)

When you have this kind of mind-set, school is much more appealing, and work can be fun. Plus, having a basic understanding of how things are made and how the parts work together helps you learn how to maintain things that are in your care. This kind of curiosity and understanding is how John-David has acquired such excellent mechanical ability.

WORKING TOGETHER

While we were living in Little Rock after Josie's birth, I brought a bunch of the children back to the Springdale house for a few days to take care of some appointments, and also because we had some jobs to do. For one thing, it was late March and the Christmas decorations were still up! We had left in such a rush after Josie was born that we hadn't taken time to put them away.

I wanted everything to be nice and clean when Michelle and the baby finally came home (which turned out to be nearly four months away), so I marshaled the troops and declared a cleaning day. I told them, "Let's get the house cleaned up so it looks nice for Mama and Josie when they get to come home, and then we'll do something fun."

At the time, I had no idea what that fun thing would be, but the kids know I enjoy coming up with creative new things for us to do together, so they hustled to get their assigned areas cleaned. When I carried a load of Christmas garland to the garage, I happened to see an old disc swing we had taken down when we moved from our house on Johnson Road. *Hmmmmm!*

I mentioned my idea to John-David, and he went to the shop and made it happen. He got out the old, used bucket truck we had traded for several years ago, and used it to tie the disc-swing rope high up in a tree in the front yard.

It wasn't long before the Duggar army had finished the cleanup and everyone was lined up outside, waiting a turn on the grand new disc swing. And it wasn't just any ol' swing. It had about a forty-foot arc that swung out over the hillside, so riders could *really* swing high. Looking at the video shot by the TLC film crew later, I knew it was a

good thing Michelle hadn't been home to watch her children flying through the air!

The disc swing is just an example of how we make working together fun—either while we're working or in knowing there will be some kind of reward when we're finished, even if that reward is just the satisfaction of knowing we did a good job.

Of course, there *are* some challenges in kids having an attitude of discovery and an eagerness to share. Someone always has an exciting story to tell Mama and Daddy about something that happened or something that was lost or found or

We try to teach our kids by example to work hard—and then play hard too. A handful of our brave kids followed Jim Bob's bungee-jumping lead.

eaten or spilled or broken or stuck in someone's hair or found in the freezer beside the Popsicles. It takes a lot of patience and also some finesse to listen to these stories while also trying to get out the door to go to a doctor's appointment or round up all the other kids to come to the dining table or get everyone on the bus so we can go on a field trip.

Molding children into enthusiastic workers requires that we, as parents, not only make the work fun whenever possible but also that we make the children feel appreciated for what they're contributing to our family effort. We also learned long ago that there's no place for a perfectionist attitude in the Duggar domain!

When I (Michelle) was a new mom, I thought I had to keep my house in order constantly or else I just wasn't a good wife and mother. Nowadays, if I can walk through the hallway without tripping over something, I say the house is clean enough, even though there may be dust everywhere I look. I had to grow into that attitude, but my life is so much easier now that I have.

We don't fuss at our family continually about keeping the house clean, but there are chores that have to be done every day, and we're training the children that everyone needs to help. Yes, it takes extra time and work to train a seven- or eight-year-old to do a job correctly, and the truth is that he or she isn't going to do it perfectly. On the other hand, we've learned that once a clever seven- or eight-year-old figures out to do a cleaning job with that little child-sized broom and dustpan, he or she can whiz around and get into places we could never dream of getting to with our adult-sized broom.

Even the little guys like having a "jurisdiction" so that they scurry around, doing their part when our family goes into quick-clean mode. Everyone pitches in, and it feels oh-so-good to look around and see what we've accomplished. We can mess the house up in a hurry, but we can also clean it up in a hurry! That cleaned-up state might last only five minutes, but it's wonderful while it lasts!

We shower our workers with lots of encouragement, praise, and motivation—maybe including the promise of doing something fun together, like go to the park when the work is done. Or maybe each one gets a piece of candy, or perhaps just a hug and a big "Thank you. You are such a big help to me!" Other times, maybe we'll pay someone five dollars for cleaning out the van or one dollar for being the one who finds a lost item. They don't get a reward for helping every time, because a reward is a *gift*, not something that is *due*. We teach them that sometimes the reward is simply the satisfaction of knowing they did their job well.

Sometimes people ask if we give our children set allowances, and the answer is no. In general, our children earn money when they work for it. We believe that, if we gave our children what they want without helping them learn to earn it, we would stifle their drive to work. The result could be self-centered, lazy young people.

LEARNING TO SERVE OTHERS

Of all the things we want to teach our children, the two most important are (1) to love God and (2) to love others. We work hard to instill in our children a ministry mind-set and a heart for others, and we try to give them lots of opportunities to put that mind-set into action. Otherwise, it's like teaching the children about fishing but never *going* fishing. In contrast, when they "put feet to their dreams," when they go out and actually minister to others, it opens up a wonderful world of servanthood to them. They develop a desire for helping others and meeting others' needs.

The work our children, including Jill, did in El Salvador included cleaning up the debris created by a terrible hurricane-induced mud slide that had buried several villages.

We want to expose our children to a variety of ministry settings to help them realize that opportunities to serve others are everywhere. They've used their hands directly to help restore homes and villages after a hurricane-induced mud slide in El Salvador, and they used their voices to answer phones for a call-in radio telethon for Arkansas Children's Hospital. They've helped prepare and serve food for the homeless, and they've played in musical-recital fund-raisers for a variety of charitable causes. They've helped widows and disabled residents of our area with home repairs and yard work, and they've played with children in homeless shelters.

Striving to have a ministry mind-set while believing that all of life is a classroom means we're always looking for ways to help our children gain knowledge and develop skills that will help them serve others.

DUGGARS ON A MISSION

Earlier we mentioned the mission trips several of us have made to various parts of the world. That work has been tremendously rewarding, and has caused some of our children to consider becoming missionaries when they grow up.

The trips happened due to our friendship with Mike Schadt, who had been a missionary to Italy. When he got back to the States several years ago, he volunteered at a Florida college to provide free, noncurriculum classes to teach international students how to speak and read English. Because the classes were voluntary, he decided to use the Bible as the class's "textbook," so while he was teaching English to these international students, he was also exposing them to God's Word.

One of Mike's first students was Alex Lara, a Salvadorian man who had "won" a year-long trip to America to receive health training he could use back in his own country. He enrolled in Mike's English class and not only learned to speak English but also ended up developing a relationship with Christ because of Mike's kindness and his sharing the Bible. When Alex was preparing to return to El Salvador, Mike said to him casually, as so many of us do, "If you ever need anything, let me know."

A few weeks later, when Alex was back in El Salvador, he contacted Mike and asked if he might come down and help his people. Mike gathered up some friends and made the trip. What he saw inspired him to set up SOS Ministries, which has organized informal groups of Christian friends who have traveled to El Salvador dozens of times since then to provide service and ministry to the needy people there.

An attorney friend of ours, Todd Hertzberg, is one of the part-time SOS missionaries who invited me (Jim Bob) to come along on a trip to El Salvador about five years ago. Josh and I went with a Christmastime group that took food to families in one particularly impoverished area where the people lived in shacks and shanties with no running water and, at the time, no electricity. Todd and his family and the SOS group also hosted a Christmas party for the children of the area, complete with gifts for the two-hundred-plus youngsters who attended.

By that time, Mike's little ministry had constructed a community church building that also serves as lodging for the mission groups when they're there, with volunteers sleeping on mattresses on the floor. Most bring their own pillows and bedding, and they know, going in, they'll be taking cold showers and surviving on the bare necessities. Our group bought beans, rice, cooking oil, and other staples at local stores and distributed the food to several poor families.

What Josh and I saw and did on that trip changed us; it strengthened our desire to serve in that area of need. I realized that this kind of experience is worth every penny it costs us because we're doing much more than investing our financial resources in the people we're serving; we're also investing in the lives of our children as we let them see the tremendous rewards of serving others not only with their money but also with their lives.

We returned to El Salvador the next two Christmases, taking Josh, Jana, John-David, and Jill the second year, 2007, and a Duggar group of twelve in 2008 (myself plus ten of our older children as well as Anna, who by then was married to Josh).

Having heard their siblings' stories about the families they'd met in El Salvador, especially their comments about how much the children there loved to play soccer, the Duggar kids who got to go on the trip in 2008 prepared by emptying their piggy banks and family accounts to buy soccer balls. They pooled their money and bought all the balls they could afford and then packed them, deflated, in a large duffle bag along with a small air pump.

The work we did there continued to open our eyes and touch our hearts. The poverty is so deep, the standards of living so low. One afternoon as we crossed the river we saw a woman and a little girl—we assumed it was a grandmother and granddaughter—washing their clothes and their dishes. Others were drawing drinking water out of the same stream that the village sewage empties into. Realizing how these people are living made us not only more aware of the tremendous needs of those we'd come to serve but also humbled us as we thought of how easy life is for us in America, with hot running water, washing machines, dishwashers, and flush toilets.

A similar realization occurred as some of our kids helped restore an area in El Salvador in December 2009 where a huge mud slide had devastated a village. The slide had occurred without warning in the middle of the night, rumbling through the village and destroying dozens of homes before many residents had time to flee. They met one family who had lost a young mother-to-be. The rest of the family members that lived nearby had managed to escape, but the young woman, eight and a half months pregnant, couldn't get out before the house was crushed. Her family never saw her again.

Helping one resident of the village dig through the rubble of his demolished house, our kids were stunned to see how excited he was when they brought him a broken plate and a bent fork. They were the only things he was able to salvage from his former home.

Once again our group helped host a big Christmas party for the children of that area. We also delivered food to an orphanage there and enjoyed meeting the children, even though their stories are heartbreaking. Some of them had lived in the orphanage all their lives; others had ended up there due to parental abuse and neglect, or parental death.

Those children in the orphanages profoundly impacted the Duggar kids. The adolescent girls' stories were especially devastating. They cried, telling some of our children that they knew they had reached the age, usually twelve or so, when there was no hope of being adopted into a loving family, a legal process that in El Salvador can take four to six years. When they reached the age of eighteen their only choices would be to stay at the orphanage and become a nun or leave, a decision that would probably mean they would be homeless and would have to survive on their own.

Taking a Chance

December 2009 was when I (Jim Bob) stayed back in Little Rock with Michelle during Josie's birth and a Duggar group of fifteen made the Christmastime trip to El Salvador (the ten oldest Duggar kids plus my niece Amy and her friend as well as our friends Mandy, Amara, and Heidi Query).

Todd Hertzberg and his four children wanted to make the annual Christmas party even merrier for the two hundred children expected to attend. By that point, Alex had sent Todd a list of the names and ages of all the children in the village. Todd decided to attempt something a little risky: they would gift-wrap all the Christmas gifts they were taking to the children and put each child's name on his or her gifts.

It was risky because security agencies advise travelers not to bring gift-wrapped items on airplanes, warning that they may have to be opened for inspection. The Duggar kids knew that was a possibility, but with the hope of making Christmas extra special for the children, they decided to take the chance that they could make it through security with the personalized, gift-wrapped packages.

Lots of Christmas shopping occurred before the 2009 trip as the Hertzbergs and Duggars worked to accumulate enough gifts for two hundred children. During the next couple of days, as the children waited anxiously to see if Michelle's health would improve enough for them to be able to make the trip, they spent many hours working with other members of the group wrapping all the gifts, labeling them with each child's name, and attaching a personalized note that Todd Hertzberg had written in Spanish to explain the true meaning of Christmas.

In earlier years, gifts for the children's Christmas party had been hurriedly dropped into gift bags after the group arrived in El Salvador. But in 2009, Todd shared his wish that each child's gifts could be *wrapped*, making them extra special. Most of them had probably never received a wrapped Christmas gift, he said. Todd wanted them to have the joy of tearing the paper off a present. The truth was, most of the children probably had never received *any* Christmas gifts before Todd and his family started the annual Christmas party.

So all the gifts were wrapped, and the last thing each gift wrapper did was write his or her own name on the gift tag, wishing the child a blessed Christmas, adding yet another little token of personalization.

Our older children were very excited to learn on Monday before their scheduled Tuesday departure that they would still be going on the trip.

Their flight from Arkansas to Houston took off more than an hour late, but John-David had asked the gate agent at the Northwest Arkansas Regional Airport to call ahead and beg the Houston crew to hold their connecting flight for the Duggars' party of fifteen. When they landed in Houston, the airline had electric carts waiting to whisk them off to the international-departures terminal, a great relief for all of them. But still they wondered, *Will our luggage make the connection? And even if it does, will we be able to get those gifts through customs in El Salvador?*

Their flight landed in San Salvador about 11 p.m., and they were both astonished and relieved that eventually all thirty pieces of their checked luggage showed up on the baggage belt. But they still had to get through customs, and they all knew that in previous years, some of their luggage had been opened and inspected. If that happened now, they wondered, would the customs inspectors insist on unwrapping all the gifts?

As they entered the customs area, a uniformed airport employee greeted them in perfect English. Amazingly, he had been there the year before when the Duggar party had landed, and he remembered them. He told some of the group he had learned to speak English by watching American television. He helped them collect their luggage and head toward the customs line, explaining that as each incoming passenger goes through the turnstile, he or she was to press a large lighted button. The automated system selects those whose luggage will be inspected; if the light turns green, the passenger is admitted without further delay. If the light turns red, he or she is routed to the inspection area.

Given all the prayers that had been going up ever since the Duggar group left Arkansas, is it any wonder that the inspection button was broken on the night they landed in San Salvador?

Of course, customs officials could still order their bags to be opened. The Duggar kids credit their free-spirited cousin Amy with helping them through that situation. She was at the head of the group, and when she stepped up to the stern-faced custom official's podium, he asked her if she spoke Spanish.

Amy smiled her charming smile, shrugged in her good-natured way, and said apologetically, "Taco, burrito, enchilada?"

The official stared at her a long moment. Then he broke into a huge smile and waved them all through. Not a single bag was opened, and every gift remained wrapped!

El Salvador has been an extraordinary learning experience for our children, and now they're eager to take their servants' hearts to other places. As we were finishing this book, our oldest twins were returning from a month-long mission trip to Singapore, Malaysia, and Indonesia.

Michelle and I both have said that missions are among the greatest life experiences for our children. It is truly more blessed to give than to receive.

The Duggar Packing System

We've learned a lot from our mission trips and other travels, and a lot of that knowledge pertains to packing! It's quite an undertaking to plan a trip for as many as twenty-one Duggars (our nineteen children and ourselves; we're glad that when Grandma Duggar, Josh, Anna, and Mackynzie come along, they do their own packing!).

So many people have asked us for travel tips that we decided to include some of our favorites in this chapter. First, a few comments about our family's clothing preferences. We've already described our emphasis on modesty and our girls' decision to wear skirts that come below the knee and non-sleeveless tops with high necklines. Our boys usually wear long pants (although sometimes it seems they're growing so fast that long pants become high-water pants overnight!).

As our daughters Jessa and Jinger have gotten older, they have used their fashion sense to revolutionize our wardrobe. They have started their own Duggars' Modern-Modest clothing line. Given their creative ideas and enthusiasm, we expect it soon will be sweeping the country!

During their shopping trips, they have found many combinations of newer style clothing that are very cute and also modest.

They also gave the boys new hairstyles, and they're trying to get Dad to change his as well. So far they haven't been able to convince him to give up his hairspray and to start using forming crème!

Jim Bob and I plan out the trip, but when it comes to actually packing for the trip, we leave that up to the Duggar family travel experts: Jessa and Jinger, our organizational specialists. They have developed some efficient systems of planning and packing.

The system they use varies with how long our trip will be, how we're traveling, and what we'll be doing. But no matter what system they use, packing usually begins in our living room, which is just a few steps away from our laundry room and family clothes closet. (See our first book, *The Duggars: 20 and Counting!* for an explanation of how we came to use a family clothes closet and how it works.)

The girls designate a spot in the living room for every person they're packing for; since Jim Bob and I pack for ourselves, as do Grandma Duggar, John-David, and the other older girls, that usually leaves eight boys (Joseph through Jackson) and five girls (Joy-Anna through Josie) to pack for.

Once the spots are designated, they talk about how many days we'll be away and what clothes will be needed. Generally we wear the same clothes everywhere we go, whether it's a casual or dressy occasion; we just try to dress in a way that's comfortable enough for fun times but also looks nice enough for public appearances. The exception is when we're heading to a function where the guys need to wear their suits. (We buy most of our clothing at thrift stores, but the guys' suits were purchased new for Josh and Anna's wedding in 2008. They were a gift from Anna's parents, who got a wonderful bargain from a friend who owns a clothing business.)

If the children will be giving a musical performance somewhere, Jinger and Jessa will probably make note of it so that everyone can color coordinate that day.

When flying, we are typically gone for three to five days. The girls will stack and roll one day's pants for all eight boys in one plastic store bag (the kind you get at grocery and discount stores, and one day's shirts in another. These bags are given labels such as "Joseph thru Jackson pants/Tuesday." They do the same thing for the girls, selecting tops and skirts or dresses, as well as matching hair bows. Then the plastic bags are loaded into suitcases. Packed this way, all boys' clothes fit into two large suitcases, and the girls' into one. (We tie matching, bright-colored ribbons on all of our suitcases so they're easy to spot on the baggage carousel.)

When we get to the hotel, all we have to do on Tuesday is open one shirt and one pants bag, and all the boys have their clothes for that day. We usually have five rooms (preferably with two sets adjoining), and the girls deliver the next day's clothes to each room before bedtime, including a bag of underwear and a bag of socks for the boys. Everyone knows to leave dirty clothes in the corner of the bathroom. At the end of the stay all the dirty laundry is collected in white plastic garbage bags, which are tied and thrown into suitcases to be washed when we get back home.

When we're traveling by air, the last thing the girls do once everything is packed in suitcases is weigh them. We don't want to have to pay for any overweight bags! So they bring out the bathroom scale and check each bag. A typical Duggar road trip requires ten suitcases weighing a total of four hundred to five hundred pounds!

For road trips, the girls sort the clothing differently. For instance, they will use the racks in the bus cargo compartment for hanging dresses and shirts, and each boy will have his own bag for pants. We pick out the day's clothes from the compartment the night before.

The girls pack a pair of play shoes and a pair of dress shoes for each boy. Our girls like having a variety of shoes. Jessa and Jinger may take twenty pairs of shoes for the four youngest girls; their shoes need to match those cute little dresses! When we're gone more than a week or so, we plan on doing laundry every three or four days.

As you can imagine, it takes a while to get everything packed; sometimes the Duggar luggage holds as many as a hundred shirts, another hundred pairs of pants, plus more than fifty pairs of shoes! For longer trips, the girls start packing a week before we leave, which means our living room may be covered with stacks of clothes for several days. But their clever systems always work well for us.

A VERY IMPORTANT TRAVEL ITEM

A few years ago we learned about another important thing we need to take when we travel, besides a few hundred pounds of clothes, shoes, diapers, and other stuff. The lesson came when we were traveling out west and Jim Bob signed us up for a family airplane tour over the Grand Canyon.

Our flight was scheduled for early afternoon, and we had just enjoyed a big lunch at McDonald's with burgers, fries, and shakes. Then we boarded the small plane for the breathtakingly scenic experience. That day the air was choppy, and we were the last flight allowed because of all the turbulence. We bounced up and down the whole time, and most of us ended up carrying our lunches off the plane in motion-sickness bags! So now we try always to remember to bring along some motion-sickness "Sea-Bands" to wear on our wrists—with throw-up bags as backups!

PART 4

• Big Hearts, Full of Love •

Thou shalt love the Lord thy God with all thy heart,
and with all thy soul, and with all thy mind.
This is the first and great commandment.
And the second is like unto it,
Thou shalt love thy neighbour as thyself.

—Matthew 22:37–39

15

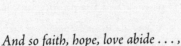

Protecting and Cherishing Our Relationships

And so faith, hope, love abide . . . ,
these three; but the greatest of these is love.
—1 Corinthians 13:13 AMP

Our goal is to base everything we say and do on God's kind of love. That kind of attitude comes easily when everything's rosy, but trials can test almost anyone's faith. We've experienced that kind of trial ourselves in the last few years as we've endured some stresses and challenges, including major and minor crises.

When Michelle's mother died in 1991, we experienced for the first time the grief that comes from losing a beloved member of the immediate family. Our oldest child, Josh, was only three years old when she died; the twins were toddlers, and Jill was just a baby. Today, none of them remember that difficult experience at all.

When my (Jim Bob's) dad got a malignant-brain-tumor diagnosis, we were relieved when Mom and Dad agreed to move in with us so we could help with Dad's care. We prayed for healing, knowing that God, who made each one of us, can heal us supernaturally if He chooses. Or He could give the doctors treatments to use to promote Dad's healing.

Except for our temporary moves to Little Rock when I was in the legislature, we had lived in the same area of northwest Arkansas as my parents throughout our marriage, and our children grew up feeling very close to Grandma and Grandpa Duggar. The kids were delighted to have their grandparents move in with us at the beginning of 2008, and because Grandpa was still able to function normally for months, the children got to spend a lot of special time building memories with him. It probably didn't really sink in until the last few months of his illness that he was, in fact, dying.

My mom devoted herself completely to taking care of his personal needs, protecting his privacy and his dignity, and asking (or allowing) us to help only when it was absolutely necessary. By February 3, 2009, when we celebrated his birthday with the Bates family after the ice storm, he was unable to stand or speak, but he knew it was his birthday and obviously loved being the center of the two big families' attention. He beamed when Josh announced that Anna was pregnant and a new generation of Duggars was on its way.

A HARD BLESSING

We grieved, knowing Dad's death was imminent, and we couldn't help but think how it would happen and how it would impact our children. After all, we were determined to honor his wish to die at home rather than in the hospital, and our home, at that time, was full of more than thirty children, our own plus the Bateses'.

All we could do was shower Dad with all the love we felt for him and ask God to prepare us and the children for what lay ahead. Then God, in His great mercy, made that hard event as easy as it could have been.

The Bateses were still staying with us the week after Dad's birthday. The ice storm had caused such devastating damage in our area, there was plenty of work for talented tree trimmers like Gil and his sons. They are our dear friends, and we loved having them there. On the morning of February 9, however, our house was almost empty—rare for the Duggars. Gil and his boys were working, and Kelly had taken the rest of the Bates family to visit a nursing home. All of our children except baby Jordyn, Jennifer, Jessa, and John-David had left for their violin group lessons.

Normally at that time of day our house would be bustling with activity and noise as the children practiced piano, harp, or violin or talked about their school assignments. That morning, when our home was empty and unusually quiet, Grandma's voice suddenly echoed over the intercom: "Jim Bob, come here!"

I rushed for the stairs, but John-David was already ahead of me, responding as instinctively as I did. Michelle followed as soon as she'd finished diapering the baby.

"He's gone," Mom said simply, looking up from Dad's body as we stepped through the door to their room.

Several days earlier, we had made arrangements for how we would handle Dad's death at home. There was no need to call an ambulance; instead our dear friend Dr. Murphy came to make the pronouncement and summon the coroner. Then the funeral home staffers removed Dad's body. While our hearts ached to know Dad would no longer be with us, we were comforted to know that, as Christians, we would all be together in heaven someday.

On that difficult morning, we were so thankful all this happened while the children were away. Still, they had to be told, and when they returned from group lessons late that afternoon, we gathered them in the girls' upstairs bedroom, where I gently shared the news that Grandpa Duggar had passed away.

All of the older ones took it as well as possible; we had tried to prepare them ahead of time, telling them Grandpa was very ill and would probably be going to heaven soon. It would be sad for us when he died, we had told them, but the Bible tells us we don't have to grieve like those who have no hope of eternal life. We believe Jesus' promise that we will see Grandpa again in heaven; Grandpa had asked God to forgive him of his sins and had given his life to Him. We are grateful to God for all the wonderful, fun times we had together.

"We're all going to die one of these days unless the world ends and Jesus comes back and takes us straight to heaven with Him," I (Jim Bob) had told them. "It's hard to lose someone we love. We'll be sad because we'll miss Grandpa; that's normal. But we have to be happy for *him* because at the very moment he dies, his spirit will be in a better place where there are no more brain tumors, no sickness at all. And someday we *will* see him again."

Despite all those preparatory talks, the news was especially difficult for our younger children to grasp. "Grandpa's down in his bedroom," said Jackson, who was four at the time.

"No, Jackson, he's not," I answered. "I'm sorry. He's not there."

"I just know he's there," Jackson said, and he wouldn't believe otherwise until he had gone downstairs to look for himself.

A couple of days later, before the visitation at the funeral home, I gathered the family again to prepare them for this new and difficult experience.

"When we get there, you're going to see Grandpa's body, lying in the casket," I said. "But remember, that's just his shell. His spirit is already in heaven with Jesus, and he's happy and healthy again. There's sadness for us, but Grandpa's not sad."

For the same reason that Josh and Anna had allowed the TV crew to film their wedding four months earlier, we invited the crew to film Dad's funeral. Both events showed the importance of our family's foundation of faith as we commemorated two emotional milestones, one joyful, one sad.

As parents, we wish we could spare our children every hard and hurtful event in their lives, but we know that's not realistic or even preferable. It's important for youngsters to grow up overcoming occasional difficulties so they learn they are capable of doing so. We know it was hard for our oldest boys, Josh, John-David, and Joseph, to serve as three of their grandpa's pallbearers. It was hard for *us* to see them in that role; but at the same time we felt proud of our sons for carrying out that job with dignity and love.

The memorial service wasn't totally sad, however. Several friends shared colorful stories about Dad's fun-loving personality, laughing about his pranks and jokes. The funeral director even joined in; he printed this picture of a ketchup bottle on the back of the service leaflet.

J.L. loved ketchup.
And just like ketchup,
he made everything
just a little bit
better, too!

Even though the service included lots of laughter, when it was my turn to speak, I told the gathering that Dad probably wouldn't have liked it. "He hated funerals," I said. "In fact, he probably wouldn't be here today if he didn't have to be."

TALKING ABOUT FEELINGS

We talked a lot about Grandpa in the weeks following his death, and some of those memories continued to produce occasional tears. I managed to maintain my composure most of the time, but I would cry when I remembered many of the special times with Dad, and sometimes I let our kids see my tears. I wanted them to know it was okay to be sad.

My dad's death was our children's first real experience with that type of grief. I wanted our kids to understand that God gave us an amazing array of feelings, and it's natural to have them. The shortest verse in the Bible, John 11:35, is "Jesus wept," which describes Jesus' response when His close friend Lazarus died. If Jesus expressed His emotions by crying, then we know it's important for us also to express our emotions during the loss of a loved one.

PUMMELED BY LIFE STORMS

Josie's premature birth and the subsequent challenges we faced as we tried to take care of her and also meet the needs of the rest of our big family was an ordeal we could never have anticipated or prepared for. It was a time when we sometimes felt as though we were lost in a maze of questions—about decisions we had already made and decisions we were having to make in emergency situations.

We prayed constantly for our little micro-preemie Josie, for our marriage, and for our family. We prayed that Josie would survive if it was God's will, and that the rest of us, by God's grace, would be able to survive our lives being turned upside down.

Our relationship with each other was strained as we struggled to cope with our need to protect and nurture our large family, and also help our sick little baby to survive. Jim Bob and I (Michelle) are accustomed to spending a lot of our time together and with our family. That closeness means we maintain a comfortable connection; we generally know what the other one is doing. But from December until July, our time together was limited. I spent many long days and nights at the hospital with Josie while Jim Bob went back and forth between the hospital and the Little Rock house, checking on our family there, or back and forth between Little Rock and Springdale, managing home and business concerns. Jim Bob and I spoke often by phone, but it wasn't the same as face-to-face communication and companionship.

Then, as one period of anguish seemed to be lifting and Josie was finally recovering, we suffered another heartbreaking loss. Shortly after Josie was discharged from the hospital the first time—and then rushed back to the NICU by ambulance less than forty-eight hours later—I received a call from my sister Pam in Ohio. She said that our father, eighty-four-year-old Garrett Ruark, had fallen and broken his hip.

Daddy's health had been fragile for the past few years after incurring serious injuries in a head-on car crash with a driver who was strung out on methamphetamines. We had just finished building our current home when the crash occurred, and we gladly moved Daddy into our first-floor guest room.

He lived with us several months. As with Grandpa and Grandma Duggar, our children loved having a grandparent nearby to talk, read, and play games with. Eventually my siblings invited Daddy to live with them in Ohio, his home turf, so he moved up there.

When Daddy fell and broke his hip I longed to rush to his bedside, but I was busy day and night helping Josie, and we knew he was in good hands. At that time, Josie's lactose intolerance had not been diagnosed, and I was still pumping milk every three hours during the day and about every six hours at night. When I wasn't in the "pumping room" at the hospital, I was in the NICU feeding Josie her bottle, talking to her doctors and nurses, or providing nonmedical care for her that I, as her mother, wanted to do.

Daddy's condition deteriorated into pneumonia, and with each worsening report I felt more anguish, torn between wanting to be with my father and my baby. By then Josie had been discharged from the hospital for the second time, and she and I were staying in the Little Rock house to be near the hospital in case problems arose.

Jim Bob and the rest of the family had left nearly three weeks earlier on the whirlwind trip out east to the homeschool conference. Their trip also included a stop at the home of the Bates family near Knoxville and a day spent in Albany, Georgia, where the children appeared as extras in a Christian movie, *Courageous*, being filmed by Sherwood Pictures, the ministry of Sherwood Baptist Church that has also produced the popular Christian movies *Flywheel*, *Facing the Giants*, and *Fireproof*.

Now they were back home in Springdale, where twelve of the kids were recovering from chicken pox.

The day Daddy died I was alone with Josie in the Little Rock house. The old, three-story mansion we rented had never seemed emptier than it did that day.

Josie had to be fed the Pregestimil formula every three hours. While she was still in the NICU, I did most of the daytime feedings but usually came home to sleep at night and let the nurses take care of her feeding until morning. After her discharge, she and I moved to the Little Rock house, where I was solely responsible for all of her care and feedings.

It was a joy to have Josie home from the hospital and thriving at last. Still, solo parenting a preemie on only three hours' sleep at a time was a challenge. When the call came about Daddy, my tears flowed in a torrent of grief and exhaustion. I poured out my heart to God, thanking Him for my daddy's life, asking Him to comfort my siblings and their families, and also asking Him to help me get through my sorrow and hold up physically for the sad and stressful days ahead.

Back in Springdale, Jim Bob loaded the family back on the bus and set out for Ohio.

I called a Little Rock friend who's also a NICU nurse at ACH; she and her husband graciously agreed to spend the night in the Little Rock house with Josie while I rushed to Ohio to attend Daddy's funeral. Arriving there, my sorrow over losing my dad was eased by being surrounded again by Jim Bob and our children. It had been nearly ten days since I'd seen them, when they had briefly stopped by the Cornish house on their way back to northwest Arkansas from their trip out east. They had stood outside on the porch, looking through the glass window, to say hello to me. It had been such a strongly poignant moment. I had longed to hold each one of them in my arms but couldn't because I couldn't risk exposing Josie to chicken pox.

The day after Daddy's funeral, I would leave my family again to fly back to Josie in Little Rock. In the little time we had

I was alone with Josie in the Little Rock house when my daddy died in Ohio. The old three-story mansion had never seemed emptier than it did that day.

together, Jim Bob and I talked to our children about this additional hard loss for our family, reminding them what death meant for Christians from both an earthly and an eternal perspective. Our family sang two songs as part of the funeral service. We spent a little time with family and friends. Then I headed for the airport, and Jim Bob and our children loaded back onto the bus for the long drive home.

FINALLY HOME

The next week, Jim Bob and some of the older boys, with strong help from our Friendly Chapel friends and other friends from the Little Rock area, brought a box truck and vans to move Josie and me from the Cornish house back home to Springdale. How wonderful it was to return to that house full of children after nearly seven months away! Not all of the kids were there, however; Jana and John-David were on their month-long mission trip to Singapore, Indonesia, and Malaysia.

In another week or so, Josie and I were alone again in a big, empty house, and Jim Bob and the rest of the kids were on the road again, traveling to Camden, Michigan, to keep a commitment we'd made months earlier. John-David and Jana, returning from their overseas mission trip, met the rest of the family in Camden. The children performed vocal music as part of a weeklong tent meeting called the "How to Be Successful" conference, organized by our friend, Camden mayor Harold Walker, with former Michigan State Trooper Tom Harmon preaching. There was a great turnout, with six to eight hundred people attending each night, which is more than the population of the whole town. Hearts were touched, and lives were changed.

After the revival, the family drove to O'Hare International Airport in Chicago, where Jim Bob got on a plane to San Antonio to meet me for the Vision Forum Baby Conference, another speaking commitment we had made the previous year. Jill flew home to Springdale to take care of Josie for the two nights I would be away. Our little preemie by then had progressed to the point of being almost like a normal baby, except for her lactose intolerance, and with Grandma Duggar's help, the very experienced Jill managed just fine.

Finally, on July 10, 2010, for the first time since December 15, 2009, all twenty-four of us—Jim Bob and me, our nineteen children plus daughter-in-law Anna, granddaughter Mackynzie, and Grandma Duggar—were together in one place, safe and happy.

Thank You, God!

SURVIVAL STORY

In a little over two years, our family lost two beloved grandfathers, gained three precious babies—granddaughter Mackynzie and our own Jordyn and Josie—and survived the upheaval of the anxious aftermath of Josie's premature birth.

There were times during those two years when we felt happy, times we felt sad, and times we felt scattered both mentally and physically. While our love for each other and for our family never waned—not one iota!—our hearts still bear the emotional scars from those moments when fear, exhaustion, and confusion seemed to muddle our thinking, steal our focus, and make us concerned about the future.

As we finish the writing of this book, we rejoice that Josie is thriving and our family is again together at

TORTILLA SOUP GRANDIOSO

4 (15.5-ounce) cans diced tomatoes
2 cans tomato sauce
4–5 cans beans (a variety of black, pinto, garbanzo, etc.)
3 large chicken breasts, cooked and cubed
4 cups frozen corn
¾ bunch fresh cilantro, chopped*
1 lime, juiced
Grated cheddar cheese, sour cream, and tortilla chips for toppings

In a large pot heat the tomatoes, sauce, beans, chicken, and corn. Simmer. After removing from heat, add lime juice and cilantro. Serve with grated cheddar cheese, sour cream, and tortilla chips!

* The fresh cilantro and lime juice add the special flavor to this soup!

home in Tontitown, healed and whole. We will be forever thankful that God brought us through our time of fiery testing. When we lost our footing, we found Him again through repeated prayer and by encouraging each other. We also felt the power of prayers being offered on our behalf by friends, known and unknown, around the world. If you are one of those friends, thank you!

16

Michelle's Heart for Children and Moms

She looketh well to the ways of her household,
and eateth not the bread of idleness.
—Proverbs 31:27

As I (Michelle) was walking in to Arkansas Children's Hospital one day, I noticed a young woman sitting outside on one of the benches. She seemed distraught, and I felt God prompting me to offer her a word of encouragement.

I stopped by the bench and asked her if I could sit down. She smiled and scooted over to make room for me. I said, "Hi, I'm Michelle. Are you doing all right today?"

She said her name was Sarah, and then she sighed. Her baby was in the NICU, just like Josie was. In fact, he had been born on March 19, one day after Josie's original due date. But like Josie, Samuel came way too early, at only twenty-four weeks gestation, near the limits of a premature baby's chance of survival. Samuel had suffered a bowel perforation, as Josie had. And now his life seemed ever so perilous.

My heart ached for Sarah. It is such a hard thing to see anyone suffer but especially a tiny, precious baby. So much of what this family was experiencing, we had just walked through ourselves with Josie. We talked some more. She was such a good listener, and we connected sincerely, from one mom's heart to another.

I asked, "Sarah, could I pray with you?"

When she said yes, we bowed our heads and linked our hearts as we prayed for little Samuel and little Josie.

What a blessing Sarah was to me that day! As a result of feeling led to be an encouragement to her, I came away from the encounter uplifted as well. That's what God means when He tells us, in his Word, to encourage one another and build each other up.

Sarah was one of dozens of parents we met at ACH who were facing extraordinary difficulties. Some of them lived far away but, like us, had a baby who had been born with problems and needed the expert care of the big hospital's NICU. Some could only be with their baby on weekends because they had to hang on to their jobs back home in order to have insurance. Some simply couldn't afford to make the long trip from some far-off corner of the state and stay in a hotel while they were there.

Moms Connecting Heart-to-Heart

I believe there's an intangible tie that binds mothers' hearts together, especially during times of stress and struggles. Whenever I see another mom out in public, perhaps herding a bunch of children through a grocery store or trying to get them to sit still in church, I always try to speak a word of encouragement to her—or at least offer her a bright smile. I remember so well what it was like when I would take five little ones under age five to the grocery store by myself!

Oh, what a special joy—and a serious challenge—that was! Sometimes

What could be more fun for Johannah and Jackson than dressing up like a cowgirl and cowboy and riding stickhorses?

my cart was overflowing with children and groceries! By the time I got to the checkout line I was usually frazzled and worn out.

But it seems that so often when I get to the end of my rope, God sends someone my way with the perfect bit of encouragement. It might be another shopper who compliments the kids on their manners or their good behavior (if we happen to be having a good-manner-and-good-behavior day). Or it could be someone who asks, "Are all of those children *yours?*" and then, after I say yes, replies, "What a beautiful family!"

Some grocery-store rules that we have implemented over the years have really helped our children know what is expected of them when we are shopping. When the children go into a store they are to:

+ Whisper quietly.

+ Sit still inside the cart or hold onto the side of the cart as we walk.

+ Not touch or pick up anything without permission or unless they've been asked to do so. (If it's candy or cookies and they're shopping with Dad, they may not have time to ask before he already has them in the cart!)

+ It's fine to make suggestions, but don't nag or we *won't* get the item.

+ Be good helpers, and you may get to go again next time.

IN MY WEAKNESS, HIS STRENGTH

It *is* exhausting being a mom, whether you have one child or nineteen. Long ago I realized I simply couldn't do it on my own. One night—actually, in the middle of the night, when I was still up, folding laundry—feelings of weariness flooded over me. That was back in the time when we had seven kids, and doing laundry by myself was a round-the-clock job. So, whenever I was up feeding a baby during the night, I was also doing laundry. I knew if I didn't stay caught up, we wouldn't have clean underwear for the potty-trainers the next day.

That night I stood in that laundry room crying. *Lord, You must have the wrong person here!* I silently prayed. *I simply can't do this. I'm not capable; I feel so overwhelmed and inadequate. I'm so grateful for these precious gifts You've given me, but, Father, I need Your help!*

My cry was like that of a helpless baby: the only way that baby's going to be helped is if a loving parent comes to meet its need.

That night I felt God saying to my heart in a soft, clear voice, *Michelle, it's easy to praise Me when things are going great—when the house is neat, the dishes are clean, the laundry's done, and your children are healthy and behaving themselves—but are you willing to praise Me right now, when it's not easy?*

Immediately to my mind came these words from Scripture: "Offer the sacrifice of praise to God continually" (Hebrews 13:15).

I said, "Father, I love You, and I'm going to praise You even when I don't feel like it. With You, I am capable; without You, I am nothing. I desperately need You." Then, through my tears, I softly began to sing, "The joy of the Lord is my strength. The joy of the Lord is my strength."

As I sang, a release came over my heart as if a burden had been lifted. I finished the laundry around 2 a.m. and went to bed.

Shortly after the laundry-room experience, my little ones were taking piano lessons at the home of an older woman we call Nana. I was sitting there drifting off to sleep while listening to their lessons when Nana asked me, "Are you okay, Michelle?"

I answered, "Yes, I'm fine. I was just up late last night doing laundry."

Nana's face seemed to light up. "Laundry? Do you need help doing laundry? I *love* to do laundry!"

The idea had never occurred to me. *Have someone help with our laundry?* Amazed, I told Nana, "Well, sure, I could use some help."

The next Saturday, Nana came to our house and said, "Just have the kids carry all the dirty laundry to the laundry room, and I'll do it." Later that day, when she was all finished, I was so touched by the gift she had given me, I cried again!

Nana said, "It's a joy for me. I love doing laundry."

God sent His angel Nana to our home twice a week for many years. What a powerful lesson it was for me to remember that God's strength is "made perfect" in my weakness—and to realize I didn't have to understand *how* He would help me; I just had to cry out in humility and believe He *would*. My job was, and is, to keep praising the Lord, even when I don't feel like it.

As an encouragement to other women, I like to share this beautiful poem by Roy Lessin. (He has also authored one of my favorite books, *How to Be the Parents of Happy and Obedient Children*.) This poem is good to keep displayed before our eyes.

CONTINUE ON

A woman fretted over the usefulness of her life.
She feared she was wasting her potential being a devoted wife and mother.
She wondered if the time and energy she invested in her husband
    and children would make a difference.
At times she got discouraged because so much of what she did
    seemed to go unnoticed and unappreciated.
"Is it worth it?" she often wondered. "Is there something better that I could
    be doing with my time?"
It was during one of these moments of questioning that she heard
    the still, small voice of her Heavenly Father speak to her heart.
"You are a wife and mother because that is what I have called you to be.
Much of what you do is hidden from the public eye, but I notice.
Most of what you give is done without remuneration.
But I am your reward.
Your husband cannot be the man I have called him to be
    without your support.
Your influence upon him is greater than you think
    and more powerful than you will ever know.
I bless him through your service and honor him through your love.
Your children are precious to me.
Even more precious than they are to you.

I have entrusted them to your care to raise for Me.
What you invest in them is an offering to Me.
You may never be in the public spotlight, but your obedience shines as a
*   bright light before Me.*
Continue on. Remember you are my servant.
Do all to please me.[1]

THE POWER OF PRAISE

Jim Bob and I both are flexible, fairly self-motivated people who set goals and try to accomplish as much as we can every day. We try to motivate our children to do well, but neither of us is a perfectionist; we don't insist that everything has to be done our way or it's not good enough. We're saddened when we hear parents wrongly using rejecting words or put-downs for correction or in a misguided attempt to motivate their children to do better or do what the parents want them to do.

Others withhold praise until their children have reached a certain high standard of accomplishment; too many children in this kind of setting grow up feeling as though they never measure up. It's easy in that situation to develop low self-worth.

Our friend Pastor Don Elmore says when expectations are high and reality is low, in between the two is frustration. As parents we

We generally serve fruits and vegetables as snacks. But occasionally, Jason (left), James, and Justin find that a hot donut is a treat worth smiling for.

want to lovingly motivate our children to do their best, but at the same time we need to give our expectations to God. We need to praise our children for whatever they accomplish, as if we didn't expect them to accomplish anything. The more we share words of affirmation in a spirit of love, the more they will want to please us, and ultimately the Lord. Then, inevitably, they will accomplish what we desire for them.

I have the following poem framed and in view where I can see it each day. It's another token of encouragement I share with young mothers when the opportunity arises. May we keep our perspective on what is most important as we nurture our little ones.

LOVE

If I live in a house of spotless beauty with everything in its place,
　　but have not love—I am a housekeeper, not a homemaker.
If I have time for waxing, polishing, and decorative achievements,
　　but have not love—my children learn of cleanliness, not godliness.
Love leaves the dust in search of a child's laugh.
Love smiles at the tiny fingerprints on a newly cleaned window.
Love wipes away the tears before it wipes up the spilled milk.
Love picks up the child before it picks up the toys.
Love is present through trials.
Love reprimands, reproves, and is responsive.
As a mother there is much I must teach my child,
　　but the greatest of all is . . . LOVE.[2]

ANGER RESOLUTION

I want our home to be a safe place where our children feel love and acceptance. I want it to be a fun place, not a house where parental anger suddenly erupts, where they have to be on pins and needles, always worrying they are making a mistake. Anger is a destructive force. Even if we take our children to church every time the doors are open, anger in us or in our home can destroy everything we are trying to teach our children. It can build a wall between them and us.

One day a few years ago, I learned an important lesson about anger and harsh words when I felt like I was at my wits' end. That day God seemed to touch my heart gently and speak calm words into my mind as I was on the verge of losing my temper. (After the laundry-room experience, I'd learned to watch for God's powerful presence in my life in the most ordinary settings and situations.)

That particular lesson was about having the proper response to my anger by speaking to my children with a soft, gentle voice. It happened because of a can of pineapple.

We probably had eleven children under the age of eleven when the incident happened. During homeschool, we were studying what the Wisdom Booklets teach on the subject of anger, how everyone feels angry sometimes and how destructive those feelings can be if they're not managed appropriately.

The lesson about anger included several Bible passages that explain the proper way to respond to anger. I began reading the passages to my children, and when I got to Proverbs 15:1, the words stood out to me and my eyes filled with tears. It says, "A soft answer turneth away wrath: but grievous words stir up anger."

Strongly impacted by that verse, I visualized several times I'd said harsh words to my children or responded quickly and abruptly, without thinking. In our faith we say we are "convicted" of something when God brings an important lesson into our minds, convincing us of its truth. That day, standing there in front of my children, I was convicted of the different times I had mishandled the anger I had felt toward them. Wiping away tears, I told them, "I am so sorry for the angry words I have spoken to you. Will you please forgive Mommy?"

They all said they would.

I silently prayed to the Lord: *Father, I don't want my children to remember me as a mama who was constantly fussing at them and raising my voice at them. I want them to remember me as a joyful and happy mama who loves being with them. God, please help me in those difficult moments to have the right response to the anger I feel welling up inside me.*

We went on with the lesson, and the more we studied the proper response to anger, the more I resolved in my heart to follow the biblical guidance.

Then God, in His wisdom, gave me an opportunity to put what I was learning into action.

A little while later, I was in the kitchen preparing a snack while mentally repeating my new anger-response plan: *A soft answer turns away wrath; but grievous words stir up strife. I'm not going to bicker, not going to nag, not going to ask the kids ten times to do something. I'm going to lovingly say it once, and if they don't obey, then I'll quickly correct them in love, encourage them in a soft voice to do what's right, and then move on. I'm going to use a soft, low voice, no matter what. If they don't listen, I'll follow through with correction, but even then, I'll stay calm and speak softly.*

I had opened a big can of pineapple chunks earlier that morning, and half of it was still sitting on the counter, waiting to be put away. One of the kids asked, "Mama, may I have the rest of the pineapple?"

I answered, "Wait just a minute. I've gotta go change sister's diaper, and then I'll come back and help you with it."

You already know what happened, don't you? I came back into the kitchen after changing the diaper, and there was the pineapple, spilled all over the floor. The sticky juice had splattered everywhere—not just on the floor but up on the doors of the cabinets and under the refrigerator—then had been tromped through and tracked into the living room by another little one. It was one giant mess.

I drew in a breath. *This is not what I need right now,* I said to myself. I couldn't even get to the mop without walking through the pineapple juice.

Then another voice came into my head: *I'm giving you grace to do what's right. Are you going to have the right response?*

The words had to have come from God, and yet it almost seemed as if they were coming from the anxious child standing before me in the middle of the mess, his little face worried, his eyes as big as giant marbles.

We looked at each other for one long moment. Then I squatted down in front of him and said, in a soft, calm voice, "What did Mommy say?"

He swallowed hard as a tear rolled down his cheek. He repeated what I had told him—to wait and I would help him get some pineapple.

"That's right. That's what I said," I told him, trying to remain calm in that same, soft voice. "Now I want you to go to your room and wait for Mommy. I'm going to clean up this mess, and then I'll be there in a little bit."

Don't think my anger was under control just because I didn't yell at him. That wasn't it at all. The attitude of my heart at that moment was, *Okay, Lord (pant, pant, pant), I'm about to explode right now. This is absolutely more than I can handle on my own, but I know You're helping me. So I'm gonna do what You say; with Your help, I'm gonna stay calm and speak in that soft, low voice.*

I cleaned up the sticky mess; it took quite a while, but it gave me time to cool down and think about the lesson I had taught the children from the Wisdom Booklet—the proper response to our anger—and suddenly I felt a surge of God's grace filling me with peace and erasing all traces of bitterness and frustration.

I went to my son, waiting nervously in his room, and was able to lovingly explain to him, in a soft, gentle voice, why he needed to always obey me: not just because he might make a big mess if he disobeyed but also because I loved him and didn't want him pulling things down that could hurt him or spill and get into his eyes or cut him with sharp edges.

"There are things you don't understand right now that Mommy does understand," I told him. "Sometimes I don't have time to explain why I'm telling you to do something or not to do something, but you can trust that it's because I love you and not because I'm trying to spoil your fun or make you wait for something you really want. God is teaching you patience—while He's teaching me how to teach you."

This heart-to-heart talk with my little guy was the beginning of a whole new level of child training for me; I was learning the value of a soft voice. Oftentimes as I spoke with my children that way while encouraging or correcting them, I was reminded of another Bible passage, a story from 1 Kings 19 that tells how, while Elijah was hiding in a cave on Mount Horeb, "the LORD passed by."

A great wind roared by the cave, "but the LORD was not in the wind." Nor was He in the earthquake that followed, or the fire that came next. But after all that, there came "a still small voice," the voice of God.

In the days surrounding Josie's birth, she and I were so sick and weak I couldn't quite imagine a day would come when we would pose for a photo like this.

That day happened many years ago, but even now, I still struggle with anger. Sometimes I feel it welling up inside of me, and my natural response is to lash out, say harsh words, and raise my voice, but then I'm reminded of the damage that kind of response causes: I can see in my children's faces that their spirits are crushed, and I feel so much guilt. It produces a damaged relationship, and I have to go back and ask them to forgive me.

Each time it happens, I think, *I don't want to have to do that again!* I realize God is training me to tame my tongue and to choose joy over exhaustion and weariness. I *choose* to smile and be joyful because my children are precious to me, and I can't think of a better way to spend my life than investing it in the lives of my children and my grandchild—and, I hope, more grandchildren and great-grandchildren to come. What I do now affects generations to come. As a reminder to me, a plaque hangs in my room that urges me to "Be a Joyful Mother of Children!"

CONSISTENCY IS KEY

ALFREDO SPAGHETTI

1 quart heavy whipping cream
1 stick (½ cup) butter
8 ounces (2 cups) Parmesan cheese
1 teaspoon salt
1 pound cooked spaghetti, drained

In large saucepan, warm whipping
cream and butter until butter is melted.
Remove from heat. Slowly blend in
Parmesan cheese and salt with wire
whisk until thoroughly blended. Cover,
let stand 10 minutes, till thickened. Stir
in cooked spaghetti. Makes 6 servings.

Another important goal is consistency. I am trying to train my children to obey the first time they're told, whether I'm asking a three-year-old to put her big sister's markers back where she found them or asking a five-year-old to sit quietly at the table for school or instructing all the youngest ones *never* to climb on the outside railing of the staircase in our living room.

Jim Bob and I aren't rigidly strict disciplinarians. We know children make mistakes and use poor judgment—and, sometimes, so do their parents. We are thankful God is patient and "longsuffering" with us. Through our own mistakes, we've learned the importance of consistently training our children according to biblical principles.

I mentioned this earlier in the book, but it's worth repeating here. If I ask a child to do something and he doesn't do it, or vice versa, or if I let a child get away with something she knows not to do, then a few minutes later there's going to be another little act of misbehavior, and a little later there will be another, bigger misbehavior. Before long there will be behavior that requires serious attention, often resulting in tears. That's not what either of us wants.

I've learned that I need to *immediately* attend to that first little incident. If it's really minor, I simply let the child know I've seen it and tell him or her to *stop*. Or if it's one of the little boys driving an "outside toy" inside the house, maybe I have the child sit at the kitchen counter for five minutes or have him or her stand quietly beside me while I'm doing dishes, cooking, or attending to something else, until I can tend to the child.

The children need to know that when Mama says something in her soft, quiet voice, she means it—and she means it the first time. I don't yell (anymore). In fact, sometimes my children say they know when I'm *really* serious because my voice gets even softer than usual! Each one must learn there are consequences for bad behavior and rewards for good behavior. All communication must be done with a gentle spirit, like a judge calmly determining the outcome of a case.

Love and consistency are the keys!

THE HEART OF HOMESCHOOLING

People often ask us why we've chosen to homeschool our children. Let me share with you the reasons. Early in our marriage, even before Josh was school age, Jim Bob and I committed to homeschooling him as well as any other children we might have.

The first reason was to fulfill the teaching of Deuteronomy 6:5–7:

> And thou shalt love the Lord thy God with all thine heart, and with all thine soul, and with all your might. And these words, which I command thee this day, shall be in thine heart: And thou shalt teach them diligently unto thy children, and shalt talk of them when thou sittest in thine house, and when thou walkest by the way, and when thou liest down, and when thou risest up.

We personally felt that homeschooling was the best way for us to accomplish the goal of training our children to love God with all their heart, soul, mind, and strength, when they get up, sit down, walk, and are going to bed as commanded in Deuteronomy.

The second reason we homeschool is that we want our children to be free to become who God wants them to become without negative peer pressure and without the influences that could lead to involvement in drugs, alcohol, and immorality.

Even though Jim Bob went to a Christian school from grades six through twelve and had a lot of godly teachers, as he looks back on his school years he sees that the kids had more social influence over their fellow students than the teachers did. In contrast, we want our children to be surrounded by positive peer pressure from godly Christian influences during their most formative years.

The third reason is that we don't want our children indoctrinated in atheism, socialism, evolution, and other worldly philosophies and behaviors eight hours a day, which is happening in many schools. We believe as parents that we are responsible for every influence we allow our children to be around. We are training our children with a Christ-centered education, and we use many resources, such as www.answersingenesis.com, which teaches not only evidence that God supernaturally created the earth but also how evolution is impossible.

The fourth reason we homeschool is that we want our children to become best friends with each other and be close as a family. Our opinion is, if you can learn to get along and resolve conflicts with your brothers and sisters day in and day out, you can learn to get along with anyone. It's a beautiful thing to see this truth lived out!

When we decided to homeschool, I loved it, but as our family grew, it sometimes seemed absolutely overwhelming. Jim Bob would be gone all day, sometimes from sunup to sundown, answering wrecker calls that came into our towing business. Even in those early years he thought he had a big family to support (little did he know!), and he felt the pressure weighing on him tremendously. Those days usually left me as the only parent available to teach, train, and correct all our little guys throughout the day.

While my intention was to teach our children, it seemed that sometimes, through our studies together, God was teaching me more than I was able to teach them. Responding appropriately to anger was just one of the lessons I was learning. I also saw how our children learn more from our responses and actions than from our words, and the importance of being consistent in training and discipline was proven to me again and again. Then came the biggest lesson of all.

One afternoon when I'd finally managed to get all of the babies down for their naps and all the school-age children seated around the table, I opened up our curriculum and suddenly felt completely inadequate for the task at hand. It just seemed to be too much to do—almost impossible. How could I possibly teach my children all the things I wanted them to know: reading, writing, math, science, history, medicine, government, and everything else? I was starting to question why I had ever thought homeschooling was a good idea.

I can't do this, Lord. It's just too much, I mentally moaned.

His answer seemed to come as quickly as my next breath: *If you can do only one thing, Michelle, do the most important thing: get My Word into their hearts and minds in such a way that they hunger and thirst for it.*

I was reminded how Jesus had summarized God's Word for His followers. Basically, He told them the most important commandments were to love God and to love others as they loved themselves. If they made those two goals their priorities, everything else would fall into place, He said. "Seek ye first the kingdom of God and His righteousness and all these things shall be added unto you."

Not long after that moment, the idea I mentioned earlier about "salting the oats" came to mind. It's the idea of making God's Word so appealing and interesting—so salty—the kids hunger for it. We began focusing more on memorizing Scripture, working on it together to put motions with the words and embedding them in our hearts.

In addition to memorizing God's Word, we also study it as the owner's manual for our lives. We read it aloud to each other just for the pure enjoyment of hearing it, or we read it silently, absorbing it into our minds. I *know* our children are absorbing it because they will come back and quote it later or refer to it when they share a situation they're struggling with.

We try to surround our children and ourselves with God's Word, and we try to get it into our heads and our hearts through as many of our senses as possible. One way we do this is to "write it upon the doorposts," using decorative lettering to copy Bible phrases, as well as encouraging quotes from Christian leaders, onto the walls of various rooms.

In addition to including Bible reading and memorization in our homeschool time, Jim Bob reads and explains Scripture passages to the children at night during Bible time. Some people ask if we skip over the Bible stories that include murder, adultery, stealing, or other sinful behavior. The answer is no. We use those stories as teachable examples of someone who did wrong and incurred God's consequences as a result. We prefer those stories to television and movie plots that sometimes feature someone doing wrong without any consequences, or even getting rewarded for committing the crime.

MEDITATE? IN *OUR* HOUSE?

At the Basic Life Principles Seminar, which we highly recommend, we heard Dr. Bill Gothard talking about the value of memorizing and meditating on Scripture. He said, "When Joshua faced the awesome giants of his day, he was given the command to meditate upon God's Word day and night, so that whatever he did would be successful" (see Joshua 1:7–9).

Remembering Dr. Gothard's words, I (Michelle) thought of an idea. I set a little CD player on my nightstand so we can listen to recordings of Alexander Scorby reading the entire King James Version of the Bible. He has a wonderfully strong but mellow voice. I set it to play continuously, with the volume barely above a whisper, and Jim Bob and I fall asleep hearing the inspiring words of the Bible.

That practice has been a great blessing to me, especially during stressful times or times of spiritual struggle. I feel like I'm being fed God's Word intravenously! Now I listen to similar recordings on my iPhone, or I turn on another CD player when I'm working in the kitchen or elsewhere in the house.

The Bible is the truth we base our lives upon, and we've taught our children to do likewise. We have only a short time with them before they're grown and living away from home, and we want to spend every possible moment filling their hearts with our love and their minds with God's Word.

The Bible says when God's Word goes out, it does not come back void (see Isaiah 55:11), and I've certainly seen the truth of that statement. I've learned that when I can't find the CD of a certain passage of Scripture, I should ask my children about it before I look further. More than likely, one of them has been listening to it through the day or as he or she falls asleep to it at night.

The Bible says, "The evening and the morning were the first day" (Genesis 1:5), which we understand as meaning that our day actually begins the evening before. Maybe that's why it seems that whatever I go to bed thinking about sets the course for the next day. Many nights, while it is quiet, I spend time alone with the Lord, pouring my heart out to Him, praying for my family and for others, and thinking about how His Word applies to every aspect of life.

This is one of the ways we meditate on Scripture in the busy, noisy Duggar family. It's interesting to see how, as we go through life and have to make important decisions, we filter our choices through those scriptures and Bible principles we've learned and studied. To me, that's what wisdom means: looking at everything in life from God's perspective.

USING THE INTERNET FOR GOOD

Speaking of wisdom, we agree with most of the world that the Internet is one of the greatest inventions in our lifetime, providing quick availability of knowledge about every subject imaginable. But the Internet also has the greatest potential to destroy souls with instant, unlimited access to all sorts of immorality. We tell our children, "Welding metal together is an incredible process. It is interesting to watch, but if you don't protect your eyes, you will go blind! Similarly, if men, young and old, do not have internet protection and accountability, they will scar their eyes, which are the windows to the soul." For that reason, we have set up multiple safeguards on our Mac computers, creating parental controls that strictly limit Internet access.

I realize that the limits we set for our children may be different than those set by others, but so many have asked us about it that I want to share our thinking with you here.

During their free time, our kids can go to more than seventy-five prescreened websites for fun and educational information and activities. Some of their favorites are lifeatthepond.com and focusonthefamily .com. The sites they're able to visit don't include any search engines or websites that have full-web search engines as part of the site. We also double-check to verify that any embedded YouTube videos on those pre-approved sites don't also have a YouTube search engine.

If the kids need to go to the open Internet to research something, they need an accountability partner to sit alongside them as they go on the web, and before they can begin, Mom or one of the older girls must type in the Internet-protection password. They're the only ones who know it.

Last year we acquired a few iPhones. They are handy and fun to use; we can check the bank balance or the ten-day weather forecast in an instant. But because they are Internet enabled, they also need to be password protected. The ones used by Dad and the boys don't have Safari or any other application that leads to a search engine.

To keep an iPhone safe from open Internet access, you have to thoroughly examine every application you are considering, as well as anything it links to and from. Even with the Safari web browser turned off, sometimes an ad on an application will lead to the open Internet. As parents we must guard our family and ourselves from wasting time on computers and allowing access to sites that could destroy our souls.

Social networks like Facebook, MySpace, Twitter, and chat rooms are quickly connecting the world. If used in the right way, they can be powerful tools for sharing God's redemption plan and for offering personal testimony about how God is working in your life. But they can also be dangerous, allowing exposure to immoral messages and images and wasting a lot of time!

Grandma Duggar has told our kids for years, "Show me your friends, and I will show you your future." Open access to social-networking sites can expose us to "friendship" that can have a harmful effect on our hearts and minds.

Consider this: Christ did not command us to go out and make friends; He told us to make *disciples* (see Matthew 28:19). We tell our kids, If your goal is to win *friends*, you'll probably end up doing a lot of compromising to keep their friendship. If your goal is to love and *disciple* others, people who hang out with you will be challenged to follow God's vision for their life, and you will have true friendships where each encourages the other to live for God!

The Learning Channel maintains a Facebook page for our series, *19 Kids and Counting*, but at this point none of our children living at home has a Facebook, MySpace, or Twitter account, even though there have been many impersonators out there pretending to be one of us.

Girl Talk

When our girls are turning twelve, or whenever it seems appropriate for them, I (Michelle) give them a little gift we call a "womanhood kit" that includes some personal feminine products, perfume and deodorant, a razor, and sanitary pads, as well as some girlie stuff: maybe some translucent powder, lip gloss, and pretty hair clips or barrettes.

Then we spend some special time together, usually beginning with lunch, where I can talk to my daughter about some of the changes that are or will be happening in her body. I explain how this is the beginning of a new and exciting season of life, and I share some of the things her big sisters and her mom know about—things like cramps and Midol, for example! I laugh, telling her about the "phenomenon" that seems to cause most of the older girls in the family to go through their menstrual cycle at about the same time. It's just one of those things that happens when a bunch of women live and work together.

I'll talk to her about how she'll soon start having those funny feelings whenever she's around boys. And how God wants her to stay pure mentally and physically until she's married; then we'll probably shop for a purity ring. It's just a simple band, but she gets to pick exactly what she wants, whether it's embossed or smooth. It's to remind her of her priority to stay pure in heart, soul, and body.

We explain to our older children, both girls and boys, that they have different areas of weakness. We share the Bible's warning about how dangerous it is to make "provision for the flesh, to fulfill the lusts thereof" (Romans 13:14). For instance, I have told my girls that romance novels are to women what pornography is to men. They stir up your emotions with unreal fantasies. In contrast, God's Word tells us to think on things that are honest, pure, lovely, and of a good report (see Philippians 4:8).

For these reasons, we try not to have things around our home that would set up our children for failure in moral purity, whether it be magazines that contain sensual ads or newspaper inserts that portray immodesty.

A PRIORITY OF PURITY

President Teddy Roosevelt said, "To educate a child without teaching morality is to educate a menace to society." In today's world, the entertainment industry glamorizes intimate physical relationships with multiple others outside of marriage as being irresistible and acceptable. But the truth is, God designed the intimate love relationship for only one man with one woman within a lifelong marriage commitment. Anything other than that is asking for painful and serious consequences.

Jim Bob loves to teach our children by telling great stories or creating analogies that they can relate to. He has an incredible ability to make a truth from God's Word come alive and become real in their hearts and minds.

To explain the importance of purity (saving yourself for the one God has made for you), he told the older children, "Imagine that your parents are going to surprise you and give you a brand-new bike for Christmas. Two weeks before Christmas, they buy your bike and hide it in the storage shed in the backyard. But then the boy next door sneaks into the shed and borrows your new bike; he stunt-rides it up and down the back alley.

"On Christmas morning your parents lead you out to the shed to reveal the special gift they bought for you, and as they open the door and say, 'Surprise!' they're just as surprised as you are. You're *all* shocked to see that the bike looks like it's been thrown off a cliff. The front fender is missing, and the front tire is warped so it rubs on the frame. It's dirty, the paint is all scratched and chipped, and the seat has a big rip in it. It looks worse than something you would have bought at a garage sale.

"I'm sure you would still be grateful for the bike, and you would have fun riding it, but it won't be in the condition your parents had hoped and dreamed it would be when you received it. You would miss out on a lot of the enjoyment they meant for you to have.

"In that same way, we don't want any boy (or girl) to come and steal your purity. It's vital to be patient and wait for the one God has for you and to not 'play around' in situations where you could be tempted to compromise your purity. What kind of gift do you want to be for your future spouse?"

Another story Jim Bob shares starts with a disgusting image: "What if we were at a meeting with about one hundred other people and the speaker asked that a large cup be passed around and that everyone spit in the cup? What if you happened to be all the way in the back—the last person on the last row—and when the cup finally came to you the speaker asked you to drink out of the cup? What would you do?"

All of our children say, "Yuck! That's nasty! Gross! That makes me sick just thinking about it!"

Then Dad explains to our older children, "That's what it's like if you have intimate physical relations with several partners. Physical relations outside marriage promote venereal disease, cervical cancer, and a host of other problems."

God can forgive any wrong choices a person is willing to confess and forsake, but there are still painful consequences to be endured. Our heavenly Father loves us, and His goal is not to take away our fun but to protect us from things that will hurt us.

MAN TO MAN

Physical purity is important to us and to our children. Jim Bob talks to our sons at about the age of eleven or twelve and discusses the facts of life to whatever degree he believes they can handle at that age (some mature faster than others).

He talks about how their bodies start to change, and he explains that the reason for their God-given attraction to girls is so that one day they will get married. He also emphasizes the importance of staying pure in mind and in body and how every man has temptations. He encourages them to come and talk to him, day or night, when they are struggling with anything, and he begins asking them on a regular basis

I (Jim Bob) work hard to maintain a strong, loving relationship with all ten of our sons so that they will feel free to tell me the concerns of their hearts.

how they are doing with their thought life and other purity issues that men face.

OVERCOMING TEMPTATIONS

We talk to our children frequently about their feelings, and we maintain an attitude of openness so they feel safe coming to us anytime about anything that's troubling them. That includes feelings and thoughts of a sensual nature, which are inevitable among adolescent and teenage children. We tell our kids, "The power of sin is in secrecy."

We say, if Satan can get you to *think* about doing things that are wrong, it's just a matter of time before he presents a situation that tempts you to *act* on your secret desires. At that point he has you right where he wants you.

You know better than to do what he tells you to do, we say. But sin can make you stupid. He tells you that doing this bad thing will bring you pleasure, and you're tempted to believe him. Sure, there may be temporary pleasure—until the consequences arrive. Then the guilt sets in as well. Once Satan has a stronghold in one area of your life, he tries to take over the rest of it too.

We've told our kids that most bank robbers don't just walk in and rob a bank on impulse. Maybe they can't pay their bills and they wonder where they're going to come up with the money. Instead of thinking about how they could work to earn what they need, they start dreaming about what they would do if they had all the money the bank has. They start coveting the bank's money, and then they start dreaming up ways they could steal it without getting caught. This mind-set could have started with something as simple as stealing a piece of candy when they were kids.

Maybe they think about robbing the bank for quite a while. Then, one day, they put their thoughts into action. They rob the bank, and they get caught and spend the rest of their lives in prison!

Where did they first go wrong? When they robbed the bank? No, the wrongdoing started before that; it started when Satan put the lazy, covetous thought in their minds. We teach our kids to "[bring] into captivity every thought to the obedience of Christ," quoting 2 Corinthians 10:5. And we remind them of something Grandma Duggar has always said: "If a person will lie to you, he will steal also." Major misdeeds and wrongdoings often get their start in what may have seemed inconsequential at the time: a wayward thought, a covetous idea, or a little white lie.

COMMUNICATING OPENLY, WITH LOVE

We explain to our children the importance of maintaining a clear conscience with God and others. We teach them how that's possible, by sharing what Jesus taught His followers: that we should confess our sins so we aren't weighed down by guilt. God's Word says, "He that covereth his sins shall not prosper: but who so confesseth and forsaketh them shall have mercy" (Proverbs 28:13).

Following that guidance, we encourage our children to share with us their mistakes and temptations as well as their troubling thoughts and feelings. We tell them if they've done something wrong (or a whole bunch of things) they need to confess it to God to be free from the guilt that will otherwise make them miserable.

We pray together with the child, asking God to wipe the slate clean and thanking Him for the wonderful gift of forgiveness. Then they go to the person they have offended, if that kind of mistake is what's being confessed, and ask for forgiveness.

When they tell us the thought or temptation that's bothering them, or when they confess the hurtful or mean-spirited thing they may have said or done, we talk to them about how harmful temptations can lead them to behaviors that damage their relationship with God and with their family and friends. Talking to us about those feelings can be freeing; once their "secret" is shared, its grip on their life is released.

Whenever our kids share their hearts with us we know it's important to keep a calm look on our faces and not to overreact to whatever they share with us. Otherwise the kids will think, *I can't tell Mom and Dad about this bad thought I've had; they'll think I'm a horrible person.*

Nothing could be further from the truth. I (Michelle) tell them there's nothing they can say, do, or think that will cause us to stop loving them.

I ask them, "Who do you think put that thought in your head?"

They acknowledge, "Satan did!"

Satan has used similar temptations throughout the centuries, planting doubt and lies in the minds of men and women as he's tried to lead them away from God's truth. I want our children to realize that *everyone* faces temptations from time to time—even Mama and Daddy. In fact, the Bible records many dramatic stories of failure as a result of temptation. From the strongest man who ever lived, Samson, to a man after God's own heart, David, biblical heroes through the ages were tempted by Satan's lies; many fell victim to those lies and failed as a result. God put their stories of failure in the Bible so we can see how the consequences played out when they listened to Satan. We pray that, by God's grace, we won't go that same route.

But the stories also tell us how God restored them to full relationship with Him when they confessed their sin and asked forgiveness. For example, when David, who committed adultery and even murder, came to repentance, God forgave him and eventually blessed him.

We teach our children these lessons so they're ready, not *if* temptations come but *when* they come. "You *will* be tempted to do wrong," I tell them. "So don't be surprised; be prepared!"

We also remind them that the Bible says they're not going to experience a temptation that hasn't already threatened someone else. In fact, I encourage them to memorize 1 Corinthians 10:13, which says, "There hath no temptation taken you but such as is common to man: but God is faithful, who will not suffer you to be tempted above that ye are able; but will with the temptation also make a way to escape, that ye may be able to bear it."

Their older siblings, and even their parents, have probably had the same thoughts or feelings they're having, I say. But by clinging to God's

Word and asking for His help, they will be able to withstand whatever temptation comes their way.

This kind of confession and discussion help keep our relationship with our children strong. But it's not just children who need to learn these kinds of communication skills. I (Michelle) tell our children, "When you learn how to share your mistakes and your temptations with your parents, who love you more than anything, you'll be laying the foundation of communication skills you'll use someday with your spouse. Then you can communicate openly and honestly with your mate just like Daddy and I do now.

"As husband and wife, we are each other's accountability partner. When Daddy is tempted, you can be sure he shares it with me. We talk about it and pray about it together. He does the same for me when I share a problem with him."

A friend of ours who has worked with juvenile delinquents tells young people, "You're going to be okay if you just keep talking, being open and honest. If you do that, you'll make it." Open, loving communication, we say, is one of the keys to strong, stable, loving relationships.

Note: Some children may not feel their parents are a safe place to share their hearts. If the child thinks that the parents will repeat what they have shared with others, they won't feel the freedom to open up.

As a parent, if you have failed in these areas you need to go back and ask forgiveness.

Our whole family helped out in the campaign rallies when Jim Bob ran for the US Senate in 2002.

17

Husbands, love your wives,
even as Christ also loved the church, and gave himself for it.
—Ephesians 5:25

Michelle and I got married in 1984, three days after my nineteenth birthday and two months before her eighteenth. I was the happiest guy in the world, having a girl like Michelle accept my marriage proposal. But most people back then probably thought I didn't have a lot going for me.

I'd been an average student in high school. I worked in a grocery store, where advancement opportunities were limited. I was a good, hard worker, but on paper, my credentials looked pretty weak. Thank goodness Michelle was able to see that my potential lay not in my résumé, but in my heart.

She knew I loved God and loved her and that I had committed my life to following God with my whole heart. Since the first night I met Michelle on a church visitation, my prayer had been that God would allow her to be mine and that I could become her spiritual leader. When the first part of that prayer was answered, I committed myself to doing all I could, with God's help, to becoming the spiritual leader husband, and eventually the spiritual leader father, that God wanted me to be. My lifelong hobby is my family. In the following pages, I'll share some of the ways this hobby has developed as I've matured. Maybe what I've learned will encourage other husbands and fathers to make their families their hobby, as well.

PRAYING ABOUT FINANCIAL DECISIONS

Although I wasn't a strong student during my youth, as an adult I've developed a passionate love for learning Bible principles. That change in me may have been triggered by a speaker I heard years ago who preached from James 1:5, which says, "If any of you lack wisdom, let him ask of God, that giveth to all men liberally, and upbraideth not; and it shall be given him."

As our family grew (baby Jinger was number six) we knew we needed a solid financial foundation to be able to live frugally and care for our children.

I prayed for wisdom and sought to become the man God wanted me to be. In the years since I heard that sermon I've attended many Christian conferences and seminars aimed at teaching men to become godly husbands, fathers, and Christian leaders. One of those seminars, Jim Sammons's Financial Freedom series, mentioned earlier, changed how we thought about and managed our family's finances (see the Resources section for more information).

Jim Sammons's goal was to be financially independent by age thirty. He borrowed money to play the stock market and did quite well— until several of the companies he'd invested in with borrowed money went broke. Instead of being financially independent at age thirty, he was completely upside down. At that point, he says now, God had him right where He wanted him. He started studying God's Word and applied it to his everyday life. As he turned his heart toward God and started applying His principles, God blessed him. Eventually he ended up paying off all his debts and gaining the financial independence he'd hoped for. His success has continued to the point that now he has paid cash to build several shopping centers.

The most important thing the Sammons program taught us was to pray about decisions relating to our personal and business finances and to base our financial practices on a biblical model. In our first book we described several of the amazing miracles we've experienced as we've followed that ideal, and each passing month seems to bring more lessons and more opportunities as we continue to follow that biblical standard.

Sammons's teaching also includes many marriage and family principles as he shares his own transparent life testimony in a humorous way. Michelle's favorite chapter is titled "Husbands, Listen to the Cautions of Your Wife."

Jim Sammons says that one way of "making ends meet" is not a matter of increasing income as much as it is decreasing expenses by utilizing present resources more efficiently. He teaches how to find God's will and how to seek His direction. So many times we have prayed about a potential investment and made an offer, and the offer was rejected or sometimes countered with a higher price than we thought we should pay. When that happens, we accept it as God closing the door on that investment at that time.

Sometimes as we pray for God's guidance about a financial decision, we see His blessings unfolding in seemingly unrelated and totally unexpected ways. For example, weeks before our extended stay in Little Rock, Josh had told me about a great deal on a fifteen-passenger van for sale by a rental-car agency. When we went to look at it, the salesman mentioned that the company was looking for a new location to rent in Springdale. We ended up buying the van, and shortly after that, I found a property on Springdale's main highway that had been on the market awhile. We were able to purchase it for a very good price, with a closing date a few weeks away in early December 2009. Right before that closing date, however, Michelle's health problems developed.

I called the company handling the closing and explained that I was in Little Rock and couldn't make it to the scheduled closing in Springdale because my wife and baby were in the hospital. They said they also had an office in Little Rock.

While I was in that Little Rock office, signing papers to complete the sale, I mentioned that we were looking for a house to rent. As we said in an earlier chapter, that comment in that place resulted in our renting the Cornish house.

Next I called the car-rental manager about the property we had just bought and asked if he would be interested in taking a look at it. Just now, as we are finishing this book, we signed a twenty-year lease with that company.

God is so good. When we let Him control our lives, He accomplishes far more than we could ever imagine.

AVOIDING DEBT, EMBRACING FRUGALITY, SAVING FOR EMERGENCIES

The second principle we adopted after going through the Financial Freedom seminars was to eliminate debt in both our personal and business finances. For more than twenty years, we've followed the principle in Romans 13:8, which says, "Owe no man any thing." Not a day goes by that we're not thankful for that lesson, especially in today's challenging economy. We've seen too many families and businesses make presumptions about the future, go into debt—and lose everything.

We've observed that when people finance big purchases, they usually pay more than they should because they're concentrating on the monthly payment instead of the total cost. They don't realize that when finance charges are added, they're paying two to five times as much for the new item as they would have paid to buy the same or similar used item that would have met their needs just as well. Too many times these debt-burdened buyers end up with a boatload of stuff they don't need or that they soon discard or set aside (sometimes having to get a rental unit to store it), but they're stuck with the payments long after the items are gone. That kind of financial pressure forces them to work longer hours and be away from their families more.

We completely understand that sometimes you want something *now*, and if you don't finance it, you have to wait, which might be uncomfortable. For instance, our house wasn't air conditioned when we moved into it. We saved our money and used window fans for about a year, until we could pay cash for a new system (and what a relief *that* was!). When three of our kids needed braces but we could afford to pay only for one, the others had to wait a little while until the budget could accommodate more orthodontia.

Saving money to buy something teaches patience and discourages impulsive purchases, so of course it's something we not only practice ourselves but also teach our children. The young ones receive money as gifts and occasionally receive monetary rewards for helping with household jobs. They save their money in a piggy bank or some other kind of container they can keep in their locker (every child has one—and a lock to go on it) or else their earnings are recorded in their account in the "family bank." When they've saved up enough to buy something, we take them shopping for it.

All our children know that the Duggar motto is "Buy used and save the difference," and they're becoming as frugal with their money as we are with ours. Some of them have gotten to the point where they really don't like to spend money! Jinger is gaining a reputation as a bargain-hunting champion. When Jinger and her older sisters go thrift shopping to buy clothing items for the family or to the store to buy some groceries, the girls usually come by my (Jim Bob's) office to say good-bye as they're heading out the door. Michelle is trying to break me of my habit of jokingly telling them, "Love you! Don't spend any money!" She says Jinger takes that message too seriously. She ends up standing at the store thinking, *This is really a good bargain. But Daddy said not to spend any money . . .*

Many people asked us whether we have accepted government assistance to help cover medical expenses with Josie's crisis. The answer is no. We have never accepted government assistance of any kind, and I pray we never have to. It's a good safety net for those who need it, but we have insurance—and savings—that so far have kept us from needing additional help.

That's not to say the out-of-pocket medical bills haven't been costly. Michelle's emergency medical flight from Rogers to Little Rock, which

Jinger is one of our thriftiest thrift-store shoppers.

wasn't covered by insurance, cost ten thousand dollars.

Josie's December 10, 2009, birth meant we had to pay her and Michelle's insurance deductible for 2009 and then pay their 2010 deductibles a few weeks later. After that, almost all of their medical expenses were covered by insurance. We had been paying thousands of dollars a year for insurance premiums over the years. With a pretty healthy family and a twenty-five-hundred-dollar deductible, sometimes I wondered if the high monthly premiums were a wise investment. After all, we really hadn't had a major health-related expense. But all that thinking quickly evaporated when Michelle (and then Josie's) health crises erupted. Also, having had an insurance license at one time, I understood the importance of spreading the risk out over thousands of people. Everyone's premiums together easily cover the costs of the relatively few major claims that occur among the policyholders.

MY MAIN HOBBY: BEING THE DUGGAR DAD

Providing financially for my supersize family could be an all-consuming, high-pressure role for me, but as we have trusted God and followed His principles, we have seen Him supernaturally provide every step of the way and meet our needs. Together we pray about upcoming decisions, and we trust God to provide the opportunities and guidance we need.

Living debt-free, I'm able to focus more of my attention on my family. I don't play golf, don't own a fancy bass boat, and don't take off for weeklong hunting trips with buddies. My family is my hobby, and I spend every minute I can enjoying it.

Because we live debt-free, I (Jim Bob) am able to enjoy more fun activities with my family— like heading to the go-cart track with (from left) Jessa, Joseph, John-David, Jinger, and the rest of the kids old enough to "drive."

Because I run our commercial rental property business from home, I'm able to mingle real estate and family responsibilities throughout much of each day. When repairs are needed on any of our properties, some of my children go along with me to help or to learn. When Michelle and I are looking at property, it's quite common for us to take along a child or two—or sometimes a whole busload. When I'm on the phone at home talking business, there is usually lots of background noise. This is not an inconvenience for me; it's what I've chosen, and I feel incredibly blessed. I like nothing better than being surrounded by my family.

I try to have a learning spirit and glean from successful fathers and businessmen. I discovered some interesting ideas recently in nearby Bentonville, where Sam Walton started the Walmart business empire.

Sam was an amazing man. He built the world's largest retail company, and that company started and is still run out of that small Arkansas town. The original store, Walton's Five & Dime, has been turned into a visitors center where "Sam's Rules for Building a Business" are on display. Reading them, I saw how Sam's built up a successful business, but I also could see how his ideas could help me build up my family. For example, just as Sam's ideas inspired his "associates" (employees) to feel ownership as partners in the company, I could see how those same ideas could help inspire my children's love and devotion to God and to each other.

Sam's rules are reprinted in the Resources section of this book. Read them and see if they don't inspire you too. For instance, Rule 1 is "Commit to your business. Believe in it more than anybody else. . . . If you love your work, you'll be out there every day trying to do it the best you possibly can, and pretty soon everybody around will catch the passion from you—like a fever."[1] I hope it's obvious to my family that I'm totally committed to them and I like nothing better than spending time with them.

I especially like Sam's "Rule 3: Motivate," which says, in part, "Keep everybody guessing as to what your next trick is going to be. Don't become too predictable."

That's what I try to do with my family when I say, "Tomorrow we're going to do something really special"—and then refuse to say what special thing Michelle and I have planned for them. Sometimes I get on our home's intercom and call, "Everybody come to the kitchen right now. I've got something to show you," and then we might do something like the hillbilly waterslide in the front yard. Or I say, "Attention, all Duggars! Everybody on the shuttle bus! We're going to go do something really fun," and we head out for some playtime at our favorite park.

Of course I work out these little (and sometimes big) surprises ahead of time with Michelle, and she helps shape the family's schedule to accommodate things like field trips to a local ostrich farm or to a historic or scenic place in our area, or, while we were in Little Rock, a trip to the zoo or a family expedition up Pinnacle Mountain. I try to fill our family with a "spirit of funness" and keep them guessing what the next fun thing will be.

Not all of the surprises are fun, however; sometimes they're challenging but rewarding. One evening in Little Rock I told our older girls (The older boys were back in Tontitown doing some home maintenance projects so they missed out on this adventure!) I had something special planned for the next day, and when they woke up I told them we were going to go donate blood! I reminded them that Josie had received more than a dozen blood transfusions, and this was one way we could give back in the same way that others had given to our family.

Now, I don't know anybody who *enjoys* being poked with needles. Our daughter Jill and I share an especially deep dread of that kind of thing, and—wouldn't you know?—I had to be stuck twice because

In thanksgiving for all the blood Josie was given during her hospitalization, the older girls and I donated blood while we were in Little Rock.

I moved while the phlebotomist was having trouble hitting the vein. But afterward, we wore our Band-Aids as proudly as our little guys do when they're showing off a boo-boo. And we all agreed that donating blood was a good thing to do.

Sam Walton's rules advise business leaders (and dads) to "communicate everything you possibly can," "appreciate everything your associates [and children] do," and "listen to everyone in your company [or family]." We look for ways to incorporate Sam's advice into the way we parent our children.

One thing Sam *didn't* listen to was the negative people who told him not to open a tenth, one hundredth, or one thousandth store, worrying that he might end up with more than he could manage. Adamantly following his core principles, he eventually became a billionaire and at one time was the richest person in America.

In the same way, by taking on the responsibility for more children over the years, Michelle and I have incurred a lot of criticism, with people questioning how in the world we would be able to take care of and provide for all of those kids. Despite that criticism, we stuck to our core principles, and God has provided and met our needs every step of the way. We consider each one of our children priceless. With nineteen children who love the Lord, we feel like the richest people in the world!

CONTROLLING ANGER

In families of any size—in fact, in any relationship—anger, especially uncontrolled anger, never produces the best results. Too often an angry dad's response to an upsetting situation causes more damage than the event itself. Sure, kids make mistakes and do dumb things, innocently or deliberately. But disciplining and correcting the child while seething with rage can cause irreparable harm to the child's heart and spirit, and cause damage to the parent-child relationship that might take years to heal. The Bible says, "The wrath of man worketh not the righteousness of God" (James 1:20).

I tell people I never had an anger problem until I had children, and then, it seemed, I'd get mad at the kids about things that would never have upset me before I became a father. Again I gained great wisdom at a seminar, one that included descriptions of how destructive a father's (or anyone's) anger can be. One of the dangers about anger is that it feeds on itself; it can easily build to an unhealthy state and become destructive.

Adopting an idea learned at the conference, I asked my family to forgive me and I gave our children permission to help me identify if I am talking with sharp words or an angry spirit. I told them when they sense that I'm mad about something and my anger is building, they have permission to touch my arm gently, whisper in my ear, and say, "Daddy, I think you're getting angry."

That sweet comment always snaps me back into "sensible mode." It's like dumping ice-cold water on a hot head. I realize what's happening, ask God to help me have the right response, and I regain control. This isn't to say our kids never do things that could make Michelle or me mad, but we try to follow the same guidance we teach our children, remembering that too often someone's response to a hard situation causes more damage than the event itself.

(A comment from Michelle: I would like to add that Jim Bob is really determined to control his anger, and this routine of the children reminding him about losing his temper is rarely needed.)

LISTENING TO EACH OTHER

Anger can also be a destructive force in a marriage, as well as in child-rearing; it's important not to let little things build into frustrations that can erupt in angry outbursts that can damage a couple's relationship.

When Michelle and I got married twenty-seven years ago, we were so in love we just overlooked each other's shortcomings. As time went on, however, it turned out that there were just a *few* little things about us that got on our spouse's nerves. We did our best to ignore them, knowing how important it is not to have a critical attitude. So those little things that bugged us stayed locked up inside our heads. Oh sure, we might make a suggestion about the spouse's behavior from time to time, but that spouse probably took it as just that: a suggestion.

For instance, when we got married, I had a fun way of taking off my socks and doing an athletic, baseketball-shooting maneuver—well, it was fun for me, though not for Michelle. I would sit down on the bed, pull off a sock, wad it into a tight little wad, and then toss it over the back of our open bedroom door (the basketball "hoop"). I was actually pretty good at getting each sock over the door and into a pile back in the corner, which made it very convenient for Michelle. She could just grab the pile of wadded-up socks and carry them to the laundry room. What a good husband I was!

Michelle liked the idea of having all my dirty clothes in a pile, but she *hated* the sweaty, stinky, wadded-up socks. Because they were wadded up so tightly, the sweaty socks didn't ever dry out while they were waiting to be laundered. They just got stinkier and stinkier, and then Michelle would have to pull and pull and *pull* to get them flattened out so they would get clean in the washer (and dry in the dryer).

She took it as long as she could—probably several months or even a year. (She is a *very* patient person.) Then she said something like, "Jim Bob, would you please not wad up your socks? It's good to put all your dirty clothes in a pile behind the door, but it's a lot of work to unwad your socks."

I said, "Okay!" And for a few days, I didn't wad up my socks. But over time I forgot, and the old habit took over again. Michelle didn't immediately comment, so the wadded-up-sock tossing continued. Then she might say, "Jim Bob, please don't wad up your socks," and I'd stop again for a couple of days and then start doing it again. Then Michelle came to me one day with a laundry basket of wadded-up socks. "Honey, this really bothers me. Would you *please* stop doing that?"

I finally got the message, and I stopped wadding up my socks.

Actually, it's hard for me to think of anything Michelle does that's annoying; she's one of the sweetest, most caring people ever. But, well, yes, there is *one* little thing. Because she's so caring and thoughtful, she sometimes sees things the rest of us miss. Instead of procrastinating, she tries to take care of those needs immediately whenever she runs across them—including when I call to her, "Hey, Michelle! Come here real quick!" She answers, "I'll be right there!" But on her way she wipes the baby's running nose, scrapes cereal off the counter and puts away the box so the kids don't spill it again, rinses her hands in the sink and then decides it needs scrubbing, and *then* she finally hurries up to me and says, "Here I am!"

I might say, "I wanted you to see something cute Jackson and Johannah were doing, but I'm sorry, you just missed it!"

Over the years, we've both tried to work on correcting our little annoying behaviors that tend to irritate each other. It's important to say that we wouldn't have known these behaviors were irritable if the spouse hadn't pointed them out. It's imperative to have good, clear communication and listening skills within a family, and we constantly work on improving them. I tell friends just a little more work, and Michelle will have me trained!

STILL LEARNING TO COMMUNICATE

Attending marriage seminars, conferences, and retreats together is a great way for married couples to enjoying a "date weekend" while also learning how to strengthen their marriage. A couple of our favorites are Whatever It Takes (for information, go to www.witministries.com) and A Weekend to Remember (www.familylifeministries.com).

Another conference that had a strong impact on our marriage was Chris and Anne Hogan's Noble Partners Marriage Conference (www .noblecall.org), which we attended about four years ago. The conference focuses on "courageous conversations" that help couples communicate with and understand each other. During the conference, couples are guided in identifying divisions that have crept into their relationship, whether they are newlyweds or have been married fifty years.

Even though we had been married twenty-three years at that point and had a good marriage, we learned new insights about how to ask each other questions to get to the heart of important issues.

During a courageous conversation, the husband is advised to ask his wife, "What is your most pressing issue?" The question seeks out what the wife wants to discuss about the need, concern, worry, fear, priority, or challenge in the marriage and the family, including its finances or its future.

She answers the question, describing what is, to her, the most pressing issue, and then it's important for the husband to rephrase what he heard her say to make sure he understood correctly. He can say, "What I think I heard you say was . . ."

When it's clear that the message has been understood, he continues, "How is this situation affecting you?" Then he listens carefully to his wife's answer, repeating and rephrasing what he has heard. The wife clarifies, if necessary.

When a woman feels she is being heard and truly listened to, she will begin to open up and share her heart—and true communication happens. In a courageous conversation, the husband's next question is, "What will the future be like if nothing changes?"

The wife's response helps him understand the consequences of doing nothing about this matter that is burdening her.

The next question gets to the real heart of the matter when, with a humble heart, the husband asks, "What do you see as my responsibility for this issue?"

This question creates an opportunity for the wife to open her heart to her husband and for the husband to gain genuine understanding of her true needs. It's crucial at this point that the husband doesn't make excuses for character flaws or imperfections but simply acknowledges what has been said.

If at this point he begins to explain, complain, or blame his wife in response to what she is saying, the conversation will fail. On the other hand, this can be a turning point in the conversation if the husband agrees to pray about and work on those areas that have been brought to his attention and the wife realizes that, while she may feel she is the victim, she also has responsibility for helping resolve the issue.

When this issue has been completely discussed, it's wise for the husband to ask, "In addition to this issue, is there something else?"

There may not be time to get to all the core issues in one sitting—in fact, husbands, you may need a pen and paper to write down a long list during your first courageous-conversation exercise! The couple may then reverse the procedure, with the wife asking the questions.

The conclusion of the conversation is the time for the couple to pray together, asking God and each other for forgiveness. Remember that, as you work through the important issues in your marriage, you are not responsible for your spouse's past mistakes, his or her hurtful words and actions. It is imperative, however, that you humbly ask God and your spouse to forgive *you* for *your* offenses. Before God and your mate, you can make *your* part right. (The *Love Dare* book is an excellent resource for those in a marriage relationship in which only one spouse is trying to make it work.)

Once your marriage issues are discussed in this way, you can work on problems and set future goals. By sharing a mutually agreed upon vision for the future and working toward it, you and your spouse can restore enthusiasm and a sense of partnership in your marriage. Then, as you see improvements as a result of your courageous conversations, you'll no doubt be motivated to work through other issues at regular intervals and to continue communicating this way.

You can also resolve to dedicate yourselves and your family to God. Without Him, we humans are naturally self-centered.

UNDERSTANDING WHAT'S IMPORTANT

During one of the marriage seminars we attended, the leaders described how, in a typical couple's relationship, a stay-at-home wife will want to tell her husband all the challenges that happened while he was at work. Hearing the wife's description of her trying day, the typical husband assumes she is asking for advice on what she could have done differently to resolve the situations that arose.

What she's really wanting, in most cases, is just for the husband to be quiet, listen as she shares her heart, and understand all the obstacles and emotions she faced that day. Then she wants him to show her compassion, love, and care, acknowledging what she went through.

ONE OF OUR FAVORITE COOKBOOK RESOURCES

Kim Cahill's *No-Guesswork Cooking Cookbook: Recipes You Can Trust* is the cookbook we grab most often. When we need to cook for a crowd or just for our family (which is a crowd!), we trust this cookbook to give us all the information we need to pull off a meal with no worries. We love the fact that it guides you through making everything from scratch if you want to—or you can use one of the variations listed to make the cooking go much faster.

It has a built-in self-standing cover and special glossy pages to protect the recipes from the messiest little chefs and helpers. Available from www.iblp.org.

She *doesn't* want "how you could've solved all the problems" advice.

Another communication issue we've encountered over the years is that I sometimes don't pick up on something Michelle is trying to tell me. There have been many times when she has talked with me (Jim Bob) about a number of pressing things that need my attention. I would make a mental list as I listened, categorizing her thoughts and prioritizing what I thought was most important to her. That system meant some things (the ones I thought weren't priorities) were left undone—and Michelle was left feeling disappointed that I didn't catch on to what she meant and, as a result, I didn't follow through with what *she* felt was a priority.

We were about twenty-four years into our marriage when we finally came up with a way to avoid these headache situations. It's a super-simple concept, but it has made a big difference in our relationship. Are you ready? Here it is: when Michelle has something to say that's very important to her, she'll make sure she has my full attention and then she will say, *"Jim Bob, this is really important to me!"*

GIVE US GODLY HOMES

Years ago we heard a song titled "A Christian Home" at another marriage conference we attended. We adopted this song as our family song, and through the years we have enjoyed singing it as a prayer to the

Lord during Bible time or at church. It is sung to the tune of "Be Still My Soul." The song opens with "Oh, give us homes built firm upon the Savior . . . Where ev'ry child is taught His love and favor." You can find the complete lyrics to the song at http://lyrics.astraweb.com/display//177/hymns..unknown..a_christian_home.html.

18

• Do the Duggars Date? •

Therefore shall a man leave his father and his mother, and shall cleave unto his wife: and they shall be one flesh.
—Genesis 2:24

We're often asked about our hopes for our children's future and how they will find eligible mates. People want to know, do the Duggars date?

The answer is yes—but only after marriage! In fact, Jim Bob and I (Michelle) just enjoyed a date night earlier this week when we went out to eat with another couple on a double date.

Before marriage? No, our children do not date—not as most people would define dating: a boy and girl getting together with little or no supervision, just going out for the temporary pleasure of enjoying each other's company. We've chosen, as a family, not to play the dating game, hoping to avoid a lot of the inherent pitfalls. (We highly recommend Joshua Harris's book *I Kissed Dating Goodbye.*) We believe that dating can lead to unstable emotional attachments, improper touching, and building a relationship solely on physical attraction rather than emotional and spiritual connection. Having a dating relationship with person after person and breakup after breakup simulates what is happening in so many marriages today. Too many couples get married with the idea that if it doesn't work out, they'll break up and find someone else.

When men and women establish a close, intimate relationship with someone of the opposite gender, they give away a piece of their heart.

Then, as they move through break-ups and new relationships, they give away more and more pieces until, when they finally find the person they decide to marry, they may have a broken heart and a load of guilt left over from wrong choices in the past.

This is a relatively new phase of parenting for us as our older children mature and enter this season of life. We are still learning, with Joshua being our only child to marry so far. Still at the beginning of this important decision-making stage, we're gaining experience about what the Bible says in regard to relationships and the healthiest way they should be established. There will be many things to learn as we walk through this season of our family's life!

We expect that finding a life partner will be a unique process for each one of our young adults, but

Josh and Anna's marriage in 2008 and Mackynzie's birth in 2009 opened a new chapter of parenting— and grandparenting—for us. We love it!

we've agreed on some basic ideas to prepare them for this stage. We are committed to guiding our young-adult children in waiting, evaluating, considering, pre-engagement, engagement, marriage, and *then* dating.

Waiting: Preparing Yourself

When the time is right—meaning, in God's timing—He will bring your intended spouse into your life. Until then you wait, preparing yourself to become the person God wants you to be in every area of your life.

Waiting begins with the idea that as a marriage-age young person, you're not involved in self-focused dating relationships but are instead seeking God's leading. It teaches contentment as you rest confidently in your belief that God has given you everything you need for your happiness.

Waiting creates a special time as God becomes your best friend. This is also a time when you seek discernment and advice from parents and friends who also are seeking God in their lives. Waiting means denying your physical urges as you hold fast to your goal of receiving God's best in His timing, not yours. Remember, the best things in life are worth waiting for! Waiting helps you appreciate that custom-made person when God brings him or her into your life to be your marriage partner.

As our daughter Jill explained it to a friend, "Often, dating is going out with guys without thinking about marriage anytime soon. *Waiting* is preparing myself to be a godly wife—the kind of girl a godly guy is looking for. That's the girl I want to be!"

Evaluating: Upfront Examining of Character

As young people get to an age when they are noticing the opposite gender, not only are they waiting, but they quickly need to learn to start *evaluating*. Even in their early teen years they need to write out a list of character qualities they want in a future spouse. It's also good to write out a separate list of negative qualities they *don't* want.

The two lists will help teenagers and young adults look past outward appearances to see who someone really is before they get emotionally involved—because once an emotional attachment forms, love becomes blind, character deficiencies are excused, and an unrealistic optimism sets in. You start believing that once you're married your spouse will become that person you said you want him or her to be. Grandma Duggar states, "A lot of people mistakenly think they can alter them at the altar!"

We've talked with our young adults about what kind of person they hope to marry. We've said there will be many "prospects" at times, but a large percentage of those candidates can be eliminated by evaluating them on their private "What I Desire in a Spouse" and "What I *Don't* Want in a Spouse" lists. By evaluating the potential spouses they encounter, they'll see that only a very few have a genuine godly focus.

One day Jana asked, "Mama, what is the most important quality a future spouse should have?"

I (Michelle) asked for time to pray about my answer, and then, later, I told her the most important thing I appreciate about her daddy is knowing my heart is secure with him. I know I can trust him to lovingly listen to whatever I need to tell him. I know Jim Bob loves God more than he loves himself, and he puts God first in his life. He shows that by expressing it in words but also in the way he lives. He shares his heart with me, including the most vulnerable things about himself; he's open and honest with me because he wants to keep his heart pure before God. That gives me a solid security that nothing else can provide; all the money in the world couldn't buy it.

A few months before Josie's birth in 2009, we renewed our wedding vows on our twenty-fifth anniversary with our eighteen children and daughter-in-law Anna as our attendants.

When we first got married, we were scraping by financially, but that didn't matter because we were deeply in love. I didn't think it was possible to be happier than I was then (little did I know!). Over the years our love has grown and matured. We have weathered many life storms together, and we're actually closer, happier, and more in love now than we were back then. I told Jana, "I love and admire your daddy so much; I still want to spend the rest of my life with him! I pray that each one of you girls find someone like your dad."

Jana listened carefully. Then she and the other older girls talked about it and they decided to put together some basic evaluations for a spouse. Their individual lists vary a little; here's a composite sample of what our older girls desire to find in a young man.

1. He has to be a deeply committed Christian with a ministry mind-set.

2. He has to love Jesus as much as I do.

3. He has to have a servant's heart and a desire to win others to Christ.

4. He needs to be emotionally and spiritually steady.

5. He needs to have common sense and constantly seek God's wisdom.

6. He needs to treat his mom and sisters with respect.

7. He needs to be a diligent worker who is able to provide for his family (but all the girls agree that this doesn't mean they expect him to be wealthy).

8. He needs to be willing to humble himself and admit his mistakes and shortcomings. Then he has to be willing to ask forgiveness and gain a clear conscience from those he has offended.

9. Even though inward character is the most important, he has to be someone they are attracted to spiritually, emotionally, mentally, and physically.

10. He needs to have a learning spirit and be a man of good character like Dad.

Here is the girls' list of what they *don't* want in a future spouse.

1. A lack of godly focus or purpose in life.

2. Quick to anger.

3. Self-centered.

4. Overly focused on hobbies.

5. Lack of manners.

6. Lack of self-control.

7. Lazy.

8. Ongoing moral issues (without brokenness.)

9. Dishonest.

10. Involved in drugs, smoking, drinking, chewing tobacco—or hangs out with those who are involved in them.

Now, this doesn't mean that someone who has had struggles in these areas would never be considered; God forgives, and so do we. But by God's grace, he would need to work on these areas to be considered a possibility.

These are not comprehensive lists; no doubt, your children's requirements will be different. We offer our girls' lists here hoping they can spark a discussion in your family and perhaps help your older children start thinking about making their own.

Until the day comes when that young man or woman appears in their lives, our children are becoming the people God wants them to be. They are learning skills that will help them support their families and create love-filled, God-focused homes. First Corinthians 7:32 says, "He that is unmarried careth for the things that belong to the Lord, how he may please the Lord." The girls are hoping to become the kind of wise and virtuous wife and mother described in Proverbs 31. They have gained great insights from Sarah Mally's book, *Before You Meet Prince Charming*, and they recommend it to every young lady.

Considering: Is This Person a Potential Spouse?

Our older sons have their own similar lists of what they're looking for in a life partner. But before one of them identifies a godly young lady who surpasses his rating checklist and might be considered as his potential spouse, he needs to make sure he also meets all the requirements on his checklist for himself. First he needs to have his own spiritual life on track with God. Second, he needs to have his life and finances in order so he can support a family. Third, if he's in the middle of training or college, he needs to consider whether this is the right time for marriage.

If all those conditions line up and after much prayer, if he believes this girl could be a potential spouse, we would encourage him to talk with the girl's dad to see if the girl would have any interest in getting to know him for the purpose of considering each other as a potential life partner. Yes, this can be kind of scary, but if it's meant to be, it will work out. If it's not God's will, it won't.

Working through the girl's father is less intimidating for the young lady than approaching the girl directly, and it gives her the freedom to express her true feelings to her father. He can then relate those feelings

We had such a good time at the Orr Family Farms in Oklahoma that we literally jumped for joy on the farm's giant jumping pillow.

to the young man. If the girl shows interest, the father and the young man can get to know each other.

Jim Bob recently shared with our older kids a wonderful example describing how a father had a heart-to-heart talk with a young man who was interested in his daughter.

This young man was a hard worker and had saved up all summer to restore an older classic car that he was driving. The dad asked about his car and about the time, energy, and money that had gone into fixing it up. The boy described how long and hard he'd worked to earn the money to buy the car and how many hours he'd spent restoring it.

The dad explained that he knew how it felt to invest his life savings and his energy into something. He told the boy he had poured his life into his daughter; she was priceless to him. All of her life he had protected and provided for her at all cost.

It is important that a dad or a godly father figure help discern a young man's character and level of spiritual maturity and evaluate his intentions.

Most of our daughters will probably wait for a guy to contact their dad; then there will be discussion and prayer about whether she is interested, or whether she wants to get to know the boy better to see if she might become interested. Potential life partners might be identified when a son or daughter spots a godly young person with good character and suggests that we include them in some family ministry or outreach activity so the two have an opportunity to interact while surrounded by our family. If the two eventually agree that they are each other's potential life partner, we probably would invite the whole family to fellowship with us so we can see the interworkings of their family dynamic. We believe you don't just marry the person; you marry into the family.

As potential life partners surface, these young adults will spend time getting to know each other in group settings to see what interests they have in common, how their personalities connect, and watching to see how each other reacts in various situations.

In our family, we're sure that lots of brothers and sisters will be weighing in and giving advice about what they think of each potential brother-in-law or sister-in-law. There is wisdom in many counselors. This "considering" time rolls along without any commitments, except the commitment to pray and seek God's will.

> **SLOPPY JOES**
>
> 1 pound ground turkey
> ½ cup ketchup
> ½ cup barbecue sauce
> ½ envelope dry onion soup mix
> 2 teaspoons liquid smoke flavoring
>
> Brown and season meat; drain. Add all other ingredients, heat through. Serve on buns; love it!

We have heard many unique, supernatural stories of how God has brought couples together, so we don't say the considering time has to happen a certain way. But we've also heard many tragic stories of couples who damaged their relationship right from the beginning by mishandling their time of getting to know each other. So we believe something like this suggestion should be considered.

The main focus is to guard the emotions of our young people so they don't prematurely give their hearts away—and then regret it later. Instead, they should be encouraged to keep their heart for the one God made for them.

Pre-Engagement: Getting to Know Each Other Better

The most important decision in your life, next to accepting Christ as your Savior, is the decision about whom you're going to marry. This decision determines your future. If you pick the right person, you can have a special relationship in which both of you give 110 percent and consistently build each other up. On the other hand, if you settle for less than God's best, it can be an "evil for evil" relationship in which there is constant back-and-forth arguing, fighting, and put-downs.

(If you are married and in that situation now, we recommend John Reiger's Intimacy in Marriage course, which helps in dealing with challenging relationships.)

So many times people don't want to give God this area of their lives because they think they can do a better job of picking out a spouse than He can.

When a couple has gone through all of the above steps, and they both believe, along with their family, that this is a possibility, then the young man would formally ask the girl's father's permission to get to know the girl and work toward possible engagement.

During this time the couple has more freedom to get to know each other in a deeper way, but always in the presence of others. It is an evaluation process. After close character and compatibility examination, a lot of couples realize this is *not* the one they are to marry.

We tell our kids, you're never going to find a perfect person because that young man or young woman doesn't exist. Still, you shouldn't settle for anything less than God's best.

Engagement

When the couple and their parents believe that this relationship is God's plan, the young man should again go to the girl's father and ask for the daughter's hand in marriage. During the engagement stage the couple probably endures more temptations than at any other time, because they are two young people in love, planning their future dreams together, and emotions and feelings are inevitably strong. That's why we recommend a short engagement and a lot of accountability!

Marriage—for Life

Marriage is not a test drive. At your wedding you're vowing before God that, for better or worse, richer or poorer, you will be together and love each other until death do you part.

How does a couple confirm that this marriage is God's will? When a man and woman who are individually dedicated to God and who love each other determine that they can do more together for the kingdom of God than they can do alone, *that* is the time to get married.

Marriage is one of the most amazing concepts God instituted, merging two people from diverse backgrounds into one being in mind, spirit, and body.

We pray that the single people who read this chapter will commit their love lives to God and then trust Him to bring into their path the spouse He intends for them. Trust is the key. "Trust in the LORD with all thine heart; and lean not unto thine own understanding. In all thy ways acknowledge Him, and He shall direct thy paths" (Proverbs 3:5–6).

JOSH AND ANNA

A few days after Josh met Anna at the concession stand of an ATI homeschool conference in 2006, he told Jim Bob that God had just revealed to him who he was supposed to marry. Jim Bob said, "Let's pray about it and see if God confirms it."

Meanwhile, Josh had also caught Anna's eye.

The Duggar girls and the Keller girls also met at the conference, and they quickly became good friends. After everyone went home, the girls started talking on the phone on Tuesday nights, usually on the speakerphone so everyone could join in. Sometimes Josh or one of the Keller boys would join the conversation too.

Early in January 2008, Anna's brother Daniel invited Josh to come to Florida to help with a week of seminars being presented by the Keller family's prison ministry. After Josh and Daniel worked on the seminar together, Josh talked to Mr. Keller about his feelings for Anna. Her dad had already asked her if there was anyone she thought might be the man God intended for her, and she had mentioned Josh. So Mr. Keller was ready that day when Josh approached him. He gave Josh permission to start talking to Anna on the phone to get to know her better.

Prayers and phone calls continued—and became more frequent. Josh and Anna talked to each other but always with their siblings listening on the speakerphone. Both became convinced that they were the ones God had intended for them, but it came as a shock to Anna, on her twentieth birthday, when Josh showed up with a diamond ring and proposed to her! He had asked permission of Anna's parents, of course, and after much prayer, all of us were absolutely certain this was God's will. An October wedding date was set.

Josh purchased a pink cell phone for Anna upon their engagement, and they were allowed to talk without siblings listening in during their many conversations from June until their wedding in October.

INTIMACY: ENJOYING YOUR PARTNER

Attention, parents: the contents of this section may be unsuitable for young children.

Jim Bob and I work hard to give our big family a solid foundation in faith, love, character, and joy. In addition, Jim Bob carries most of the responsibility for providing for our family financially. But here's something that may surprise you: our goals and responsibilities for our large family are secondary to our responsibilities to each other. Our relationship comes first!

Our children's safety and well-being are top priorities for us. But along with my (Michelle's) devotion to Christ, my relationship with Jim Bob is the underpinning of our family; it's the solid ground beneath that foundation we're building for our children. The Bible points out the disastrous difference between a house built on rock and a house built on shifting sand (see Matthew 7:24–27). We want our godly marriage to be that rock for our family, creating a foundation that points each one of them to a relationship with Jesus.

The thing that distinguishes marriage from all other relationships is the intimate spiritual, emotional, and physical connection between a husband and a wife. We've shared throughout this book many aspects of our spiritual and emotional life; now we want to address the physical aspects of a loving marriage as well. We believe too many of modern culture's messages about this very special relationship are warped and twisted.

Physical intimacy is one of the delights of marriage. Right before Jim Bob and I were married, Dr. Ed Wheat, a well-known Christian author and also our family doctor at the time, counseled us and gave us copies of his incredible books and audio messages, which include insights about physical intimacy and pleasure in marriage. (We recommend that every married couple read his books *Love Life for Every Married Couple* and *Intended for Pleasure*.)

Dr. Wheat taught us from a medical and spiritual perspective how to maximize our special time together as a couple. We quickly found out how much fun it is for a married couple to learn together, discovering God's amazing design and enjoying the wonderful gift of pleasure He has given husbands and wives! Twenty-five years later, we passed along to Josh and Anna as a wedding gift the same books and materials Dr. Wheat had given us when we got married.

After Jim Bob and I were married, a Christian friend of mine, Gayla, gave me some more great marital advice. She had been married about eighteen months earlier, and she told me, "Michelle, when the honeymoon is over, and the newness wears off, here's something to remember: men are geared differently than women. They need the physical relationship more often than we women. Keep the perspective that you are the *only* one who can fulfill that special need in his life." Through the years those words would ring in my ears at the end of a long day when I was exhausted.

The marriage relationship is all about yielding to each other's needs. We belong to one another. I am his, and he is mine! With God's grace we can do for each other what we ought to do, even when we don't feel like it. Without His grace we are selfish and tend to foster an evil-for-evil response toward each other that will destroy our relationship. The reward that comes to both of us as we choose to be unselfish toward each other is that our love deepens and we keep the home fires burning.

Most of us women probably build intimacy more through loving communication and spending quality time together than through being physically intimate. At the top of my intimacy list is how Jim Bob treats me, how he talks to me, and how he shows me that he cherishes me. *Cherishing* means seeing great value in someone, protecting her and praising her to others, and that's what Jim Bob does throughout the day. He shows his love for me by *telling* me he loves me, by calling me just to say hi whenever we're apart, or by showing respect by doing things like opening doors for me or planning a date night for us to go to my favorite restaurant.

Early in our marriage we learned more about understanding each other's needs, in part, through two Bible study booklets: *Seven Basic Needs of a Wife* and *Seven Basic Needs of a Husband* (see the Resources section for ordering information).

By far the most precious way Jim Bob demonstrates his love to me is by protecting and guarding our relationship as he willingly shares his heart with me. A man's natural tendency is to not share his real needs with his wife; he wants her to admire him as a success. But before honor must come humility. A husband wins his wife's love more by sharing his specific failures than by reporting his successes. We strive to be totally open and honest with each other by sharing our thoughts and struggles as well as our hopes and dreams.

It's vital that a husband and wife share everything in their hearts with each other. We experience great freedom when we both release before God and each other any thoughts, struggles, or temptations we are having. In our marriage, we both realize that freedom doesn't give us the right to do what we selfishly *want* but the power to do what we selflessly *ought*. Personally, I feel this freedom allows for the deepest intimacy a husband and wife can experience together. I'm so grateful to God for Jim Bob's honesty and humility. It gives me a deep love, admiration, and respect for him and a real sense of security in our marriage relationship. We realize how much we need each other.

The Bible instructs husbands and wives not to withhold physical intimacy with each other "except it be with consent for a time"

(1 Corinthians 7:5). We do agree to abstain from physical intimacy during certain times. As mentioned earlier, we choose to follow Old Testament guidelines of abstinence for forty days after the birth of a boy and eighty days after the birth of a girl. We also abstain for seven days after the start of my menstrual cycle.

We practice self-control during those times of abstinence, and for me it's a time of rest (except for struggling with menstrual cramps!). We find that the time of abstinence builds anticipation and excitement, and when we come back together, we enjoy renewed passion and an increased desire for each other. We personally believe it is wrong to touch oneself for sexual pleasure because God wants us to wait for each other and learn self-control. Only a husband and wife together should meet those needs for one another.

Our children grow up feeling secure and confident that nothing will shake the bond their parents are seeking with each other and with God. With a broad smile and a happy tone, Jim Bob tells the kids, "I love your mama, and I'm so grateful to God she married me!"

Josie, our miracle baby, on her first birthday.

Our children understand that Dad and Mama have dedicated their lives to loving and serving God and each other, and that is the foundation of our love for them. We let them see that love played out as we show appropriate affection to each other throughout the day with quick kisses and hugs or by holding hands as we sit and talk. For our intimate affection, however, we have a good, strong lock on our bedroom door!

Our love has deepened over the past twenty-seven years of marriage.
I love Michelle more now than ever!

P.S. Answering the Big Question

I have set before you life and death, blessing and cursing;
therefore choose life that both thou and thy seed may live.
—Deuteronomy 30:19

A couple of months after Josie was born, we started hearing the question "So, are you going to have more children?" The best way to answer that question is to reaffirm what we continue to believe.

For several years now, sharing our beliefs publicly has put us in a different light than most of our nation's culture. As we joyously celebrate the birth of each new child, we realize that there are people who condemn us for the choices we have made. In fact, *People* magazine in mid-February 2010 put our picture on the cover with a line asking, "How many kids are too many?"

We are glad to live in a land where everyone can express his or her opinion. We don't let the negative opinions bother us. Nor do we let them influence what we continue to believe, including what God says about children: they are a gift and a blessing and a reward from Him. It's probably impossible for anyone to fully understand the depth of His love for His children, but those who have endured the death of a child, experiencing the deepest grief and sorrow, might come a little closer in understanding. God knew that agony as He watched His only Son die on the cross—on our behalf. Imagining (or remembering) yourself in the midst of such a heart-wrenching loss gives you a much clearer picture of how precious life is. The value of that one life is worth more than all the riches in the world. We are so thankful for each one of our children.

God's love truly does multiply! We are experiencing it as we enjoy the family He has given us.

We write these words not knowing what the future holds for us; but we know who holds the future, and we place our trust in Him. It might be that by the time you read these words, I will be pregnant again, if that's God's will for us. Or it may be that Michelle's child-bearing days are over due to menopause or simply because it's God's will. It's true that there are risks involved, perhaps greater risks than we've faced before. But the truth is, our hearts haven't changed. We are grateful to God for each child He has blessed us with, and our love for children has grown deeper with each passing day. We still desire to love children the way God loves them, and we consider children one of His greatest gifts.

So to answer the question "Are the Duggars going to have any more children?" we say, "If that is God's will for us, we would love to have more!"

We believe children are a gift from God, and with nineteen children, a daughter-in-law, one granddaughter (and, as of this writing, our first grandson on the way), we feel incredibly blessed!

• Resources •

For more resources we have found helpful, go to www.duggarfamily.com.

AUDIO AND VIDEO RESOURCES

Christian movies by Sherwood Pictures, the ministry of Sherwood Baptist Church that has also produced the popular Christian movies *Flywheel, Facing the Giants, Fireproof,* and *Courageous.* www.sherwoodpictures.com

Pastor S. M. Davis preaching videos. www.solvefamilyproblems.com

The principles taught by Jim Sammons in his Financial Freedom series have been life-changing for us. www.iblp.org/iblp/discipleship/financialfreedom.

Other websites we like as a source of audio and video resources:

www.titus2.com
www.unshackled.org
www.saicff.org
www.wallbuilders.com

BIBLE STUDIES

Seven Basic Needs of a Wife and *Seven Basic Needs of a Husband.* http://store.iblp.org/products

BOOKS

Randy Alcorn, *Does the Birth Control Pill Cause Abortions?* (Sandy, Ore.: Eternal Perspective Ministries, 2007). Available from www.epm.org/store/product/birth-control-pill-book/.

Kim Cahill, *No-Guesswork Cooking Cookbook: Recipes You Can Trust*. Available from www.iblp.org.

Alex Kendrick and Stephen Kendrick, *The Love Dare* (Nashville: B&H Books, 2008).

Sarah Mally, *Before You Meet Prince Charming* (Cedar Rapids, Iowa: Tomorrow's Forefathers, 2006, 2009), 40–41.

Dr. Ed Wheat and Gloria Okes Perkins, *Love Life for Every Married Couple* (Grand Rapids, Mich.: Zondervan, 1997).

Dr. Ed Wheat and Gaye Wheat, *Intended for Pleasure: Sex Technique and Sexual Fulfillment in Christian Marriage* (Grand Rapids, Mich.: Revell, 1976).

Other websites where we find Christian books:

www.christianbook.com/

www.visionforum.com/

CHILDREN'S RESOURCES WEBSITES

www.jonathanpark.com/

www.majestymusic.com/

www.visionforum.com/news/enn//

www.whitsend.org/

CONFERENCES AND SEMINARS

A Weekend to Remember (www.familylifeministries.com)

ALERT Academy Homeschool conferences (www.alertacademy.com)

Basic Life Principles seminar (www.iblp.org)

Journey to the Heart http://iblp.org/iblp/discipleship/journeytotheheart/

Noble Partners Marriage Conference (www.noblecall.org/conferences/)

Whatever It Takes (www.witministries.com)

ENCOURAGEMENT RESOURCES

Free daily success e-mails: http://iblp.org/iblp/discipleship/dailysuccess/

Vision Forum Family Resources: http://www.visionforum.com/

Other websites where we find ideas for sharing encouragement:

www.bbnradio.org/

www.oneplace.com/

www.tdharmon.com/

www.livingwaters.com/

www.focusonthefamily.com/

Homeschool Resources

Accelerated Christian Education. www.aceministries.com.

The Advanced Training Institute, source of the Wisdom Booklets we use as well as other homeschool materials. http://ati.iblp.org/ati/.

Christ-centered homeschool materials that teach how God supernaturally created the earth and how evolution is impossible. www.answersingenesis.com.

CollegePlus! is a Christian-based distance-learning program that helps students earn their fully accredited bachelor's degree in a fraction of the time and cost of the traditional university system. www.collegeplus.org.

Home School Legal Defense Association is a nonprofit advocacy organization established to defend and advance the constitutional right of parents to direct the education of their children and to protect family freedoms. www.hslda.org.

Oak Brook College of Law, a Christian law school providing education and training in law and government policy in the context of a biblical and historical framework. www.obcl.edu.

Switched on Schoolhouse (SOS) software from Alpha Omega Publications. www.AOPhomeschooling.com.

Verity Institute, another Christian-based distance-learning program that offers dual high school and college enrollment in association with Thomas Edison State College, Indianapolis, Indiana. www.verityinstitute.org.

Internet Filter Service

American Family Online: http://www.myafo.net/

Ministry Opportunities

SOS Ministries International is a faith-based, not-for-profit ministry that desires to minister to the physical and spiritual needs of people throughout the world by feeding the hungry, clothing the poor, embracing the orphan, providing education and medical attention to the destitute, and giving hope to the hopeless through the Word of God. This is the group that organizes the mission trips to El Salvador in which we participate. www.sosminternational.com.

Other websites offering ministry-opportunity ideas and resources:
www.gospelink.org/
www.gfa.org/
www.reversalministry.com/
www.ican-online.org/

Modest Clothing Resources

We find modest clothing at these websites or retailers:
Swim Wear: www.wholesomewear.com
Skirts: Cato Fashions & Accessories: www.catofashions.com
Tops: Christopher & Banks affordable fashions: www.christopherand banks.com

Sam Walton's Rules for Building a Business[1]

RULE 1: COMMIT to your business. Believe in it more than anybody else. I think I overcame every single one of my personal shortcomings by the sheer passion I brought to my work. I don't know if you're born with this kind of passion, or if you can learn it. But I do know you need it. If you love your work, you'll be out there every day trying to do it the best you possibly can, and pretty soon everybody around will catch the passion from you—like a fever.

RULE 2: SHARE your profits with all your associates, and treat them as partners. In turn, they will treat you as a partner, and together you will all perform beyond your wildest expectations. Remain a corporation and retain control if you like, but behave as a servant leader in a partnership. Encourage your associates to hold a stake in the company. Offer discounted stock, and grant them stock for their retirement. It's the single best thing we ever did.

RULE 3: MOTIVATE your partners. Money and ownership alone aren't enough. Constantly, day by day, think of new and more interesting ways to motivate and challenge your partners. Set high goals, encourage competition, and then keep score. Make bets with outrageous payoffs. If things get stale, cross-pollinate; have managers switch jobs with one another to stay challenged. Keep everybody guessing as to what your next trick is going to be. Don't become too predictable.

RULE 4: COMMUNICATE everything you possibly can to your partners. The more they know, the more they'll understand. The more they understand, the more they'll care. Once they care, there's no stopping them. If you don't trust your associates to know what's going on, they'll know you don't really consider them partners. Information is power, and the gain you get from empowering your associates more than offsets the risk of informing your competitors.

RULE 5: APPRECIATE everything your associates do for the business.

A paycheck and a stock option will buy one kind of loyalty. But all of us like to be told how much somebody appreciates what we do for them. We like to hear it often, and especially when we have done something we're really proud of. Nothing else can quite substitute for a few well-chosen, well-timed sincere words of praise. They're absolutely free—and worth a fortune.

RULE 6: CELEBRATE your successes. Find some humor in your failures. Don't take yourself so seriously. Loosen up, and everybody around you will loosen up. Have fun. Show enthusiasm—always. When all else fails, put on a costume and sing a silly song. Then make everybody else sing with you. Don't do a hula on Wall Street. It's been done. Think up your own stunt. All of this is more important, and more fun, than you think, and it really fools the competition. "Why should we take those cornballs at Walmart seriously?"

RULE 7: LISTEN to everyone in your company. And figure out ways to get them talking. The folks on the front lines—the ones who actually talk to the customer—are the only ones who really know what's going on out there. You'd better find out what they know. This really is what total quality is all about. To push responsibility down in your organization, and to force good ideas to bubble up within it, you *must* listen to what your associates are trying to tell you.

RULE 8: EXCEED your customers' expectations. If you do, they'll come back over and over. Give them what they want—and a little more. Let them know you appreciate them. Make good on all your mistakes, and don't make excuses—apologize. Stand behind everything you do. The two most important words I ever wrote were on that first Walmart sign: "Satisfaction Guaranteed." They're still up there, and they have made all the difference.

RULE 9: CONTROL your expenses better than your competition. This is where you can always find the competitive advantage. For twenty-five years running—long before Walmart was known as the nation's largest retailer—we ranked number one in our industry for the lowest ratio of expenses to sales. You can make a lot of different mistakes and still recover if you run an efficient operation. Or you can be brilliant and still go out of business if you're too inefficient.

RULE 10: SWIM upstream. Go the other way. Ignore the conventional wisdom. If everybody else is doing it one way, there's a good chance you can find your niche by going in exactly the opposite direction. But be prepared for a lot of folks to wave you down and tell you you're headed the wrong way. I guess in all my years, what I heard more often than anything was: a town of less than 50,000 population cannot support a discount store for very long.

CHARACTER QUALITIES[2]

Operational Definitions of Character Qualities

TRUTHFULNESS vs. Deception — Earning future trust by accurately reporting past facts. Ephesians 4:25	**ALERTNESS** vs. Unawareness — Being aware of that which is taking place around me so that I can have the right responses. Mark 14:38	**SELF-CONTROL** vs. self-indulgence — Instant obedience to the initial promptings of God's Spirit. Galatians 5:24-25	**WISDOM** vs. Natural Inclinations — Seeing and responding to life situations from God's frame of reference. Proverbs 9:10	**RESOURCEFULNESS** vs. Wastefulness — Wise use of that which others would normally overlook or discard. Luke 16:10	**ORDERLINESS** vs. Disorganization — Preparing myself and my surroundings so that I will achieve the greatest efficiency. 1 Corinthians 14:40	**ATTENTIVENESS** vs. Unconcern — Showing the worth of a person by giving undivided attention to his words and emotions. Hebrews 2:1
OBEDIENCE vs. Willfulness — Freedom to be creative under the protection of divinely appointed authority. II Corinthians 10:5	**HOSPITALITY** vs. Loneliness — Cheerfully sharing food, shelter, and spiritual refreshment with those God brings into my life. Hebrews 13:2	**REVERENCE** vs. Disrespect — Awareness of how God is working through the people and events in my life to produce the character of Christ in me. Proverbs 23:17-18	**DISCERNMENT** vs. Judgment — The God-given ability to understand why things happen. 1 Samuel 16:7	**THRIFTINESS** vs. Extravagance — Not letting myself or others spend that which is not necessary. Luke 16:11	**INITIATIVE** vs. Unresponsiveness — Recognizing and doing what needs to be done before I am asked to do it. Romans 12:21	**SENSITIVITY** vs. Callousness — Exercising my senses so that I can perceive the true spirit and emotions of those around me. Romans 12:15
SINCERITY vs. Hypocrisy — Eagerness to do what is right with transparent motives. 1 Peter 1:22	**GENEROSITY** vs. Stinginess — Realizing that all I have belongs to God and using it for His purposes. II Corinthians 9:6	**DILIGENCE** vs. Slothfulness — Visualizing each task as a special assignment from the Lord and using all my energies to accomplish it. Colossians 3:23	**FAITH** vs. Presumption — Visualizing what God intends to do in a given situation and acting in harmony with it. Hebrews 11:1	**CONTENTMENT** vs. Covetousness — Realizing that God has provided everything that I need for my present happiness. I Timothy 6:8	**RESPONSIBILITY** vs. Unreliability — Knowing and doing what both God and others are expecting me to do. Romans 14:12	**JUSTICE** vs. Fairness — Personal responsibility to God's unchanging laws. Micah 6:8
VIRTUE vs. Impurity — The moral excellence and purity of spirit that radiate from my life as I obey God's word. II Peter 1:5	**JOYFULNESS** vs. Self-pity — The spontaneous enthusiasm of my spirit when my soul is in fellowship with the Lord. Psalm 16:11	**THOROUGHNESS** vs. Incompleteness — Knowing what factors will diminish the effectiveness of my work or words if neglected. Proverbs 18:15	**DISCRETION** vs. Simple-mindedness — The ability to avoid words, actions, and attitudes which could result in undesirable consequences. Proverbs 22:3	**PUNCTUALITY** vs. Tardiness — Showing high esteem for other people and their time. Ecclesiastes 3:1	**HUMILITY** vs. Pride — Recognizing that God and others are actually responsible for the achievements in my life. James 4:6	**COMPASSION** vs. Indifference — Investing whatever is necessary to heal the hurts of others. I John 3:17
BOLDNESS vs. Fearfulness — Confidence that what I have to say or do is true and right and just in the sight of God. Acts 4:29	**FLEXIBILITY** vs. Resistance — Not setting my affections on ideas or plans which could be changed by God or others. Colossians 3:2	**DEPENDABILITY** vs. Inconsistency — Fulfilling what I consented to do even if it means unexpected sacrifice. Psalm 15:4	**LOVE** vs. Selfishness — Giving to others basic needs without having as my motive personal reward. 1 Corinthians 13:3	**TOLERANCE** vs. Prejudice — Acceptance of others as unique expressions of specific character qualities in varying degrees of maturity. Philippians 2:2	**DECISIVENESS** vs. Double-mindedness — The ability to finalize difficult decisions based on the will and ways of God. James 1:5	**GENTLENESS** vs. Harshness — Showing personal care and concern in meeting the needs of others. I Thessalonians 2:7
FORGIVENESS vs. Rejection — Clearing the record of those who have wronged me and allowing God to love them through me. Ephesians 4:32	**AVAILABILITY** vs. Self-centeredness — Making my own schedule and priorities secondary to wishes of those I am serving. Philippians 2:20-21	**SECURITY** vs. Anxiety — Structuring my life around that which is eternal and cannot be destroyed or taken away. John 6:27	**CREATIVITY** vs. Under-achievement — Approaching a need, a task, an idea from a new perspective. Romans 12:2	**CAUTIOUSNESS** vs. Rashness — Knowing how important right timing is in accomplishing right actions. Proverbs 19:2	**DETERMINATION** vs. Faint-heartedness — Purposing to accomplish God's goals in God's timing regardless of the opposition. II Timothy 4:7-8	**DEFERENCE** vs. Rudeness — Limiting my freedom in order not to offend the tastes of those God has called me to serve. Romans 14:21
PERSUASIVENESS vs. Contentiousness — Guiding vital truth around another's mental roadblocks. II Timothy 2:24	**ENDURANCE** vs. Giving-up — The inward strength to withstand stress to accomplish God's best. Galatians 6:9	**PATIENCE** vs. Restlessness — Accepting a difficult situation from God without giving Him a deadline to remove it. Romans 5:3-4	**ENTHUSIASM** vs. Apathy — Expressing with my spirit the joy of my soul. I Thessalonians 5:16,19	**GRATEFULNESS** vs. Unthankfulness — Making known to God and others in what ways they have benefited my life. I Corinthians 4:7	**LOYALTY** vs. Unfaithfulness — Using difficult times to demonstrate my commitment to God and to those whom He has called me to serve. John 15:13	**MEEKNESS** vs. Anger — Yielding my personal rights and expectations to God. Psalm 62:5

• Notes •

Chapter 7. Living Under the Microscope

1. For a more detailed analysis of how birth-control pills work, see Randy Alcorn, *Does the Birth Control Pill Cause Abortions?* (Sandy, Ore.: Eternal Perspective Ministries, 2007). Available as a PDF download from www.epm.org/store/product/birth-control-pill-book/.

Chapter 16. Michelle's Heart for Children and Moms

1. "Continue On," © 2011 Roy Lessin. Used by permission. All rights reserved.

2. "Love," Jim Fowler. Used by permission of Jim Fowler, Christ in You Ministries.

Chapter 17. Jim Bob's Lifelong Hobby

1. Sam Walton, *Made in America* (New York: Bantam/Doubleday/Dell, 1993), p. 314.

Resources

1. From *Sam Walton: Made in America* by Sam Walton, copyright © 1992 by Estate of Samuel Moore Walton. Used by permission of Doubleday, a division of Random House, Inc.

2. Used by permission of Institute in Basic Life Principles. www.iblp.org

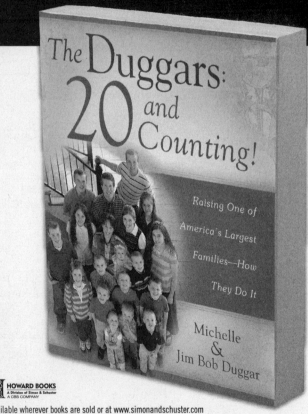